Chinese Divide:
Evolving Relations
Between Taiwan and
Mainland China

Chinese Divide: Evolving Relations Between Taiwan and Mainland China

Edited by J.W. Wheeler

Hudson Institute
Indianapolis, Indiana

Hudson Institute

Indianapolis, Indiana

Library of Congress Cataloging-in-Publication Data

ISBN 1-55813-057-8

Printed in the United States of America

This book may be ordered from:
Hudson Institute
Herman Kahn Center
P.O. Box 26-919
Indianapolis, Indiana 46226
(317) 545-1000

CONTENTS

SECTION IV: Bilateral Interaction with the U.S., Japan, and Southeast Asia, and the Evolving Cross-Strait Relationship

SECTION V: Alternative Scenarios

Chinese Divide: Evolving Relations Between Taiwan and Mainland China

PREFACE

With the recent news clips of China launching missiles near the main seaports of Taiwan, and the warning to the U.S. to stay away from an island China regards as a renegade offshore province, information on the complex, mercurial relationship between the two nations is at a premium. Thus *Evolving Relations Between Taiwan and Mainland China*, edited by J. W. Wheeler, arrives at a most important time for international policymakers in the U.S. and abroad.

The Hudson tradition in the analysis of international relations includes a skepticism about the conventional wisdom and a willingness to look realistically at threats to the international order. *Evolving Relations Between Taiwan and Mainland China* continues this tradition, by noting both the gravity of the problem and the existence of possible solutions. As co-author and editor J. W. Wheeler notes, an outbreak of violence between China and Taiwan would have devastating consequences for the region and the international order, and the U.S. has an essential role in helping to keep the peace in the region.

Evolving Relations Between Taiwan and Mainland China comprises a series of essays that grew out of an international conference cosponsored by Hudson Institute and the School of Advanced International Studies of Johns Hopkins University. The authors consider the past, present, and possible future relationships between the Asian giant and its prosperous island neighbor, and provide a thorough overview of the complex issues that divide the two nations. The introductory essay sets the tone with an overview of the major findings of the conference and identifies the important risks, opportunities, and policy implications of the tension between the two nations. It also considers whether tension across the

Taiwan Strait "is likely to remain an immutable fact of international life" or, through the increasing web of economic and other relations, Taiwan and the mainland can reach constructive conflict resolution.

Other essays examine the domestic roots of the policy differences between the two nations; analyze the effect of bilateral interactions between Taiwan and three important powers in the region—the U.S., Japan, and the Association of Southeast Asian Nations—on the evolving cross-Strait relationship; and consider possible scenarios for the future of this strained relationship.

As all the authors make clear, the relationship between China and Taiwan will continue to evolve, with serious consequences for the world economy and world peace. U.S. policy will have a powerful effect on the outcome, and *Evolving Relations Between Taiwan and Mainland China* attempts to give policymakers a solid understanding of the issues, ideas, and events that underlie the conflict and should drive U.S. efforts toward peace and prosperity in the region.

Many generous contributors to Hudson have helped to make this book possible. Although these organizations bear no responsibility for the ideas and conclusions of this work, Hudson Institute gratefully acknowledges their assistance.

Leslie Lenkowsky
President
Hudson Institute

SECTION 1
Summary and Outlook

CHAPTER 1
Evolving Relations Between Taiwan and Mainland China

*Ralph N. Clough, Karl Jackson,
and J. W. Wheeler*

Introduction

The Competitiveness Center of Hudson Institute and the School of Advanced International Studies of Johns Hopkins University hosted a conference in Washington, D.C., during late August 1994, in order to examine one of the more enduring problems in the international system, the evolving relationship between Taiwan and mainland China. This chapter provides an overview of the major findings and speculates about the major risks, opportunities and policy implications.

Background

The early 1990s witnessed several remarkable international transformations. The Cold War ended, Germany was reunited, both Koreas were admitted to the United Nations, and a UN peacekeeping mission reunited Cambodia. Many problems thought beyond resolution have, in fact, been settled.

Since 1949, tension between the PRC and ROC (Taiwan) has been a constant in world politics. Yet both societies have evolved, economically and politically, along lines making them nearly unrecognizable to the original protagonists of the conflict. New forms of interaction and cooperation have become a reality—from Taiwan's tourists on the Great Wall, to formal talks in Singapore, to Taiwan's investment on the mainland, to simultaneous involvement in the IBRD (1971-80), ADB, APEC and, in time, perhaps the GATT (MTO).

In light of both altered international circumstances and the increasing web of economic and other relations between Taiwan and the mainland, it has become important to examine whether tension across the Taiwan Strait is likely to remain an immutable fact of international life or if an opportunity arisen for constructive conflict resolution?

Key Issues

Conference participants were charged with examining a number of key issues, with the ultimate goal of sketching out the most likely scenarios for interaction between Taiwan and the mainland over the next decade.

1. How will domestic politics in Taiwan and on the mainland contribute to continued conflict or its resolution? How will differing views of the People's Liberation Army, the governing elite, and the new business elite shape policy toward Taiwan during the coming succession crisis on the mainland? Given the military might of the mainland and the ongoing opposition of the KMT elite to an independence strategy, what is the likelihood democratization and economic growth will push Taiwan towards the independence option? Is a condominium possible between the KMT and the DPP on the reunification option? What is the likelihood of resolving issues dividing Taiwan and the mainland through direct and formal negotiations? Does evidence exist indicating that either Taiwan or the mainland would significantly modify or give up its distinctive political system as a result of an agreement between the two elites? What is the likelihood that each elite would follow a course that would precipitate an international crisis?

2. What will be the likely economic scope and political impact of rapidly increasing economic interaction between Taiwan and the mainland? As Taiwan becomes an increasingly important source of capital and high level manpower for the modernization of China, will this result in greater toleration for Taiwan's

4

economic, social, and political system on the part of ruling elites on the mainland? Will economic interaction with the mainland decrease fear of reunification on the part of Taiwan? Do investments on the mainland serve as a brake on any Taiwanese independence movement?

3. How have the perceptions of Taiwan and the mainland been changing in among other nations? Will Taiwan upgrade its diplomatic relations with more states? Will the mainland continue to use its leverage to prevent the expansion of Taiwan's international role? Can democratic pressures on Taiwan tolerate only a gradual expansion of Taiwan's international role, or will domestic politics force more aggressive goals? Can the mainland accept *any* expansion of Taiwan's role, even far short of formal recognition of Taiwan as an independent state?

4. With the disappearance of the bipolar world and the increasing importance of international trade, is it likely that an economy the size and vitality of Taiwan will remain isolated and uninvolved in major international institutions? Will mainland China continue to view Taiwan's participation in multilateral organizations as a threat to reunification? Is a community of interests emerging between Taiwan and the mainland which might lead to their cooperation and common voting record on a variety of issues within international organizations? At what point can mainland leaders begin to perceive Taiwan as an ally rather than as an automatic adversary within international organizations? Can interaction within the ADB, APEC, and at some point in GATT (MTO) lead to cooperation?

Did we reach a consensus on answers to this long menu of questions? Of course not. But the authors, discussants, and other participants brought a clarity of debate to these complex issues that is rare in discussions of cross-Strait relations. We only hope this chapter captures a part of the richness of the conference interchange. The next section outlines major conclusions and observations, organized more-or-less along the lines identified in the four key issue areas. This will be followed by a discussion of the principal scenarios against which contingency planning must occur. The chapter will end with a presentation of some of the more important policy implications.

Mainland Taiwan Policy: A Holding Pattern

Lowell Dittmer's paper clearly presents the underlying continuity of the mainland's Taiwan policy. The fundamental principles of its Taiwan Policy, ultimate reunification and the indivisibility of sovereignty, have remained unchanged, while strategy and tactics have evolved over time. Even the policy framework has remained constant with a rigid international dimension (maximal isolation of Taiwan) and a somewhat more dynamic intranational dimension (cross-Strait threats and inducements to prevent independence and improve the likelihood of reunification). In part, this reflects a continuity of control concentrated at the top of the PRC power structure, in part a broad consensus among the key elites.

Following Mao's death China's policy reduced its emphasis on military threat, adopting a peaceful reunification as the strategy (while retaining the "right" to use force). A number of innovative proposals were floated and debated in the early 1980s, which ultimately coalesced into what is now known as "one country, two systems"—the model China seeks for Taiwan, Hong Kong and Macao. Since then, Beijing's Taiwan policy has remained essentially unchanged. (Compare Deng's 9 point proposal in 1981 and 6 point proposal in 1983 to the Oct. 1992, Jiang Zemin political report to the 14th CCP Congress.)

Why change? After all, their policy has been working. Despite large changes in the international environment and a few setbacks, such as with the U.S.-Taiwan Relations Act and the parallel participation in the ADB and APEC, China's relentless pursuit of Taiwan's isolation continues to progress. Further, except for the U.S., where success has been mixed, Chinese intimidation has seriously limited Taiwan's access to imports of advanced military systems. Finally, China's opening to commerce with Taiwan helped induce an extraordinary growth in indirect trade and investment, and a more accommodative Taiwanese intranational policy posture.

China's future Taiwan policy, however, will have to deal with a variety of challenges, uncertainties and internal contradictions. Two stand out. First, the use of nongovernmental entities permits both sides to finesse the disagreement over the status of the government on Taiwan (recognition as an equal vs. subordinate to Beijing) in cross-Strait affairs, but this will not work in most international arenas. China has taken advantage of this in its efforts to increase Taiwan's political isolation. Can it continue to do so? Is it worth the effort? Despite the mainland's diplomatic successes, Taiwan's trade, investment, travel, and social and cultural

6

interaction around the world continues to expand with virtually no hindrance. Moreover, this nongovernmental fiction weakens as the cross-Strait relations become ever more complex. Dealing with the various problems is gradually ceding to Taiwan greater explicit recognition as a separate political entity.

Second, a reunification policy that promises Taiwan considerable autonomy in foreign affairs, independent military and police forces, and noninterference after reunification, stands in an increasingly glaring contradiction with current Chinese policies and practices. The contrast is highlighted by the evolution of events leading up to the 1997 transfer of sovereignty in Hong Kong. Beijing has clearly demonstrated its aversion to democracy and to capitalism that is not subservient to socialism, as well as revealing a view of autonomy that entails considerable detailed interference in local policy.

Taiwan policy on the mainland, however is unlikely to change much in the near-term. Not only is the policy still working in most respects, but there appears to be a broad consensus among the elites on core elements of the strategy (if not always the tactics). At the same time, the various leadership groups are highly adverse to change while in the midst of a drawn-out succession crisis. Until the succession is resolved, and perhaps until after the Hong Kong absorption, no innovation in China's policy can be expected. Afterwards, Dittmer and other participants believe that a more appealing reunification package will be offered. It might even adopt a variation of Taiwan's rhetoric of "one country, two governments." The components of such a package might well include Beijing dropping the military option, cutting way back or stopping its efforts to isolate Taipei, and offering convincing security guarantees. Such a package would place great pressure on Taipei and indeed on Washington, since it is essentially what was requested in the first stage of Taiwan's Guidelines for National Unification (adopted March 1991).

Taiwan Mainland Policy: Democracy Resurgent

Taiwan's cross-Strait policy, until recently was controlled at the top of the KMT and the military, among a group with a strong consensus on the same broad goals as the PRC—eventual reunification and the indivisibility of sovereignty—with the obvious disagreement about who was to end up in charge. As explored in Michael Ying-mao Kau's paper, mainland policy changes since the early 1980s have come to reflect domestic as much as international or cross-Strait forces. Indeed, the emergence of democracy has fundamentally and permanently altered the political dynamics of mainland policymaking.

Until the 1980s the KMT ran Taiwan under a highly efficient Leninist style political network, with an effective patron-client economic structure. Under this authoritarian structure no opposition was permitted, especially on mainland policy. The one-China policy was simply too important to KMT ideology and its political legitimacy. Mainland policy was far from stagnant, however. It adapted rather effectively and pragmatically to the growing diplomatic isolation of the period, especially to the U.S. shift in recognition to Beijing, to the various initiatives launched by the PRC, and to the beginnings of cross-Strait economic interchange.

The extraordinary success of the government's earlier economic policies laid the foundation for collapse of authoritarian rule, as a new wealthy and politically active middle class and other autonomous social groups emerged seeking a say in government policymaking. Combined with a KMT that had become increasingly stagnant, inefficient, factionalized, and corrupt after four decades of continuous rule, even a small organized opposition was able to take advantage of international and domestic trends to force remarkable changes on the system. Self identity, nationalism, and mainland policy inevitably became key issues of debate, particularly in light of the Taiwanization of politics. For better or ill, mainland policy is now subject to domestic politics.

Cleavages over mainland policy cut across several different dimensions. Age is important, in that most of the voting public today have no personal memories of the mainland and are rightfully proud of their own economic and political accomplishments. The ethnic cleavage between native Taiwanese and the descendants of the mainlanders (the nationalists) is even more important than age. The loss of the nationalist monopoly over the power structure is having far-reaching impacts on policy orientation and debate over national identity. The native Taiwanese always tend to look to "Taiwan first" rather than "unification first," which greatly alter their perception and articulation of national priorities in setting policy. The political cleavage has two dimensions. The first is between the KMT and the DPP—the first effective opposition party. The DPP began as primarily a party of the native Taiwanese, calling the KMT an "alien regime" from the mainland, with a strong Taiwan independence policy platform. The second dimension is within the KMT itself. There is less and less agreement within the party itself over many issues including mainland policy.

Mainland policy differences have settled into three well articulated positions during the past eight years of political debate and controversy. On the right of the political spectrum lies the CNP (a small party splintered off from the KMT) and the so-called non-mainstream faction of the KMT. They espouse the more-or-less traditional one-China policy, insisting that Taiwan is part of China and should be reunited. They advocate deepening trade and other links in order to lay the foundation for future political unification, and promote a policy shift from permitting only indirect to stimulating direct trade, shipping, and communications. This is essentially the Beijing position and is most commonly advanced by the mainlander old guard and second-generation mainlander activists. It is often referred to as the "pro-unification" or the "mainlander" faction.

On the left of the policy spectrum lies the DPP's strong "one Taiwan, one China" stand. It advocates complete and de jure independence from China, but increasingly is willing to recognize the risks of doing so quickly. Dealing with the risks lies behind the party's efforts to internationalize the Taiwan issue on the world stage. They have come to believe that Taiwan must be involved in the international arena, especially the UN, if it is to insure the Nation's security and survival during it move to independence. They also strongly oppose any party-to-party negotiations between the KMT and CCP, assuming that the Taiwanese will be sold out.

Somewhat in the middle of these two extremes falls the mainland policy position of the so-called mainstream KMT, as articulated in the official Guidelines for National Unification. This is a three-stage, gradualist approach, building up from indirect, unofficial interaction, to direct interaction and official contact, to negotiations over the framework and timing of ultimate unification. This process is hinged to Beijing's "positive" response, rhetorically and in implementation, at each stage, and Taipei will not accept any predetermined timetable. Taipei also rejects Beijing's "one country, two systems" model, insisting upon equal political status for both governments.

Over time, the KMT and DPP positions have moved closer together, as the DPP has toned down its inflammatory rhetoric, and as the KMT has accepted the need to seek UN membership and moved closer to DPP's "one China, one Taiwan" model, a position analogous to the former "two Germanys" or today's "two Koreas." For now this seems to be what the voters want. Kau is convinced that the issue of independence vs. unification will remain one of the core political issues in Taiwan for the foreseeable future, even as pragmatism will dominate Taiwan's approach to economic and societal relations across the Strait. If this convergence can result in real bipartisanship on cross-Strait policy, Taipei will be able to present a far more effective resistance to China's efforts to impose its one-China view.

Economic Integration: Both Stability and Risk

Since China's opening to the world in 1978, indirect economic exchange across the Strait has grown explosively. This growth in intra-Chinese investment and trade has stimulated widespread speculation about the implications of "greater China." J.W. Wheeler's paper examined the issues that will determine if this informal "Chinese Economic Zone" might provide the stabilizing backdrop that is needed for eventual accommodation, even reunification. Both sides have supported growing economic interchange for their own reasons, yet both also are concerned about potential risks—especially Taiwan.

The future impact of economics on the cross-Strait relationship will cut across several dimensions: economics and relative political power, the trade off among goals as economic growth continues in both economies, and response to events that might dramatically alter the priority of economic gain relative to other political, security, or nationalist goals.

From the mainland's perspective, economic relations with Taiwan helps achieve at least four critical long-term goals. First, Beijing's leadership hope to create a domestic constituency on Taiwan favorable to accommodation with the mainland. Second, Beijing seems to believe that closer economic ties will mute calls for independence and fears of unification among the rest of the population on the island. Third, Taiwanese trade and investment offer significant benefits to China's economic growth objectives. Finally, China believes that it gains more political leverage than it loses through interdependence. China's sheer size makes it far less vulnerable to economic leverage than Taiwan. There are risks. Some are concerned about the potential influence resulting from the thousands of individual business and personal relationships among mainland and Taiwan citizens. Beijing's propaganda attacks against Taiwan meddling following the Tiananmen Square confrontation reflect this sensitivity. Another concern is to prevent Taiwanese firms from reaching a dominate position in any critical industry or niche, not too difficult to achieve in light of Taipei's own restrictions on investment and trade in key high technology areas.

On their own terms, China's policy of inducing asymmetrical interdependency with Taiwan has been highly successful. Yet, it is a political lever deterred by huge potential economic and political costs.

Blatant use of trade and investment ties to pressure Taiwan would have far greater consequences than just on Taiwan. It would raise fears and uncertainty among all foreign partners about the safety of their contracts, no matter what China declared. It is harder to assess success of the goals designed to influence domestic politics on Taiwan. It is not at all clear whether growing economic interdependence has created more *or* less political support for reunification on Taiwan. Clearly, fears of dealing with China have been reduced. Yet at the same time, the pro-unification faction in Taipei's politics is shrinking, while the mainline KMT and the DPP are converging towards a consensus on unification policy that elites in Beijing are unwilling to accept.

Taipei's goals concerning economic opening to the mainland have been more reactive and thus more difficult to assess. There were strong domestic pressures to let Taiwanese firms take advantage of the opening Chinese market after 1978. Not only was there great complementarity between the two economies, but proximity, language, preferential treatment, and other factors gave Taiwanese firms unique competitive advantages. Taiwan's own domestic economic and political successes increased the leadership's confidence that the communist propaganda message would fall on deaf ears. Indeed, they came to see growing interchange as one of the best means of communicating Taipei's message to citizens on the mainland. Moreover, Taipei hoped to be able to use the network of contacts in the provincial governments developed through economic interchange to help moderate extremes of mainland policy towards Taiwan. Finally, Taipei sees a China embedded in web of complex economic relationships as potentially more stable and less threatening. The main risk has been and continues to be seen as excessive economic dependency that could be manipulated by Beijing for its own political ends. Efforts to diversify notwithstanding, the dependency ratio on China trade continues to rise.

Economic progress is a high priority on both sides of the Strait. As long as this is true, both parties will consider alternatives and costs before taking actions that will seriously disrupt such mutually beneficial ties. Economic benefit, however, still will yield if China sees a conflict with nationalist or ideological objectives. Nowhere is this more obvious than in the contrast between the progress in pragmatic economic exchange across the Strait and the lack of significant gains on the international front. China has shown virtually no flexibility on Taiwan's involvement in multilateral organizations, even for purely economic purposes. China's

11

position is to block any semblance of international legitimacy, regardless of the circumstance, and will admit no precedent to such parallel participation as in the ADB and APEC.

Economics can and is helping develop an ongoing dialogue across the Strait, as well as a limited habit of pragmatic cooperation. Barring a political or security crisis, this economic pragmatism can be expanded into more areas in a gradual effort to reinforce the growing, though fragile, mutual perception of trust. For example, if Beijing can be convinced to offer a package acceptable to the U.S. and other industrial states, bringing both Taiwan and China into the GATT (MTO) will be an important step in inducing cooperation and discussion about broader policy issues than just managing cross-Strait trade and investment.

Third Parties in the Cross-Strait Relationship: Bit Players, but Critical to the Play

The international community has always played a key role in the competition across the Strait, over diplomatic recognition, over trade and investment relations, and as a constraint on aggression. These will continue to be key, but except in extreme circumstances will never be the driver of change. The U.S., Japan, and the ASEAN states were identified as both having important national interests at stake in, and having some potential influence on the outcome. Authors were tasked to assess the current state of affairs, examine prospects for change in the status quo, and identify critical policy issues.

The United States

Ralph N. Clough took on the task of analyzing the unique relationship between the U.S. and Taiwan that gives American actions special importance to cross-Strait affairs. This began with the U.S. decision at the beginning of the Korean war to step in and prevent the PRC from taking over Taiwan. From that point, the U.S. became Taiwan's principal sponsor in international affairs, its primary source of economic, technical and military assistance, and its source of strategic protection. Over the next 20 years, a complex set of bilateral economic, political, and personal relations evolved. Even following the decision to recognize the PRC as the legal government of China in 1979, the bilateral relationship was embodied in a unique piece of legislation—the Taiwan Relations Act—essentially granting de facto recognition. Not surprisingly this special relationship with Taiwan has complicated management of U.S.-China affairs.

Post-World War II relations with China have been driven almost exclusively by strategic considerations. The initial decision to defend Taiwan was primarily to contain Sino-Soviet expansionism in Asia. Nixon's decision to establish a diplomatic relationship in 1971 was designed to take advantage of the Sino-Soviet split, and facilitate the withdrawal of U.S. forces from Vietnam. Carter completed the process begun by Nixon by shifting official recognition to the mainland in 1979, again primarily to strengthen the ability to check the USSR in Asia and in an effort to contain Vietnamese expansionism. The 1982 Agreement to limit arms sales to Taiwan had a similar basis.

The collapse of the USSR, the growth of the mainland's economic interaction with the rest of the world, and the reduced confrontation across the Strait has fundamentally altered the strategic equation once again, forcing U.S. policy towards China and Taiwan out of focus. Clough presents a clear economic, political, and security case for keeping China an important component of U.S. foreign policy, paralleled by an equally compelling case to maintain good relations with Taiwan, with a principal goal of encouraging peaceful coexistence. Inevitably, the U.S. will become involved in some of the international and the intranational aspects of the cross-Strait competition. Dealing with these requires a delicate balancing act, while keeping as far away as possible from any involvement in the detailed management their bilateral relationship. He argues that only by maintaining a cautious dual track policy can the U.S. hope to influence both sides in the direction of a peaceful resolution.

The Clinton administration policy review towards Taiwan, completed in September 1994, revealed the extreme caution with which this relationship is viewed. Basis policy was left unchanged. Some process issues were modified that scarcely justified a policy review, such as easing restrictions on high-level visits and on meetings in government offices. The major decision was changing the name of Taiwan's office in the U.S. from the Coordination Council for North American Affairs to the Taipei Economic and Cultural Office.

Considerations in policy towards either side of the Strait relations must increasingly take into account the other, as the economies become more intertwined. Economic sanctions, such as considered withdrawal of most-favored-nation treatment of mainland exports to the U.S., would have had a major impact on Taiwanese firms (as well as those from Hong Kong, Japan, even the U.S. itself). Such unintended consequences was one of the considerations that ultimately blocked imposition of this sanction. Criminal activity is another challenge as cross-Strait relations, when firms and individuals across the Strait cooperate to break U.S. law, the existing limited intranational agreements greatly impede effective combined law enforcement responses. Similarly, regional operations of American multinationals would be greatly facilitated if some of the strictures on direct links across the Strait were eased.

None of these concerns argue for major policy change to protect U.S. interests. However, the domestic political dynamics on Taiwan which are forcing Taipei to seek improvements in the island's international status may well present the U.S. with difficult choices. Prolonged failure could well strengthen popular support for Taiwan independence, which in turn could force the U.S. away from the studied ambiguity that has served U.S. interests so well for the past 15 years. Clough believes that major change in U.S. policy could only serve to disrupt the process of peaceful coexistence. However, he feels that the U.S. should work to help develop formulas for Taiwan's participation in the IMF, the World Bank, and certain technical intergovernmental organizations affiliated with the United Nations, but that it would be counterproductive to confront China on Taiwan's admission to the UN General Assembly. Whatever the U.S. does, it will be primarily indirectly through contacts and interaction with moderate officials on both sides of the Strait.

Japan

Robert Scalapino took on the task of examining the challenges facing Japanese policymakers in their efforts to deal with cross-Strait affairs. Japanese relations with both sides are plagued by a history that forces the Japanese to be highly defensive. Nonetheless, China policy is second to U.S. policy in Japanese foreign priorities.

The ongoing sorting out of domestic political affairs in Japan appear to preclude virtually anything except a reactive foreign policy over the immediate future. Eventually, the debate about Japan's role in Asia and the world will have to come off of hold. But as long as weak governments persist, they will avoid raising the divisive issues that such a debate would entail.

With regard to China, Japan recognizes the mainland, but runs a de facto one China, one Taiwan economic policy, that is accepted by both sides. There are economic grievances, but overall the major difficulties have been managed fairly effectively. With its arms export ban, Japan avoids having deal with one of the major issues in mainland-Taiwan relations. Other aspects of the political and strategic environment are more complex for Japan to deal with. Japan gives every indication of pursuing the status quo with at most modest incremental changes. It will focus first on the U.S. and the retaining a U.S. security commitment in Asia. This will set the tone of Japan's policy toward China and Taiwan. China's long-term goals are viewed with some alarm in Tokyo, just as Beijing views Tokyo with suspicion. Japan is China's main contender for regional influence and many in Beijing do not believe that the economic might of Japan will not translate over time into more traditional forms of political and military power. In light of these concerns Japanese China-Taiwan policy will be cautious.

Japan has no incentive to alter the status quo. Relations with the PRC are more extensive and better than at any time in this century, while the economic relationship with both sides of the Strait has evolved in ways very positive to Japanese interests. The wild card seems to be the confrontation between the PRC and the ROC over the latter's efforts to expand its international role. This is becoming more troubling to the Japanese and almost certainly will induce Japan to creep down the one China, one Taiwan path, especially in economic arenas—but always carefully calibrated against the impact on Sino-Japanese relations. Scalipino's observation that believable one-China policies of Japan and the U.S. serve as the principle external constraint on the Taiwan independence movement is an issue close to the center of Japan's policy thinking.

Southeast Asia

Southeast Asia is vulnerable to the risks of potential conflict across the Taiwan Strait, and a major beneficiary of continued economic dynamism on both sides. Sarasin Viraphol and Umphon Phanachet tackled the challenge of sorting out the various crosscurrents in the complex interactions among Southeast Asian states, Hong Kong (due to its pivotal economic role), China, and Taiwan.

Much has changed in China relations over a very short period of time. Trade and investment flows have grown as China has opened to the world. And, despite concerns about China's military buildup and its extensive claims over the South China Sea that conflict with some members claims, all six ASEAN states now have normal diplomatic relations with China, and it is only a matter of time until ASEAN will invite China to become a dialogue partner.

Taiwan's role in the region expanded as the region's economy has boomed, becoming a major trading and investment partner little hindered by the absence of diplomatic ties. Southeast Asia has been a primary target in Taipei's diplomatic offensive to enhance its international political standing, with some limited success. It has not resulted in, nor is it likely to result in any formal re-recognition of the Taipei regime. However, it has served to counter some of the mainland's efforts to diplomatically isolate the island's government.

Both Taiwan and China interact with ASEAN under the APEC umbrella on economic issues, but so far only China participates as an invited guest in the annual ASEAN Ministerial Meeting or in the newly formed ASEAN Regional Forum as a framework for regional political and security discussion. In light of the mainland's opposition, Taiwan's exclusion is not likely to change soon. Even so, from the ASEAN perspective, having China at a regional multilateral table set up to discuss political and security issues should help to establish a more predictable and constructive pattern of relations among Asia-Pacific states, including over cross-Strait relations.

The key future trend seems to be that economic interaction will move faster than political initiatives. Hopefully, the demonstrated gains through cooperation will continue to outweigh the tensions caused by ideological and geopolitical disputes. ASEAN and its member states seem to be committed to supporting this peaceful evolution based on economic exchange, while avoiding overt involvement in cross-Strait politics. For example, Indonesia did seek (unsuccessfully) to invite President Lee to the Jakarta APEC Summit. However, such efforts will be carefully gauged. China is simply too large, potentially too dangerous, and too large an economic opportunity to confront openly on the Taiwan issue.

New Directions

Taiwan-mainland relations are in a state of flux while at the same time remaining locked in a fairly rigid pattern. The final session of the conference focused on possible future direction in the course of both direct cross-Strait negotiations and intranational interaction in the international arena.

Cross-Strait Negotiations

Bob Li focused on the directions in cross-Strait negotiations. He rightly observes that the realm of the possible is limited by the perceptions of the major stakeholders on both sides. On the mainland the major constraints on flexibility are the old-timers in the party who participated in the long march during the civil war, and those close to the central government. In both cases, the Taiwan issue is a matter of ideology and legitimacy. Other groups with potentially more flexible views simply have no significant voice on Taiwan or any other issue of "high" politics at present or for the immediate future. On Taiwan, the constraint has come on the one hand from the old guard KMT, who for similar reasons seek a one-China policy, and on the other from a highly conservative populace showing great caution towards the more radical independence views of the DPP. As discussed in Dr. Kau's paper, the old line KMT group has dramatically lost power, while the DPP has moderated its rhetoric. Taipei's policy has thus become more flexible, yet the consensus is heading towards a policy that is, for now, unacceptable on the mainland.

Since serious (as opposed to symbolic) negotiations can only occur if common interests are on the table, these trends suggest to Dr. Li that success will result only if three conditions are met:

- The negotiations are focused upon practical issues between individuals and organizations, avoiding political purposes and discussions,
- The negotiations avoid defining China, using a "one China but not trying to define it now" model, and
- Both sides have a sense of security about the broader relationship, the negotiations themselves, and the uses to which any outcomes will be put.

These three conditions suggest that success is most likely to occur in cases that are based on low-key, behind the scenes personal contacts. The main challenges, of course, are (1) how to build trust in the context of threats of the use of force and other confrontational rhetoric, (2) how to engage the international community in a way that is not seen by the mainland as adversarial, (3) can such low-key negotiations keep up with the necessary practical problem-solving required but the dramatic growth in economic interaction across the Strait, and (4) does this go far enough to be acceptable politically among the Taiwanese electorate?

The International Arena

Gerrit Gong moved us beyond the great changes in cross-Strait relations to examine possible new directions in the international arena. He sees any new direction in participation in international organizations accommodating or reflecting changes in certain basic premises.

Beijing's de jure assertion of a single, inviolable sovereignty and Teipei's de facto assertion of separate, co-existing political entities.

- The cross-Strait relationship has been handled as part of an essentially political, dynamic relationship.
- Because both sides have defined their cross-Strait relations in competitive, political terms, there has been some room for political compromise and maneuver.
- For both, some cross-Strait contact in international fora may be necessary to demonstrate and advance their respective "one China" assertions.
- The essential interest and purpose of participation in international organizations needs to be ascertained. Only then can standards be set to judge success or failure.

Based on ongoing practices and policies, both sides seem to see scope for positive interaction, even though it remains embedded in a competitive, still largely zero-sum political paradigm. Looking ahead, Gong argues that even without transforming this competitive political context, there is scope for political pragmatism to lead both sides to adopt a recognition that greater international "breathing space" is in both Taipei's and Beijing's interests. Indeed, there may even be issues of common interest in the international arena in which neither have direct political interest, or in which their direct interests are subsumed in greater concerns. Scope, of course, is only a potential for action, not a requirement.

A number of conditions would have to be met for both sides to see greater common participation in international organizations to be seen as beneficial by both sides. A simplistic summary includes:

- the efforts cannot be taken primarily as a way to jockey for political advantage.
- it is neither desirable nor practical to wait until political competition disappears before attempting such joint efforts.
- in some cases, virtue will have to be its own reward. To succeed the political and other credit must be claimed within the cooperative framework.
- such joint efforts must go beyond the symbolic, if they are to build maximum confidence

Beyond the current pragmatic working out of problems in the growing cross-Strait economic and personal relations, Gong sees a number of largely transnational issues as potential opportunities to broaden common cross-Strait interests within a wider international arena. These opportunities fall in four broad areas, humanitarian fora, development fora, economic fora, and even security fora.

In many ways the humanitarian fora are the easiest in which to build parallel, even joint, multilateral participation. The possibilities go well beyond straightforward disaster relief, to such areas as limiting of drug trafficking and crime control, contributing to the resolution of major international women and children issues, and cooperation in the control of major diseases, among others.

Development and economic fora offer similar opportunities, especially since both can build on their common membership in the ADB and APEC as the basis for identification of common interests and a possible expansion of a working relationship into the GATT(MTO), World Bank, IMF, etc.

The security arena is more difficult and joint participation in multilateral fora less likely. However, open communication channels via multilateral organizations, venues to permit Taiwan's voice to be heard in political and security discussions, and means of indirect cooperation—if only symbolically—are all important to enhancing both cross-Strait and regional perceptions of security.

The bottom line is that there are potential nonzero-sum opportunities for Taipei and Beijing to create and pursue broader common interests in international fora. Because of its newly vocal and somewhat flamboyant democratic opening, Taipei faces a serious domestic education imperative, in order to clarify and explain the options and what they imply, in order to limit the politicization of such initiatives. Success depends upon both sides finding low-profile, less political, more substantive approaches to selected international organizations.

Scenarios

Specific events could evolve in a large number of directions. However, these events tend to cluster into a relative small number of plausible scenarios, if we exclude massive external shocks to the system (implosion of Russia into chaos, a catastrophic U.S.-Japan trade war, a renewed Korean war, etc.). The scenarios are not predictions, instead that are the result of plausible political and economic interactions triggered by a set of initial conditions. Reality undoubtedly will fall somewhere in between the pure cases presented.

Status Quo

In this scenario, both sides of the Strait continue their current policies with only incremental change. The PRC continues its efforts to isolate Taiwan internationally, while seeking to co-opt it economically. It offers no compromise in its strict one-China interpretation. Taiwan also continues its "pragmatic" dollar diplomacy, accepting no compromise on its one China, two systems approach. Future integration is contemplated only with the emergence of major systemic change on the mainland.

Stability?

In general, this scenario was seen as relatively unstable. The driving forces are the evolving domestic political situation on both sides of the Strait. The present ambiguous arrangements have been highly successful at preserving peace and permitting the expansion of economic interaction, but they are being overrun by political events.

The longer Taiwan remains democratic, rich, and de facto independent, the more difficult it will be for Beijing to alter the situation. Beijing's leaders certainly know this. The fundamental question is how long will the PRC tolerate a status quo in which the prospects for reunification on Beijing's terms continue to diminish. After all Beijing is in the midst of a fundamental transition of power to post-revolutionary generation leaders. The government will have a more collective nature than has been the case previously, in which the military will play a vital role. And it is military leaders who have taken among the most rigid public positions towards Taiwan. Harsh military positions, however, have not prevented limited flexibility on Taiwan investment issues and on resolving jurisdictional questions regarding highjacking.

Across the Strait, President Li Teng Hui has embarked on a campaign to join the UN, primarily as a result of competition with the DPP, who advocate Taiwan independence. Certainly the KMT has received diminishing majorities at the ballot box and the polls taken just following the Thousand Lakes incident revealed a growing support for independence. The President cannot stand still on issues of international presence and prestige and retain the KMT's political dominance. A spirit of flexibility has followed President Li's initiative as the DPP has moved towards a more moderate stance on independence issues—essentially wait and see. However, continued blocking of progress by the PRC almost certainly will harden not only the pro-independence forces on Taiwan, but also the Taiwan-unique nature of the island's democratic institutions.

What appears to be in the realm of the possible on the mainland and what is needed for a KMT-DPP consensus remains far apart, raising the potential of highly unstable action and reaction political dynamics across the Strait.

Conflict Resolution Driven off the Tracks by Internal Politics in Either Society

On the Taiwan side the primary trigger would be a DPP win in national elections, or a KMT win in which it had to adopt or outbid the DPP on issues of cross-Strait affairs. Even if the DPP declares it will not seek formal independence, its ascendancy to power (win or lose) would create a sense of crisis on the mainland.

On the mainland, the key triggering event would be the triumph of militant nationalism. For now government and party legitimacy is based upon economic success and Chinese nationalism. A unique character of China's economic success to date is its dependence upon international trade and investment (no other large country has seen its growth so reliant upon interdependence), a great deterrence to hostile actions. Yet China is also nearly unique in having a territorial dispute with almost all of its neighbors. Indeed, aggressive pursuit of its South China Sea claims seems more restrained by meager military projection capabilities than by concern about the negative impact of such actions on their trade and investment prospects.

Stability?

A positive outcome can result from these preconditions if China's new leaders feel they have the flexibility to redirect Taiwan policy—renounce the use of force, allow both autonomy and democracy on Taiwan, an attenuate the campaign to isolate Taipei in the international community. This would cut the ground out from under the political independence movement on Taiwan, especially if variations of such policies were implemented towards Hong Kong and Macao. Taipei then declares that it remains part of China, with two de facto governments but with accelerating economic and other integration.

The great concern, of course, is the risk of a negative evolution. Nationalists within the mainland military elite almost certainly will play a crucial role in insuring the succession and the continued central role of the CCP. In the absence of Deng as a restraining force, increasingly prominent international activities of the KMT and DPP could draw forth a series of reactions that result in a major crisis. Leadership is the crucial variable here. Social change is so rapid that events with the potential to become as destabilizing as Tiananmen are virtually certain to occur. Skilled leadership can balance the tremendous tensions these changes imply, while incompetent leadership could well set off uncontrollable forces of nationalism resulting in illogical, undesirable, even devastating outcomes.

Political Crisis Leads to Military Crisis

This is less an independent scenario than an outcome of one of the first two scenarios taking a negative turn. Even then, the likelihood of a military crisis remains low, though not implausible. There are a number of possible ways in which a military crisis might evolve.

The PRC renews shelling of the offshore islands that was stopped in 1979. This would symbolize the threat of the use of force, perhaps without panicking the international system. It is an ideal method of testing the resolve of the United States. Would the U.S. bring the Seventh Fleet to bear?

- At the next level of escalation, the PRC declares a state of hostilities, begins massing military force across the Strait, and initiates intrusions into Taiwan's sea lanes and air space. Even without open conflict, the U.S. is forced into major political decisions due to the TRA, which in turn faces Japan, ASEAN, and Vietnam with choices that tend to preclude neutrality. No matter what the outcome, it would be almost impossible to return to the pre-crisis international status quo. The economic shockwaves would begin with panic on the Taiwan, Shanghai, Hong Kong, and possibly other regional stock exchanges. Real investment from Taiwan to the mainland halts along with most other offshore Chinese investment. All international trade and investment with both sides of the Strait pauses. Major businesses world wide with significant "Greater China" exposure would see immediate impacts on their stock prices, risk perceptions by creditors, order flow, shipping costs and, insurance premiums.

- The next step could be a PRC engineered incident, such as sinking a Taiwan vessel, or blocking commercial shipping bound for Taiwan on the high seas. The circumstances, of course, would be important. Sinking a naval vessel would send a more ambiguous signal than a noncombatant freighter. Analogously, warning commercial shipping away from an area of potential conflict is more ambiguous than declaring a blockade.

- Finally, of course, the crises could escalate into an open conflict with the declaration of a blockade or an attack across the Strait.

Such an escalation has low probability (lower at each step). But it is not implausible if the respective political elites fail to effectively manage their domestic political evolutions, and if the U.S. fails to make it unambiguously clear to China that use of force is totally unacceptable.

Improved Status Quo

The conference participants came to a broad consensus that a preferred and perhaps even the most likely scenario can be characterized as improved status quo. However, such an outcome will not occur without deliberate policy decisions on the part of the major players—third parties as well as both sides of the Strait. This scenario includes aspects of two other scenarios that were downplayed in the discussion as not independently viable—resolution through negotiation, and gradual alignment through international interaction.

Basic third party scenario elements include:

- The U.S., backed by other key states, make it clear to China that force is unacceptable.
- These same states also make it clear that, as long as the transition is peaceful, the issue of independence or unification is purely a Chinese decision.
- At the same time, these states demonstrate as desire for participation of both parties in those international activities where such participation has great practical value and can be organized without prejudice to the question of sovereignty.

Policies to implement these changes tend to put the U.S. in a pivotal role. The small changes released in the Clinton Administration's Taiwan policy review will be quickly, if without public fanfare, emulated by other major countries. As a result Taiwan will gain more of the substance of sovereignty (i.e., the ability to more openly conduct its international relations). Further, a firm U.S. commitment to peaceful resolution will be backed by others.

Basic cross-Strait scenario elements include:

- The respective political transitions on both sides of the Strait are competently managed, and extremely bad luck is avoided.
- Both side accept and adopt a longer term flexibility over the issue of sovereignty with the goal of conflict resolution.

Key policies to implement these changes tend to fall most strongly on Beijing, though important changes are required on both sides of the

Strait. There must be an informal collaboration among policymakers on both sides to contain extremists. Confrontational rhetoric must be toned down as both sides begin to demonstrate constructive cooperation to deal with issues of common interest and erode the conflict over sovereignty.

Certainly as the density of economic relations across the Strait rises, the mainland faces growing difficulty in asking other countries to avoid direct relations with Taiwan. Moreover, China needs to take the initiative and create an excuse for Taiwan to participate more in international organizations. This will include various opportunities as they continue to devolve more authority to the Provinces, and as areas of common interest can be identified and pursued, as explored in Gong's paper.

Conclusion

Paradoxically, there is both an increase in the fundamentals leading towards resolution of the conflict across the Taiwan Strait and in the risk of confrontation. This raises the premium on good policymaking and clarity of communication among the players. It also raises the importance of avoiding rigid positions and maximizing behind the scenes flexibility. Clearly constructive ambiguity must continue to be the guiding principle in cross-Strait policy and by third parties toward the cross-Strait relationship. Nonetheless, events on both sides have changed too much to maintain the status quo. Efforts to do so not only are likely to fail, but the outcomes could be destabilizing.

The participants in this conference outlined a series of possible actions, by Taiwan, the mainland, and third parties that could lay the foundation for an improved status quo that not only reduces the risks to stability, but could create the dynamics of a virtuous circle of political interaction across the Strait.

SECTION II
The Domestic Roots
of Policy Differences

CHAPTER 2
The Evolution of China's Policy Toward Taiwan

Lowell Dittmer,
University of California at Berkeley

It is hard to overestimate the importance of Taiwan and the issue of national reunification in post-Liberation Chinese foreign policy. Because the Nationalist government had previously gained legitimacy in international affairs for "China," its ability to stave off defeat by taking refuge on this small offshore island enabled it to continue to claim that status for the next two or three decades, thereby symbolizing an incomplete civil war, an incomplete revolution, an incomplete arrival in the comity of nations. Taiwan also represented a continuing ideological challenge to the regime, the more as the nationalists proceeded to establish and run a highly successful market economy. Because the United States interjected the 7th Fleet into the Taiwan Straits in the wake of the outbreak of the Korean War, the Taiwan question became inextricably connected to Sino-American relations, leading to a long period of isolation of Beijing and a difficult emergence. Because it was the Soviet threat to both countries that provided the pretext for them finally to finesse the issue of Taiwan and reach a preliminary accommodation, Taiwan became indirectly involved in China's Great Power diplomacy. Because it was the Third World that provided the first international recognition facilitating China's escape from ostracism, and because Taiwan has in more recent years pursued its comeback in international politics along similar lines, the

Third World also became embroiled. Finally, as in other nations split apart by the Cold War, Taiwan symbolizes a truncation of national identity, leading through the mechanism of prodigal kinship, grievance, envy, curiosity and occasional rage.[1]

China's Taiwan policy is also methodologically interesting in the sense that it provides an unchanging Archimedian point from which to view a blur of otherwise constantly changing policies. For there are several aspects of the policy that have been adhered to with amazing tenacity. First, both sides have clung to the goal itself; moreover, uniquely among divided nations, both sides have consistently insisted upon the indivisibility of sovereignty (though Taiwan has gradually begun to break free of this through "flexible diplomacy" in the past few years). One may say that the framework in which the goal has been pursued has remained constant as well, consisting on the one hand of the international dimension (who diplomatically recognizes and supports which side), and on the other of the bilateral, intranational dimension. Although the tactics have shifted periodically (see below), the repertoire has remained relatively constant, consisting of the use of violence on the one hand and stratagem on the other, one usually emphasized over the other but neither ever relinquished. There has even been considerable continuity in personnel: China's Taiwan policy has been formulated by the Central Leading Group on Taiwan Affairs, set up under the CCP Central Committee, a group of veteran cadres led in turn by Ye Jianying, Li Xiannian, Deng Yingchao, Yang Shangkun, and (currently) Jiang Zemin, with Foreign Minister Qian Qichen as deputy head. To preclude the possibility that Taiwan could respond on a state-to-state basis (and thus acquire national legitimacy), policies have however typically been announced via such "popular" assemblies as the National People's Congress or the Chinese People's Political Consultative Conference.[2] There have also been certain thematic continuities: the relentless contest for "face" is perhaps to be expected in view of the fact that indivisible sovereignty is what is at stake, but it seems rather odd in a system in which informal politics seems to prevail everywhere else to see hairsplitting attention to such nominal distinctions as that between "Taipei, China," and "Taipei, Chinese"[3]—and to behold such expressions of dismay when formal agreements are not rigorously adhered to. But of course there are variations as well, such as the waves from quiescence to crisis in the issue's priority, or the wide gaps in the schedule for its fulfillment.[4]

The evolution of China's Taiwan policy may be divided into three basic periods. The first, the period of "continuing revolution under the dictatorship of the proletariat," from 1950 to 1976, was one in which the main emphasis was on struggle, with a minor emphasis on "peaceful Liberation." The second period, from 1978 to the mid-1980s, was one of the most creative in China's Taiwan policy, when several conceptual innovations were introduced and elaborated with unprecedented detail and considerable plausibility; the major emphasis was on "peaceful reunification with the motherland," and the minor emphasis was on armed force. The third period, from the late 1980s to the present, is defined not by the introduction of major policy departures from the second but by the transformation of the international and domestic environment and by the development of a more active and effective counterpolicy by the government of Taiwan. We proceed to examine these periods in chronological sequence, dealing however with the first period only briefly.

The Period of Continuing Revolution

During the "Maoist" period the focus on continuing the revolution, and the threatening international environment, permitted only temporary interludes of diplomatic maneuver. Mao was a professional revolutionary with great faith in the historical dialectic who did not hesitate to fight for "principle," and in a letter written during the Cultural Revolution (to explain his alliance with Lin Biao) he said "This is the only time in my life that I made myself agree with another on a major matter of principle." Taiwan represented the class enemy with whom struggle was inevitable.[5] According to recently declassified CCP documents, Mao started preparing for an invasion of Taiwan to follow up the victories on the mainland even before the founding of the nation in October 1949. In June 1949 the CCP Central Military Commission ordered the Third Field Army and East China Bureau to establish a special organization to study the issue of "liberating Taiwan." Mao was alert to the need for air superiority,[6] and the Center authorized CCP vice-chairman Liu Shaoqi (visiting Moscow in July-August) to secure Soviet help in buying jets and establishing an air force. Mao seemed convinced by mid-1949 that U.S. intervention was unlikely, and although an attempt by Admiral Ye Fei to take Jinmen in October 1949 was repulsed with heavy losses, the CCP did succeed in taking Hainan Island in May 1950 and was a heavy favorite to take Taiwan in the summer of 1950 (American diplomats asked—and received— permission to evacuate family members). But of course the Korean War broke out on June 25, apparently because Kim Il Sung preempted the agreed schedule, and Truman promptly put the 7th Fleet in the Taiwan Straits.[7] The American presence was decisive in preventing an immediate resolution of the struggle, probably in Beijing's favor.

After the Korean War ended in July 1953 and the Geneva peace agreement on Indochina was signed in July 1954, Beijing again turned to the Taiwan issue. The peace conference had scarcely ended before Mao sent a telegram to Zhou Enlai in Geneva, criticizing him for not raising the issue of Taiwan in the peace talks. The PLA was mobilized, a railroad and airport built to facilitate travel to Fujian. On September 3, 1954 Beijing began bombarding the islands of Jinmen and Little Jinmen, precipitating the signing of a Mutual Defense Alliance between the U.S. and Taiwan on December 2. The offensive resulted in the capture of Yijianshan I, off the Zhejiang coast, as well as Dachen Island, whereafter American nuclear threats made clear no further progress could be achieved.

Beijing then shifted to a peace campaign. In April 1955, addressing the Afro-Asian Conference in Bandung, Zhou Enlai introduced the option of "peaceful liberation" (repeating the idea at an NPC Plenum in June 1956), and offered to discuss the matter with the U.S. It was at this time that China also made its first effort to escape diplomatic isolation by cultivating support within the Third World. The strategy was to split Taiwan from the U.S. by making plausible offers while also isolating Chiang Kai-shek within the KMT by appealing to other members of the old guard. Although Chiang rejected the offer, he was sufficiently interested to send a secret envoy (one Song Yi-shan, a former student) to Beijing in 1957 to explore the options; Song was in turn so favorably impressed by his talks with Zhou and other CCP officials (Zhou offered a "high degree of autonomy") that he was not permitted to return to Taiwan. But neither the Bandung spirit nor the Warsaw talks they initiated with the U.S. resulted in any progress on Taiwan, leading Beijing to flip-flop back to a military option.

There has been a good deal of controversy over Mao's intention in launching a second shelling of the offshore islands in August 1958. Gromyko's argument that Mao intended to initiate a major war with the U.S. that the Soviet Union could then finish with nuclear weapons is perhaps the most extreme of the range of interpretations suggested. Clearly the campaign—among the most ambitious of the 1950s, with air and sea battles and landing attempts—involved not only Taiwan but the two superpowers (e.g., Wang Bingnan claimed it constituted an indirect repudiation of Khrushchev's appeasement policies); it was most likely a probe, with a range of options depending on how circumstances unfolded. American nuclear threats (and Soviet refusal to reciprocate them very convincingly) brought the issue to a close in September, and the failure of the Great Leap Forward followed by the turmoil of the Cultural Revolution precluded another serious threat from the Chinese side. There was a serious threat of invasion from the Taiwan side in 1962, while the PRC was barely surviving the "three bad years," but Kennedy, still smarting from the Bay of Pigs (and under heavy pressure from Chinese diplomats in Warsaw, who had wind of KMT preparations) vetoed the gambit. Hostility and intermittent bombardment continued across the straits until the end of 1978, despite the relative improvement of Beijing's international status that followed the 1972 opening to the United States.

Reform and Reunification

The reform era was immediately preceded by a turning of the tables in the international arena. The situation began to shift to the Chinese advantage beginning with the famous Nixon opening to China, which opened the floodgates for recognition by a large group of countries who had previously been inhibited by American patronage of Taiwan. The diplomatic isolation of Taiwan began with its displacement by Beijing in the UN in October, 1971; Taiwan was consequently expelled from the WHO, ILO, IAEA, IMF, World Bank, IFC, IDA, and all UN specialized agencies. Before this time Taiwan had been officially recognized by more countries than the PRC. But between 1971-75, 53 countries switched recognition: 16 in 1971 (mostly Third World), 18 in 1972 (now including Germany, Australia, New Zealand), 2 in 1973, 8 in 1974, 9 in 1975, 3 in 1976. Taipei maintained official diplomatic relations with only about 20 countries, mostly small states with little political influence. One reason for this isolation was Taiwan's continued inflexibility—immediately before its expulsion from the UN the leadership rejected U.S. suggestions of two seats for two Chinas. But Beijing, too, insisted that severage of diplomatic ties with Taiwan was a precondition for formal relations with Beijing from the very outset.

The reform era was distinguished by Beijing's innovation of new, unprecendentedly magnanimous intranational proposals, coupled with a continuation of its successful drive to isolate and weaken Taiwan in the international arena. During the Maoist era, whenever "the east wind prevailed over the west wind" internationally, the regime would utilize its advantage by resorting to force bilaterally, as in 1958. But Mao died in 1976; Chiang Kai-shek predeceased him by one year. Under Deng, while the regime never relinquished its right to resort to force, in fact repeatedly making threats to use it or mobilizing troops in military exercises to ensure

31

that it did not lose its credibility[8] (as the superpowers' nuclear deterrent lost is credibility in the course of détente), the shelling of the offshore islands was unilaterally terminated in January 1979 and there has been no recurrence of inter-Strait violence.[9] This two-pronged strategy has been aimed at making Taiwan's independent existence uncomfortable, perilous, ultimately untenable while making its reunification with the mainland maximally attractive.

The first PRC peace initiative coincided with the focus on modernization as what Mao would have called the new "general line," beginning at the 3d Plenum of the 11th Central Committee in December 1978. Not only would a peaceful environment (including across the Straits) be useful for domestic modernization, the new domestic economic program proved quite compatible with the new Taiwan policy. With the adoption of market methods the ideological conflict would be blunted—the use of external trade and export policies already successfully used by the KMT (e.g., Export Processing Zones) enhanced the Taiwan regime's claim to have created a model Chinese province. The decentralization of economic planning corresponded to Beijing's promised financial autonomy for Taiwan after reunification. The modernization of the coastal provinces would raise living standards at least locally and hence reduce the difference in living standards between the Taiwan and China's "gold coast." The decision to postpone the modernization of the PLA until after a more general modernization of the Chinese economy reduced the threat to Taiwan.

The new Taiwan policy also coincided with normalization of relations with Washington, hitherto the most powerful obstacle to reunification: the communiqué of the 3rd Plenum stated that normalization of Sino-American relations "further places before us the prospect of the return of our sacred territor, Taiwan to the embrace of our motherland and the accomplishment of the great cause of *reunification.*" [N.B., the phrase "peaceful liberation of Taiwan" was officially dropped at the Plenum, along with "class struggle" and "mass movements."] Deng promised in a November 1978 interview with a foreign correspondent that "after a peaceful reunification of the country is achieved, Taiwan may still retain non-socialistic economic and social systems." The bombing of Jinmen [Quemoy] and Mazu [Matsu] was officially ceased on January 1, 1979, and on the same day (coinciding with official normalization of Sino-American relations) the Standing Committee of the National People's Council (NPC) issued "A Message to Compatriots in Taiwan." This message inaugurated the call for *santong siliu* (3 links & 4 exchanges):

the three links were direct postal, trade, and transportation; the four exchanges were of relatives and tourists, scientists, cultural groups and performances, and athletic teams. Later in the year the offer was made more generous, with assurances that Taiwan could retain its own local economic and political arrangements: now it was the "three upholdings, three links, and four exchanges." [three upholdings would be an unchanged social system, economic system, and local and provincial administration]. Although the message was in the realm of "people-to-people" diplomacy, addressed to Taiwan compatriots, it also suggested talks between the PRC government and the Taiwan authorities—presumably not the KMT but the government (this implication was later retracted).[10] Taiwan responded with its "three noes policy" [*san bu*]: no contact, no compromise, no negotiation.

But the Carter administration had proceeded with normalization talks in secret and unilaterally, emerging with a final settlement relatively favorable to Beijing, and when the results were unveiled in late December this triggered a backlash from Taiwan's supporters in the U.S. Congress. The result was the Taiwan Relations Act (TRA). The principal problem from Beijing's perspective was the fact that the U.S. was to continue providing military assistance to a state with which it had no formal relations. Also objectionable was the language containing a U.S. commitment "to resist any resort to force or other forms of coercion that would jeopardize the security, or social or economic system of the people on Taiwan." The act itself was incomprehensible from the PRC perspective: how could the agreements they had reached in good faith be altered by Congress? They asked State Department officials to "tell" Congress to vote in line with the joint agreement. On March 16, 1979, three days after the bill passed both houses of Congress, Foreign Minister Huang Hua informed U.S. ambassador Leonard Woodcock that the situation was "unacceptable to the Chinese government."

By 1980 Beijing had become increasingly vexed, as they saw the TRA give Taiwan more comprehensive protection than the 1954 Mutual Defense Alliance via the creation of a CCNAA (Coordination Council for North American Affairs) with virtual ambassadorial status, as they saw the U.S. sell Taiwan some $800 million worth of arms, as the Taiwan authorities continued to claim legal ownership of the former ROC embassy in Washington and other facilities. This reversal of what had initially seemed a diplomatic victory came in the context of accumulating difficulties for Deng's reform faction. By the December 1980 meeting of the Politburo the CCP was able to replace Hua with Hu as Party chair and Deng as CMC chair. The Deng group also succeeded in repudiating Hua's Maoist ideological platform at the 6th Plenum (June 27-29, 1981)) and formalizing this shift. But lingering fallout from the Vietnam incursion, lack of unanimity on dumping Hua and the election of his replacement (Ye Jianying withdrew to Guangzhou for a 6-month exile), the postponement (again) of the 12th CCP Congress, and deferring further economic reform until 1985 indicated that Deng disposed of only a bare majority. Economic growth, which the reformers had made their defining issue, was basically nil in 1981, and the media discussed a "crisis of faith" among the youth. Meanwhile Taiwan proceeded with elections to the National People's Congress, in which the KMT polled 82 percent of the vote against a legitimate nonpartisan opposition [*dangwai*], suggesting that even if only 20 countries recognized them the regime had domestic legitimacy. At the 12th Congress of the KMT (March-April 1981), the Chiang regime introduced its own plan for peaceful "reunification under the Three Principles of the People."

It was in this political context that the famous 9-point initiative was launched, which may be seen as both a pragmatic adaptation to strategic weakness and the first step in the counterattack. On September 30, 1981, one day before the 32nd National Day anniversary, Ye Jianying, in an "interview" with the NCNA, set forth Beijing's most systematic plan yet, already anticipated in early reports in the pro-Communist papers of Hong Kong. To review briefly: The first point proposed talks between CCP and KMT toward formation of a "third United Front," making possible talks without explicitly recognizing the sovereignty of either side. In the second point Beijing repeated its challenge to develop cross-channel trade. The third point proposed for the first time that Taiwan's future status would be that of a Special Administrative Region with a considerable degree of autonomy, including its own administrative personnel and military, with a "guarantee" that the central regime would not interfere in local affairs. (It is however implicit that Taiwan must give up sovereignty and recognize Beijing as the central authority.) The fourth point reiterates the "three upholds" with a guarantee of proprietary rights, the right of inheritance, unchanged social system, etc. Point five offers positions to Taiwan officials in PRC administration. Which positions is left unclear, but it leaves open the possible interpretation of a coalition government. (Hopes were further buoyed by Bo Yibo's statement shortly thereafter that Chiang Ching-kuo would receive a post "higher than a vice-premier's.") Point six, which offered help in Taiwan's possible financial difficulties, when the per capita income of Taiwan in 1980 was estimated to be at least nine times that of the PRC, indicated either that Beijing was out of touch or that this was aimed at the domestic audience. Point seven, which guarantees Taiwanese the right to travel or settle on the mainland without discrimination, is in effect an amnesty for internal opposition on the mainland (no corresponding right is mentioned for mainlanders to migrate to Taiwan). Point eight encouraged Taiwanese investment on the mainland—a tribute to Taiwan's industrial achievements. The final point emphasizes the honor that prompt realization of the sacred mission of reunification will bring to our ancestors, appealing not only to Chinese nationalism but ancestor worship, belief in destiny, and other myths. The note that reunification was "in the interest of peace in the far east and the world" subtly renewed the threat of force—refusal would not be in the interest of peace. This threat was reinforced by the holding of military maneuvers in the Taiwan Straits in the same month and by large PLA parades in Fuzhou.

Taipei rejected Beijing's offer promptly and firmly. But the PRC paid no attention and continued to propagandize the offer—they were aiming at another audience. Although mainly addressed to Taiwan, the document was also addressed to the U.S., and specifically to the TRA. Ye Jianying's claim that "the situation in the Taiwan Straits...has relaxed" was directly addressed to the paragraph of the TRA in which the administration adverts to the importance of stability in the region. Also the offer of "great autonomy" and the repetition of the "3 upholds" and the guarantee of retaining their own military forces corresponds to TRA demands (in Section 2(b), par. 6). The Reagan administration responded positively: Secretary of State Haig "expressed open approval...of Beijing's 9-point framework...seeming to stop just short of publicly advising Taiwan to change course and at least explore the proposal."[11] For the rest of the year Beijing continued to seize upon various symbols of national unity to champion a third united front. They celebrated the 70th anniversary of the Hsinhai revolution in high style, and the death of Song Qingling inaugurated a vast commemoration of her erstwhile husband Sun Yat-sen, celebrated in films, articles, displays, a renovation of his Najing mausoleum, culminating in the erection of a huge portrait (flanked in red flags) in Tiananmen Square. Chiang Ching-kuo and 13 other prominent personalities were invited to the funeral on May 29. In March the NPC Standing Committee decided to free interned KMT officers and officials, and more than four thousand were in fact released from prison.

Thanks to this successful propaganda campaign, by the fall of 1981, Beijing was in a favorable position to pressure Washington to cut arms sales from the TRA. In the first meeting between Reagan and Zhao Ziyang at Cancun, the former expressed his "understanding" of Chinese concerns in the light of Zhao's explanation of the 9 points. In December Liao gave an interview to *Sankei Shimbun* in which he tried to explain the discrepancy between Beijing's policy toward arms sales before and after reunification: "we will not send even a single man of the Chinese PLA into Taiwan...Taiwan can maintain its armed forces, police and even secret service organizations...The arms sales issues has nothing to do with Taiwan's maintenance of armed forces." Finally, in August 1982, the arms issue was resolved in the third of the "three communiqués" (1972, 1979, 1982) that have since defined the Sino-American relationship and determined the fate of Taiwan. In par. 5, this document referred to post-nine-points developments as a "new situation" that offered "favorable conditions to set aside differences...on the weapons sales issue" and emphasized that there was no intention to practice a "two Chinas" policy (thus putting to rest Reagan's electoral campaign rhetoric). But par. 6 was decisive, promising to reduce and eventually to end sales gradually over time as the situation permits. In par. 7 American weapons sales were called a "legacy of history" that "after a period of time will lead to a final solution." In the parallel interpreting comments the differences were etched more clearly: Reagan called the communiqué consistent with the TRA, Beijing said it was not; Reagan spoke of continuing arms sales, Chinese called for their early termination. The 17 August communiqué came as a great shock to Taiwan, who had considered Reagan a "friend."

The third major CCP conceptual innovation, the "one country, two systems" idea, was implicit in earlier proposals but now spelled out more fully as a solution not only to Taiwan but to Hong Kong and Macao. The major innovation was in formal recognition of the legitimacy of two "systems," which was to be sure implicit in the 1979 and 1981 offers, but assumed to be a "united front" tactic designed to assuage anxiety about communization. Deng himself coined the phrase in a meeting with a foreign friend in January 1982, when he said the 9 points "embodies the 'one country, two systems' principle." The full implications of the idea were elaborated at a closed conference of the CCP Central Committee on February 13, 1982, at which Hu Yaobang noted that since Hong Kong and Macao would be returning to China's jurisdiction soon, they should be embraced under the same schema as Taiwan. The integration of HK, Macao and Taiwan should by the year 2050 lead to an economic giant of international significance, "a more important commercial pole in Asia than Japan," according to Deng. Reunification thus becomes a step in the modernization of China.[12] Deng and others now used the phrase frequently, including Deng's meeting with Margaret Thatcher during her September 1982 visit to Beijing and in other meetings leading to the disposition of Hong Kong in the September 1984 Sino-British Joint Declaration. Deng told Thatcher in December 1984 that "the one country, two systems proposal did not begin with Hong Kong, but with the issue of Taiwan. Although the 9-point statement...was not called 'one country, two systems,' in fact, that was what it was."[13] Taiwan was also the source of the Special Administrative Region (SAR). There were painstaking attempts to give the proposal a firm constitutional foundation, enabling Beijing to claim that the existence of capitalism in the SARs was "guaranteed."[14]

The problem is that the Constitution also stipulates, especially in the preamble and in Articles 1, 5, and 6, that the political, economic, and legal systems are based on socialism and governed by the Four Cardinal Principles of the CCP. Also, unlike the Autonomous Regions such as Tibet (where the law of the Regions is to be enacted by the NPC), the relationship between the central government and the SARs is not stipulated in the Constitution. What about the Four Cardinal Principles? Deng has insisted that they are a nonnegotiable *sine qua non* without which "one country, two systems" proposal could not have been born, but they would not be applied in the SARs.[15]

Because the ideological implications of the "two systems" are agnostic—both systems are assumed to have a certain validity—Chinese theorists were invited to find a sound basis in Marxism-Leninism for this new doctrine. They argued that it reflected dialectical materialism, the theory of (nonantagonistic) contradiction, the unity of opposites (socialism being the principle aspect of the contradiction), Mao's dictum of seeking truth from facts, Lenin's NEP, China's Bandung diplomacy. Some Chinese scholars tried to elevate the concept into a new theory of the state—a state that is essentially unitary, but has some features of federalism.[16] Sovereignty is indivisible, but the sovereign government authorizes the existence of local units with the right to govern and rule areas with a different system, granting in fact more powers than under a federal system.

Deng continued to participate in the discussion, contributing for example a "6-point" policy on June 26, 1983, that elaborated on the 9 points. All of Deng's statements on the matter were summarized and presented systematically in an October 1984 article in *Liaowang Zhoukan* [outlook weekly].[17] From Deng's perspective, whereas Taiwan and Hong Kong could be treated with the same formula, since both were capitalist irridenta left by history, reunification with Taiwan would be simpler in legal terms because it was already defined as a domestic problem while Hong Kong was a foreign colony. But Taiwan was in the past more alienated from the mainland, more deeply divided by a history of civil war. So Taiwan would be more independent: its own armed forces, administrative personnel, even secret police. After reunification Taiwan could purchase arms from abroad, have independent legislative power provided it did not go against the Chinese constitution.[18] In 1983 Zhao added that "the mainland will not collect any tax or impose any levies of money on Taiwan...Taiwan may also develop its trade relations, exchanges and cooperation with foreign countries in economics, technology and culture." But Taiwan would not be completely autonomous, Deng noted in a conversation with Winston Yang of Seton Hall University in June 1983. Taiwan would be a local government under a unitary system, not a federal, not to mention a confederal system. Only Beijing could represent China in foreign affairs.[19] Taiwan's armed forces could "not constitute a threat to the mainland." Coexistence of two systems does not mean parity: socialism on the mainland would be dominant and capitalism would be a transitional, subsidiary system used to complement the development of socialism. The two systems would coexist only for a limited transition period—50 years for Hong Kong, 100 years for Taiwan (according to the Yang interview). The goal is not some sort of convergence of socialism and capitalism, but the assimilation of capitalism by socialism. It would seem that the limits of autonomy are defined by the limits to the CCP's ideological self-confidence: "Without the dominance of socialism, capitalism will gobble up socialism."[20] This concern about the survival of socialism leads to an emphasis on the subsidiary, supplemental roles of Taiwan, Hong Kong, and Macao.

With the introduction of "one country, two systems," Beijing's spate of policy innovation seems to have drawn to a close. There has been very little change in PRC Taiwan policy between the 9 points and 6 points in 1981 and 1983 and what was contained in Jiang Zemin's political report to the 14th CCP Congress in October 1992. One recent ideological innovation is the "primary stage of socialism," which does not represent a change in Taiwan policy but rather a change in reform policy bringing it into line with Taiwan policy. Although the idea was mentioned as early as the 6th Plenum of the 11 Central Committee and again at the 12th CCP Congress, it was only at the 13th Congress (November 1987) that Zhao Ziyang fully expounded it. Zhao explained that China was at the beginning of the socialist road and it would be at least 100 years (from the 1950s) before socialist modernization would be achieved. In the meantime, China must emphasize reform, opening, public ownership playing the dominant role, private property a minor role. This new theory enhances the acceptability of SARs where capitalism is practiced under autonomous conditions.

Taiwan Policy in the New World Order

The international system is currently undergoing its most basic transformation since the end of the last World War half a century ago. But although it is clear that the old, bipolar system is coming to an end, the nature of the New World Order emerging to take its place is not yet entirely clear. The Asian Pacific region seems to have been marked by more continuity than the international system as a whole. Although the popular upheavals that were to dismember the Communist world began in China, the Tiananmen demonstrations met with a firm "No" from the generation of revolutionary veterans that still clings to the reins in Beijing. Thus, Communism survived here, as in North Korea and Indochina. Yet, ideology does not cleave the Asian region as sharply as the European Iron Curtain, thanks to China's lurch Westward in the early 1970s. Instead of facing an ideological monolith, the United States confronted the Soviet nemesis with the equivocal assistance of the other major Communist power, which permitted monitoring stations on its territory, contested Soviet expansionism in South and Southeast Asia, and seemed bent on assimilating capitalism to its still vigorous economy. The Asian political geometry was "triangular" rather than bipolar, providing a wider range of diplomatic options not only for the great but for the smaller powers.

Although the onset of change in Asia has been less dramatic than in the West it has also been quite profound. The collapse of the Soviet threat meant that China's value as a triangular "card" became much less vital to Western defense strategy, and this in turn meant that Taiwan's leverage in its own triangular relationship with Washington and Beijing increased. The Tiananmen massacre made clear to the West that any evolution toward bourgeois democracy was firmly opposed by China's leadership, who took ideology far more seriously than many imagined. At the same time, economic reform experienced only a brief and temporary hiatus (1989-91), as China resurged in an impressive display of East Asian hypergrowth, becoming the world's second leading recipient (after the United States) of foreign direct investment. The decline of ideology gave rise to economics in command, for which China's brand of socialist reform proved reasonably well adapted, with the proliferation of corruption being perhaps only an overreaction to unwonted economic opportunity.

As far as Taiwan policy is concerned, Beijing launched no new initiatives but endeavored to implement the old ones amid major changes in domestic and international environments. China's Taiwan policy may be divided into international and intranational dimensions, which we review in sequence.

Internationally, China has continued to pursue the isolation of Taiwan with relentless determination. By 1988, Taiwan had lost recognition from 55 countries, 80 percent of its previous total, while establishing new diplomatic relations with only 9 countries. By June 1992, Taiwan managed to increase its list to 31, but countries such as Niger, Vanuatu and Grenada were poor and small, and in August South Korea broke relations, leaving South Africa as the only country of international importance having relations with Taiwan. Taiwan had (by 1988) retained its seat in only 8 international government organizations, the most important of which was the Asian Development Bank (where they were forced to adopt the name "Taipei, China," the exact parallel of the "Hong Kong, China" colonial formula. In its attempt at diplomatic comeback, the Lee Deng-hui regime, adopting an idea first proposed by the DPP several years ago, attempted in 1993 to enter the United Nations under the "one nation, two governments" formula first used by the two Germanys and two Koreas. But Beijing repudiated the idea in its August 1993 *White Paper*, "The Taiwan Question and the Reunification of China," even arguing "in principle" against Taiwan's inclusion in any international governmental or nongovernmental organizations. And Beijing has thus far prevailed, despite the Taiwan regime's adroit use of "flexible diplomacy," "dollar diplomacy" and "vacation diplomacy" to try to short-circuit Beijing's objections. China's growth surge following Deng's 1992 voyage south carried the PRC for the first time beyond Taiwan in total trade volume, and despite the latter's huge trade surplus and currency reserves few were willing to risk Beijing's diplomatic reprisals by recognizing Taipei. Nevertheless, the activity of the Taipei government in pursuit of a more secure place in the international system has accelerated indefatigably, now largely driven by domestic electoral politics.

Beyond isolation, Beijing has tried to render Taiwan helpless as well as interdicting arms sales. This was achieved (on paper) with the August 17 communiqué in Sino-American relations. In 1981, Beijing downgraded diplomatic relations and ordered the Hague to recall its ambassador for selling to submarines to Taiwan; only after Holland rejected Taipei's request for four more subs did the PRC agree to restore official relations.[21] In May 1991, the mainland protested Belgium's sale of aircraft and rocket parts to Taiwan. France's attempt to sell frigates has long been frustrated. Yet, the United States and France both sold advanced fighters to Taiwan in 1992, and though Beijing cracked down on Paris, it hesitated to move against Washington. Many Taiwanese claim that the relentless pressure to reunite or disappear from the diplomatic map may force the country to proclaim its independence, while Beijing avers the opposite—only the threat of force deters independence.[22] Taiwan has meanwhile been building its own defense industry. In the late 1980s, over 30 percent of the Taiwan government's budget went for defense, despite a cutback in the number of members of the armed forces from 600,000 in the early 1950s to 400,000 by 1989. Hau Pei-ts'un in May 1988 announced that Taiwan could withstand an attempted mainland invasion—Taiwan's very smallness meant that China's numerical advantages could not be brought into play, but would have to attack in waves. Outside military analysts seem to believe that invasion would be successful, but too costly to realistically contemplate, while a blockade (also frequently threatened) would be a more feasible option.[23] The reaction of the U.S., still legally bound by the TRA, cannot be predicted in that event.

But the most dynamic developments have been in the intranational arena, which has seen real movement toward a "Greater China." Here there is good news and less good news. The good news is that the initiatives of the early 1980s have paid off big for Beijing, as its offer of *santong siliu* ended up being completely accepted by the Taiwanese, at first cautiously and under constraints but with constantly growing momentum. An economic and to a somewhat lesser degree cultural and social interdependency has developed between Taiwan and southern China, and although the Taiwan government has taken various steps to insulate itself from the political repercussions—such as allowing only indirect contact, via Hong Kong, and by erecting "nongovernmental" agencies to mediate developments—it has also made concession after concession in response to popular demand. By July 1985 the Taiwan government was obliged to shift to a new "three noes": no contact, no encouragement, and no interference. In November 1987 Taiwan lifted its ban on travel to the mainland, and by 1993 about a million Taiwan residents were visiting the mainland each year. By the same year, bilateral trade had soared to $14.39 billion (estimates are only approximate, but Taiwan figures underestimate the amount of capital involved), making Taiwan China's 4th largest trade partner while China became Taiwan's 5th largest. Investment started in earnest in 1988 and by the end of 1993 Taiwan businessmen were running ca. 10,000 enterprises on the mainland with a contract value of some US $10 billion, making Taiwan the 2nd largest source of foreign investment after Hong Kong. Medium and small entrepreneurs were the pioneers; when early ventures turned out to be profitable, large companies plunged in, particularly in late 1991 and early 1992, when a new wave of economic reform in Beijing opened the door wider. The first investments were very short-term and labor-intensive, but later became more capital and technology intensive, also spreading from Fujian and Guangdong to interior regions as wages were bid up along the coast.

This interdependency has been mutually profitable, bringing together the capital surplus and managerial and technological skills of Taiwan with cheap and abundant mainland labor and resource markets. In Taiwan there has been concern about a "hollowing out" effect as capital forsakes the domestic economy, which the government has tried to remedy by permitting only relatively labor-intensive and low-tech investments abroad. But in economic terms the investments have been highly profitable from the Taiwanese perspective, resulting in a very large trade surplus and permitting Taiwan to reduce its trade surplus with the U.S. by exporting it to the mainland. The suspicion has been that these exceptionally favorable terms[24] will have a political price, but it is hard to see how Beijing can make political capital of these assets without damage to its own economy. While the perhaps politically inspired favorable terms of investment have contributed to the headlong momentum of economic synergy, they have also given rise to a certain suspended paranoia among business people, a sense that once the process is consummated the holiday may be over—better to remain perennial girlfriend than bride.

Beijing's initiative has also been successful in producing some of the institutional "spillover" effects predicted by Deutsch and Haas in their studies of Western European integration: Taiwan established the Straits Exchange Foundation (SEF) in 1991 under Koo Chen-fu, and the following year Beijing followed with ARATS (Association for Relations Across the Taiwan Straits, headed by Wang Daohan). High level talks between Wang and Koo were held in April 1993, reaching a number of agreements concerning document verification and registered post. Taiwan also pressed the mainland on legislation to protect Taiwan investors' interests on the mainland, and by the beginning of 1994 the NPC passed a law with the express purpose of protecting Taiwanese investment on the mainland. Beijing also pressed for extradition of hijackers, leading to a complicated dispute about legal sovereignty before both sides were finally able to agree to extradition "in principle" in January 1994. Thus practical problems have been driving both sides to cooperate on a widening range of issue areas. With this cooperation has come as well a sense of shared interests on a widening range of issues—Taiwan was not among the most vocal critics of the Tiananmen crackdown, nor of Chinese claims vis-à-vis Tibet or the Spratleys; it has quietly supported China's MFN status (in which it has a stake), the Beijing Olympic bid, and so forth.

The less good news is in the modality of the Hong Kong retrocession. The Hong Kong precedent is for Taiwan purely analogous, but it is not a misplaced analogy, for the Chinese made plain from the outset that Taiwan could expect like treatment. During the Sino-British negotiations on Hong Kong, China's commentators were at pains to point out the parallels for Taiwan—Taiwan's economic troubles in the mid-1980s were blamed on its diplomatic isolation and uncertain future, from which Hong Kong would be spared! Since the Sino-British Joint Declaration was signed in December 1984, the NPC established a rather elaborate apparatus for the formulation of a Basic law, which it finally approved after much consultation and revision in April 1990.[25] Local reception of the Basic Law, which added an antisubversion clause (Art. 23) and decreed that only about a third of the Hong Kong SAR's legislature would be chosen by direct elections in 1997, suggests that certainty is not necessarily an antidote to uncertainty. Since that time, preparations for the transition cannot be considered smooth. On the one had, it must be said that the economy has continued to perform very well, despite rising brain drain and an unknown amount of capital flight, as Hong Kong has become every more fully integrated into Guangdong province, shifting its manufacturing base northward (30 percent of Hong Kong's currency is circulating in China) while undergoing an economic transition to management, commerce, and financial services. On the other, Beijing has made clear its aversion to democratic elections and given ample reason to doubt that Hong Kong will have a considerable degree of autonomy, interfering constantly for example not only in Patten's quite modest reform proposals but in the arrangements for construction of a new airport. The argument they have used for such interference at a time when Britain was promised they would continue to have exclusive political jurisdiction is that developments in Hong Kong must converge with the Basic Law, displaying a CCP obsession with the "path" analogy that goes back to historical materialism, the proletarian and capitalist roads, and so forth: in view of the facts that "one country, two systems" is only transitional one may wonder whether capitalism will also be regulated to converge with its eventual socialist destination. Of course, the timing for retrocession has not been ideal, as Tiananmen evoked both great anxiety in Hong Kong and an obsession with populist "chaos" in China, and Beijing has been locked in a pre-mortem succession crisis that seems to have impeded political flexibility. Moreover, Taiwan has been promised that it would be spared some of Hong Kong's concerns, such as a local PLA base or integration of its police force with that of the mainland.

Conclusions

China's Taiwan policy, maintained with essential fidelity since the founding of the PRC, has been on the whole quite successful. There has been a certain merging of views. Both now support peaceful reunification (albeit with qualifications on PRC side). Both sides are willing to negotiate at an unofficial level, though democratization in Taiwan has outdated talk of party-to-party negotiations or some sort of bipartisan coalition government. They do of course continue to differ on the status of the government in Taipei. Taipei claims it is an independent entity, a legitimate government ruling Taiwan and the neighboring islands. Beijing insists it is a province under jurisdiction of Beijing, albeit with considerable autonomy. This has consistently hampered contact: Taiwan insists on recognition as an equal, which Beijing refuses. In their bilateral relations they have been able to finesse this through the creation of "nongovernmental" proxies. But in the international arena, the difference cannot be fudged. Since Beijing took over Taipei's UN seat in 1971, Taiwan has suffered one blow after another.

The "three links and four exchanges" Beijing introduced at the outset of its reform era seem to have been the most successful tactical innovation in China's Taiwan policy since Liberation, launching a self-reinforcing juggernaut toward economic integration. There are three logically conceivable political implications of this centrifugal dynamic. The first is null: no political implications at all (i.e., economic integration continues without loss of political autonomy); second, economically determinist: politics follow economics (i.e., economic integration leads to political integration, eventuating in "Greater China"); and third, contrarian: political implications compensate for the dominant economic trend rather than complementing it (i.e., economic integration precipitates political resistance). The "null" possibility is the one that Beijing has chosen to stress in its "one country, two systems" propaganda. But if Hong Kong is a valid test case, it does not seem realistic. Since the approval of the Sino-British Joint Declaration, two countervailing political reactions have emerged: on the one hand, a democratizing trend, whose thrust has been to reinforce autonomy; and on the other, Beijing's response, whose thrust has been to constrain democracy and reassert its authority. Political realities indicate that the latter is fated to prevail in 1997 (though Beijing may have to pay an economic price). In Taiwan, there has been some indication that the "contrarian" possibility might come into play, but at this point the likelihood of this (i.e., DPP electoral victory) does not seem high, due both to limited domestic appeal and the bleak international outlook for this option. Thus economic determinism seems plausible there as well. Should a centripetal backlash occur, however, it could derail the locomotive of political integration. This might happen for any number of reasons—succession "turmoil" in China, a "blackmail" attempt by Chinese political authorities, even a less rational "last gasp" resistance to the final relinquishment of sovereignty similar to what we have seen in Europe since Maastricht. Taiwan would put the brakes on and resistance might even erupt in Hong Kong, despite the irreversibility of formal retrocession. Two distinct political entities might then continue to coexist for an indefinite time span, cooperating on some economic issues but continuing to disagree on the issues of national sovereignty and security. Taiwan's sovereignty could in that case be expected to continue to diminish, as it continues to lose the struggle for diplomatic recognition or representation in international and regional forums. As China's market grows its economic magnetism seems likely to outdraw that of Taiwan. The bottom line is that however humiliating Beijing's diplomatic stranglehold, it has not had any perceptible material impact on a country that has retained functional economic relations with nearly as many countries (around 150) as formerly recognized it. And as economic integration between the two sides increases the prospect of hostilities or blockade would logically also decline.

Barring an explosive event that would derail the economic integration train, it might still not reach its destination, simply because the passengers decide they like the ride too much to risk getting off the train. There are reasons for Taiwan to think courtship might be preferable to marriage (to mix metaphors). There are certain telltale signs: In the international arena Beijing plays hardball, reducing Taiwan to a diplomatic nonentity, but this also tends to discredit Beijing's promise of a certain degree of Taiwanese autonomy in foreign affairs. There is also a certain incongruence between the promise of complete autonomy and noninterference after reunification and Beijing's adamant insistence on the right to use military force against Taiwan before then. Or between

Taiwan's right to buy weaponry after reunification and Beijing's attempt to cut Taiwan out of the arms market before that time. Thus Taiwan will no doubt follow the fate of Hong Kong, whose treatment has already deteriorated since its betrothal, very closely.

There is reason to believe that there are political actors in Beijing who are aware of the discrepancies in their Taiwan policy and interested in putting together a more appealing package.[26] The CCP leadership has been in a delicate phase of its succession crisis when new initiatives are temporarily unlikely, but it is not hard to imagine that they will be forthcoming once succession has been negotiated. If Beijing drops its military option, stops trying to isolate Taiwan diplomatically (under, say, a "one country, two governments" formula) and offers convincing guarantees of Taiwan's future security, they would have a very cogent package. If Beijing were officially to renounce the threat of military force, that would place great pressure on the Taipei, who would lose its strongest argument for continued American arms sales and TRA security guarantees, and international (and American) sympathy for Peking's intentions would increase. Taiwan would find it more difficult to defend its somewhat contradictory stance (continued independence without claiming independence) internationally or its heavy arms spending domestically.

CHAPTER 3
Democratization in Taiwan and its Impact on the Relationship to the Mainland

Michael Ying-mao Kau,
Brown University and 21st Century Foundation

On August 3, 1994, Tang Shubei, vice chairman of China's Association for Relations Across the Taiwan Strait (ARATS), arrived in Taipei for the fifth round of negotiations on functional matters related to interactions between Taiwan and China mainland with his counterpart Chiao Jen-ho, vice chairman of Taiwan's Straits Exchange Foundation (SEF). While the two negotiating delegations kept a low profile with courteous and correct posture, Taiwan's mass media bombarded Tang with political admonitions that Beijing should be more pragmatic and realistic by accepting Taiwan as an equal "political entity" in the world arena and committing to the policy of "peaceful coexistence" between the two sides (*Chung-kuo shih-pao*, July-August, 1994).

Small forces of demonstration, representing the interests of the mainlanders and the China New Party (CNP), took the occasion to express their enthusiastic support for the negotiations and the prospect of future unification. However, the main opposition party, the Democratic Progressive Party (DPP), was straightforward and forceful in expressing its dissent. The DPP's "welcome party" met Tang and his delegation at the Chiang Kai-shek International Airport in Taoyuan shouting anti-China slogans such as "Taiwan belongs to the Taiwanese" and "China, get out!" Violent confrontations were avoided only through police intervention and well-planned tactical management of the event by the hosting SEF (*Lien-ho pao*, August 2-10, 1994; *T'ai-wan Kung-lun pao*, August 3-9, 1994).

This latest incident, which was extensively covered by the mass media, vividly reflects the ongoing drama of Taiwan's democratization process and its impact on the island's delicate relationship with the mainland.

For over four decades, sensitive political issues such as "Taiwan Independence" and the demand for political democratization were effectively silenced in Taiwan under the authoritarian rule of the Kuomingtang (KMT). Public challenges to the doctrine of "one China" or the KMT's absolute rule carried a high risk of arrest, imprisonment, or even death (Tien 1989, 4-12).

Today, however, Taiwan has emerged as a dynamic and assertive civil society. All issues, including the most sensitive political matters that were traditionally treated as "sacred taboos" are now openly debated before the public and aired freely in the media. Government conduct and adoption of public policy are rigorously scrutinized by the legislature and by public opinion (Simon and Kau 1992, 3-42).

This paper will first examine, from a macroscopic perspective, the model of authoritarianism established in the 1950's by the KMT in Taiwan as well as the pattern and stages of its ensuing development. It will then analyze how the process of democratization affected the structural erosion of the KMT and touched off the process of "Taiwanization" in the island's political system. Finally, the paper will assess the impact of Taiwan's internal political change on the evolving relationship between the Republic of China (ROC) on Taiwan and the People's Republic of China (PRC) on the mainland. It should be noted that this paper is not intended to be a detailed analysis of the historical process. Rather, it will focus specifically on the major characteristics of the structure and process of politics at various stages of Taiwan's political development and assess how the island's changing patterns of politics affected Taiwan's interactions with the mainland.

The KMT Model of Authoritarian Rule in Taiwan

Soon after the KMT retreated to Taiwan in 1949, Chiang Kai-shek began to reorganize his one million political followers and military forces into an efficient political machine creating a corporatist state based on a close alliance of party, government, and military (*tang-cheng-chün*). Patterning itself after the Leninist Communist system, the KMT functioned as the core of the body politic and penetrated systematically into every sector of society (Clough 1978; and Tien 1989).

Within the government, power was concentrated strictly in the hands of the executive branch. The legislature was reduced to a rubber-stamping "legislative bureau" of the executive branch of government. Judicial independence and the due process of law existed only in name and not in practice.

The adoption of "Temporary Provisions during the Period of Mobilization for Suppressing the Communist Rebellion" by the National Assembly in 1948 practically placed the nation under "emergency rule." The Temporary Provisions provided the "legal basis" for suspending normal constitutional governing processes and citizens' civil and political rights. With the imposition of the infamous "three controls"—martial law, a ban on the formation of opposition parties, and tight restrictions on the freedom of the press—in the name of national emergency, the state had a free hand to do practically anything it saw fit over society. The state's unrestrained power was further reinforced by the party's absolute control over military and police forces (Simon and Kau 1992).

Under the pervasive corporatist system of KMT leadership, elite recruitment amounted to a straightforward top-down process of political cooptation and hierarchical control. Even though limited local elections were instituted early on in the 1950s, candidates were always carefully screened for political loyalty, and elections were skillfully "supervised" to ensure a KMT majority. Hence, the Party managed to develop a perfect model of a patron-client network among political appointees and elected representatives at all levels.

Signs of political opposition or dissident movements were invariably treated with harsh measures of intimidation or imprisonment known as "white terror." The systematic elimination of indigenous political leaders during and after the 228 incident of 1947, the political persecution of Lei Cheng, publisher of the *Free China* magazine, in 1960, and the imprisonment of Professor Peng Min-Ming, chairman of the Political Science Department at Taiwan University, in 1965, typified the widespread practice of political oppression. It is clear that the KMT model of authoritarianism was built not only with positive incentives for its supporters provided by the patron-client relationship, but the system also was fortified with the negative sanction of political coercion against its potential adversaries (Tien 1989).

The KMT model of authoritarian control extended beyond the core of the political system. The Party apparatus also penetrated into labor unions, farmers' associations, student and youth organizations (through the China Youth Corps in all high schools and universities), professional organizations, state enterprises, and the business community. Party cells were established in all social groups at all levels. Under such an omnipresent network of Party control organized along functional and geographic lines, there was no room for the development of subsystem autonomy and activism of civil society.

In the economic realm, the state carried out its regimentation through regulatory control. As has been pointed out frequently by the political economist, an authoritarian government often exercises control of the economy through such methods as state licensing, foreign currency allocation, tariff regulation, and public work contracting. Taiwan's authoritarianism was no exception. The Party was able to bring the business community and private sector in line with Party policy and political command through judicial use of economic reward and punishment. In addition, the government also maintained an enormous sector of state and party enterprises that was used systematically by the government to enforce its industrial policy and political discipline (Gold 1986; and Wu 1987).

In the 1950s the unique historical circumstances arising from the Japanese withdrawal from Taiwan in 1945 and the transfer of control of the island to the ROC government gave the KMT a rare opportunity to superimpose its authoritarian rule. When the Japanese colonial elites withdrew from all sectors of Taiwanese society at the end of World War II, the nascent local leaders and social forces were simply too young and too weak to compete against the KMT takeover forces. The political vacuum was quickly filled by the occupying KMT elites who moved in with powerful military forces. Practically all top positions in the corporatist structure of the party-government-military pyramid were filled by mainlander officials who came with Chiang Kai-shek. Hence, the ethnic homogeneity and solidarity of the ruling elite also made the KMT power structure even more invincible (Tien 1989).

From Predatory Authoritarianism to Developmental Authoritarianism

KMT authoritarianism in the 1950s was often characterized as "predatory authoritarianism," mainly because the Party was so preoccupied with regaining control of the mainland that Taiwan was treated simply as a stepping stone for recuperating its strength to return to the mainland. The welfare and development of Taiwan for its own sake was not the primary concern of the Party's long-term political strategy (Cheng 1989; and Cheng and Haggard 1992).

In the 1960s, however, emerging new circumstances forced the leadership to reexamine its basic mainland-oriented strategy. As Communists on the mainland further consolidated their position, refusing to disappear as a "passing phenomenon," the KMT had to rethink its sojourn on Taiwan as a matter of long-term survival. The Quemoy Crisis of 1958 forced the KMT to squarely face the difficult reality of long-term survival on Taiwan versus the short-term dream of counterattacking to retake the mainland. Hence, the concept of economic development began to carry increasing weight and moved into the center of the KMT's political game plan.

There was a new realization that economic development was critical not only for support of military buildup but also for improving the living standard of the people in order to enhance the legitimacy and popularity of the Party and state. Moreover, by allotting certain arenas for the private sector and business community to engage in industry and commerce, the state under KMT tutelage would be able to achieve an unique division of labor between a government specializing in political control and a private sector devoted to economic matters (Cheng and Haggard 1992; and Wu 1987).

To the ruling elite, the new game plan clearly made a lot of political and economic sense, especially at the initial stage of economic development. The success of its implementation, however, produced many unforeseen and unintended consequences which eventually complicated the KMT's monopolistic control.

Schematically speaking, in order to make economic plans and industrial policy work and to push for an effective execution of economic development, the government would have to enhance the role of planners, technocrats, and entrepreneurs, and concede to them a higher degree of professional autonomy and independence based on their professionalism and expertise. Such a trend ultimately strengthened the hand of the professionals and technocrats and eroded the monopolistic comman of the power holders and party functionaries. In short, economic progress gradually increased the power and influence of the new social and professional groups in the political arena (Shiau 1994).

In this respect, modernization theory that emphasizes the functional linkage between economic development and political liberalization is quite on the mark. The Taiwan experience strongly verifies its validity. There is indeed a dialectical relationship in the interaction between political development and economic modernization. The rise of socioeconomic pluralism, as concomitants of Taiwan's "economic miracle," provided some of the most critical ingredients for the ensuing phase of the island's political liberalization and democratization (Cheng and Haggar 1992; and Aberbach, Dollar and Sokoloff 1994).

From Developmental Authoritarianism to Competitive Democracy: The Structural Transformation of Taiwan Politics.

The period between 1986 and 1988 constituted a critical watershed in Taiwan's political transformation. Several landmark events are worth noting. In September 1986, opposition forces formally established the DPP in explicit defiance of existing law and KMT policy. In the summer of 1987, the government formally lifted martial law, control of the press, and the ban on contacts and trade with the mainland. In January 1988, Chiang Ching-kuo died of a heart attack. The departure of the strong man, who controlled Taiwan politics single-handedly for over a decade between 1975 and 1988, symbolized the end of the era of KMT political monopoly. A native-born Taiwanese, Lee Teng-hui, managed to succeed Chiang Ching-kuo as president of the Republic and chairman of the Party after a brief power struggle within the Party, and the gate of political reform was swung wide open (Kau 1989; and Simon and Kau 1992).

The jury is still out on the causes of, as well as the credit for, the critical political developments during the period of 1986-88. Were they due to Chiang Ching-kuo's vision and initiative for political reform? Or did they represent the fruits of the arduous struggles by opposition forces? What is of particular significance for the purpose of this analysis is that the critical developments did take place, and Taiwan was ushered into a new era of political democratization. Three major aspects of Taiwan's political transformation since the mid-1980s deserve special attention.

I. The Structural Erosion of the KMT Corporatist Party State

Before the 1980s, as discussed earlier, the KMT was able to maintain a highly efficient political machine based on a massive Leninist organizational network in the political arena and skillful management of patron-client politics in the economic sphere. The structural and functional integration of the state, the military, the economy, and society under the centralized command of the Party was further reinforced by the imposition of the "three controls." The model of authoritarian rule as designed and developed by the KMT was almost a perfect one.

After four decades of continuous authoritarian rule, however, the Party also accumulated problems and baggage: self-complacency, corruption, abuse of power, and arrogance all set in and spread. As in most authoritarian systems, there were no institutionalized mechanisms of self-cleansing and reform in effect. Within the system, power corrupted; personal gain and bureaucratic politics replaced the call of ideolology and political causes. It is revealing to note that by the late 1980s, even though the Party claimed to have an enormous membership of more than 2.5 million, the Party invariably failed to demonstrate its commensurate strength at times of elections and political mobilization (Tien 1989).

The process of economic development also complicated the KMT's monopoly of power. The ascendance of the wealthy and assertive middle class and other autonomous social groups, for instance, confused the established electoral system based on Party patronage. When elected officials and representatives could succeed in the political arena without depending exclusively on the Party's resources and support, they began to gain their own autonomy. By the 1990s, many elected leaders of the KMT dared to declare publicly that when orders of the Party clashed with the wishes of their constituents, they would have no hesitation to side with the voters (Huang Teh-fu 1994).

Within the structure of the government, the institutional shift of power and leadership was even more conspicuous. The mandatory retirement in 1990 of "senior representatives" of the national parliamentary bodies and the elections of all members of the Second National Assembly and the Second Legislative Yuan solely from Taiwan in 1991 and 1992, respectively, made these parliamentary organs the new center of power and legislation. Asserting their constitutional power over appointment of high officials, the national budget, and legislative bills, they demanded their autonomy from strict Party control. The momentum of constitutional reform and democratization also raised objections to the Party's penetration into and interference with government operations. Under the principle of "administrative neutrality," the KMT was asked to withdraw from the government bureaucracy, the armed forces, the judicial system, and educational institutions (Huang Teh-fu 1994).

Within the Party, the emergence of power struggles, factional disputes, and political fragmentation also contributed greatly to the decline of the KMT's authoritarian control. Suffice it to point out that following the death of Chiang Ching-kuo, the troubles of power struggle and political succession surfaced quickly. Liberal and reform-minded leaders, especially among the elite of Taiwanese origin, rallied to support President Lee Teng-hui, while the conservative old guards of mainlander origin formed coalitions first around Premier Li Huan and later around Premier Hao Po-tsun. These two broad power constellations were generally referred to as the "mainstream" and the "non-mainstream" faction, respectively (Tien 1994).

The power struggles from 1988 through 1993 represented more than just personality contests. They were intimately connected with the fundamental issues of the redistribution of power and the future direction of Taiwan's political development in the post-authoritarian era. At the forefront of the power struggles, the dispute involved the method, process, and criteria for selecting the Party chairman and vice chairman, as well as the premier and cabinet members of the Executive Yuan. On the policy side, the leaders were bitterly divided over such crucial issues as constitutional reform, Party restructuring, and mainland policy (Feldman 1991).

On the eve of the 14th Party Congress in August, 1993, the KMT leadership was so divided that six legislators and some old guards formally left the Party to form a separate party known as the China New Party (CNP). They publicly criticized the mainstream faction's "undemocratic" leadership style and its "traitorous" mainland policy. Although many mainlander leaders chose to stay with the KMT establishment, they formed anti-mainstream groups, such as the New Revolutionary Alliance (*Hsin-t'ung-meng-hui*), to continue their factional struggles from within (Hsia and Zeldin 1994).

In the parliamentary bodies at all levels, a wide variety of political factions or coalitions, known as "subgroups" (*tz'u-chi t'uan-t'i*), also mushroomed within the KMT (see Table 1). Some were based on personality and leadership factors; others were organized for shared political interests, policy alliances, and/or money politics. In the Legislative Yuan in recent years, for example, roughly a dozen or so such competing "subgroups" have emerged; they all tried to claim some degrees of political autonomy from the central leadership (Huang Teh-fu 1994).

The growing trend of factionalism and fragmentation naturally further corroded the Party's discipline and solidarity under a centralized leadership. On several critical occasions, the minority DPP was able to exert its leadership on such major issues as the Civic Organizations Law, the Sunshine Law, the Health Insurance Program and the National Pension Program and even outvote the majority KMT at the Legislative Yuan. Obviously, the KMT's disunity and fragmentation was to blame. There

TABLE 1
Subgroups in the Legislative Yuan, 1989-93

Period	No. of Subgroups	Membership Range	Party Affiliation	
			KMT	Nonpartisan
Prior to 1989 Election	11	5-42	5	6
Between 1989 and 1992 Elections	8	8-20	7	1
Post 1992 Election	7	7-25	6	1

Source: Data are adapted from Huang Teh-fu 1994.

is no doubt that by the 1990s the KMT's corporatist party state had been seriously eroded both structurally and functionally. The Party is no longer capable of enforcing its traditional authoritarian command (Tien 1994; and Huang Teh-fu 1994).

II. Taiwanization of the Power Structure

The takeover of Taiwan by the Nationalist government in 1945 following the unconditional surrender of Japan and the retreat of Chiang Kai-shek from the mainland to Taiwan in 1949 gave the KMT an unique opportunity to monopolize all leadership positions of political significance in Taiwan in the 1950s. Ever since, the ethnic factor has played a crucial role in the distribution of power in Taiwan. Before the mid-1970s, power at the pyramid of the party-state-military alliance was tightly held by the mainlander elites. As Tables 2-5 show, although Taiwanese constituted 85 percent of the island's population, only a very minute percentage (ranging from zero to 13 percent depending on period and organization) of the high positions in the state and party hierarchy were occupied by local Taiwanese. While a handful of Taiwanese managed to get to these high positions, they were mainly used as a token of political participation. They rarely sat in positions of genuine significance or substance (Tien 1989).

As the natural attrition of aging and death depleted the strength of

TABLE 2

Composition of the KMT Central Standing Committee, 1952-1994

Election Date		Chairman*	Total*	Taiwanese		Military		Legislature	
Year	Date		No.	No.	%	No.	%	No	%
1952	10/23	Chiang Kai-shek	10	0	0.0	3	30.0	4	40.0
1954	8/5		10	0	0.0	2	20.0	5	50.0
1955	3/3		10	0	0.0	3	30.0	4	40.0
1956	5/8		10	0	0.0	1	10.0	5	50.0
1957	3/3		10	0	0.0	1	10.0	5	50.0
1957	10/26		16	1	8.3	4	25.0	5	31.3
1959	5/19		16	2	12.5	5	31.3	6	37.5
1960	10/2		16	2	12.5	6	37.5	6	37.5
1961	11/16		16	2	12.5	6	37.5	6	37.5
1962	11/15		16	2	12.5	5	31.3	6	37.5
1962	11/23		16	2	12.5	6	37.5	8	50.0
1964	11/28		18	2	11.1	6	33.3	6	33.3
1966	12/29		19	2	10.5	6	31.6	8	42.1
1967	11/23		19	2	10.5	6	31.6	9	47.4
1969	4/10		21	2	9.5	5	23.8	7	33.3
1972	3/10		21	3	14.3	5	23.8	5	23.8
1973	11/15		21	3	14.3	4	19.0	5	23.8
1976	11/19	Chiang Ching-kuo	22	5	22.7	4	18.2	6	27.3
1979	12/10		27	9	33.3	6	22.2	5	18.5
1981	4/6		27	9	33.3	5	18.5	4	14.8
1984	2/14		31	12	38.7	4	12.9	6	19.4
1986	3/29		31	14	45.2	4	12.9	6	19.4
1988	7/14	Lee Teng-hui	31	16	51.6	3	9.7	9	29.0
1993	8/23		35	20	57.1	3	8.6	9	25.7
1994	8/26		35	21	60.0	3	8.6	7	20.0

Source: Data are adapted from Huang Teh-fu 1994; Chung-kuo shih-pao, August 27, 1994.

*The total membership does not include the chairman. For the period 1957-64, the statistics includes Chen Cheng as party vice chairman, and the period after 1993 covers four vice chairmen, Li Yuan-tsu, Lien Chan, Hao Po-tsun, and Lin Yang-kang.

TABLE 3
Composition of the KMT Central Committee, 1952-1993

Election Date Year	Date	Congress Date	Taiwanese No.	%	Military No.	%	Legislature No.	%	Total No.
1952	10/19	7th	1	3.1	10	31.3	5	15.6	32
1957	10/23	8th	3	6.0	11	22.0	15	30.0	50
1963	11/22	9th	4	5.4	16	21.6	14	18.9	74
1969	4/8	10th	6	6.1	16	16.2	16	16.2	99
1976	11/17	11th	19	14.6	21	16.2	15	11.5	130
1981	4/3	12th	29	19.3	15	10.0	30	20.0	150
1988	7/12	13th	62	34.4	21	11.7	37	20.6	180
1993	8/17	14th	112	53.3	8	3.8	67	31.9	210

Source: Data are adapted from Huang Teh-fu 1994.

the mainlander elite, particularly after the KMT shifted its gears from "predatory authoritarianism" to "developmental authoritarianism" in the 1970s and 1980s, the policy of "Taiwanization," or "indigenization" (*pen-t'u-hua*), started under Chiang Ching-kuo recruited more indigenous Taiwanese into government services. As a result, the ethnic composition of Taiwanese at the national level increased markedly, from 20 percent to 30 percent levels. As a rule, however, Taiwanese were assigned to positions of lesser importance. Take the cabinet post appointments, for example: Key posts for national defense, finance, economic affairs, education, and foreign affairs never went to Taiwanese before Lee Teng-hui's ascent to leadership in 1988 (Lin 1993).

Table 5 below shows that in the last year of Chiang Ching-kuo rule (1987), even with the declared policies of elite "indigenization," important positions in high echelons of the Party, government, military, and police were still predominately controlled by mainlanders (ranging from 86 percent to 96 percent). Statistically, the Taiwanese still played a very insignificant role in Taiwan's political arena (ranging from 4 percent to 14 percent) as late as 1987.

Lee Teng-hui's succession to Party chairmanship and the state presidency in 1988 after Chiang Ching-kuo's death symbolized a new era in Taiwan's political power structure. The ethnic balance of power

TABLE 4
Ethnic Composition of the Executive Yuan Cabinet, 1950-1994

Period	Premier	Taiwanese		Mainlander		Total
		No.	%	No.	%	No.
1950	Chen Chen	1	5.0	19	95.0	20
1954	Yu Hung-chun	1	5.3	18	94.7	19
1958	Chen Cheng	2	10.5	17	89.5	19
1963	Yen Chia-kan	2	8.7	21	91.3	23
1966	Yen Chia-kan	3	12.5	21	87.5	24
1969	Yen Chia-kan	3	13.0	20	87.0	23
1972	Chiang Ching-kuo	6	26.1	17	73.9	23
1976	Chiang Ching-kuo	6	26.1	17	73.9	23
1978	Sun Yun-suan	6	30.3	16	70.0	20
1984	Yu Kuo-hwa	7	36.8	12	63.2	19
1988	Yu Kuo-hwa	11	45.8	13	54.2	24
1989	Lee Huan	11	45.8	13	54.2	24
1990	Hao Po-tsun	10	47.6	11	52.4	21
1993	Lien Chan	9	45.0	11	55.0	20

Sources: Data are Based on Lin 1993; and Huang Teh-fu 1994.

began to shift decisively from the mainlanders to the Taiwanese. It took four rounds of fierce power struggle and delicate political maneuvering, however, for Lee to loosen the tight political grip of the old guards and establish his personal leadership within the Party and government (Hsia and Zeldin 1994).

The departure of Li Huan and Hao Po-tsun (leaders of the mainlander, non-mainstream faction) from the premiership in 1991 and 1993, respectively, and the appointment of Lien Chan as premier—the first Taiwanese to occupy that high office in KMT history—constituted another major watershed in Taiwan's political transformation. As shown in Tables 2-5, the ethnic ratio of the elite composition under Lee Teng-hui shifted greatly in favor of the Taiwanese in both statistical and substantive terms. The traditional ethnic pattern of the distribution of cabinet posts and major party jobs was broken. Taiwanese now occupied not only about 50 percent of the top positions in the Party and government hierarchies, but they also were assigned to posts of real significance and power.

The shift of ethnic balance within the parliamentary bodies of the National Assembly and the Legislative Yuan was equally conspicuous. Before the complete overhaul of the membership of the National Assembly in 1991 and the Legislative Yuan in 1992, the overwhelming majority of seats, ranging from 70 percent to 95 percent at various time periods, was occupied by "senior representatives" elected on the mainland in 1947. After the general elections of 1991 and 1992, as shown in Tables 6-7, the pattern of ethnic composition was completely reversed in the central parliament. Currently, Taiwanese constitute 81 percent of the National Assembly and 78 percent of the Legislative Yuan, respectively (Copper 1994). Given the fact that the mainlanders represent only 13 percent of the island's population, the shares of their representation (19 percent and 22 percent) are still proportionately high. For historical reasons, obviously, the KMT leadership under the Taiwanese majority still gave special consideration to ensure an appropriate mainlander representation in the political arena. The "nationwide constituency" and the "overseas Chinese quota" based on the proportional representation of the popular vote (crafted through constitutional reform) was designed to protect the declining representation of the mainlander population in Taiwan politics (Hsu and Chang 1992).

TABLE 5
Ethnic Composition of Top Positions, 1987

Category	Taiwanese		Mainlander		Total
	No.	%	No.	%	No.
Party	33	13.6	210	86.4	243
Government	21	14.0	129	86.0	150
Parliament	220	16.9	1080	83.1	1300
Military	15	4.3	335	95.7	350
Police	11	7.3	139	92.7	150
Combined	300	13.7	1893	86.3	2193

Sources: Kung-lun pao, March 6, 1987; and Yuan-chien tsa-chih, July 1, 1987, p. 19.

TABLE 6
Ethnic Distribution of Seats in the National Assembly, 1986 and 1996

Year	Constituency	Taiwanese NO.	%	Mainlander No.	%	Total No.
1986		101	10.8	834	89.2	935
1992	Regional	192	85.3	33	12.6	225
	Nationwide	70	70.0	30	30.0	100
	Combined	262	80.6	63	19.4	325

Sources: Kau 1989; Huang Teh-fu 1994; and Copper 1994.

The ethnic cleavage in Taiwan has for a long time played a crucial role in politics. In the past, the KMT's absolute rule was deeply rooted in the ethnic homogeneity and political identity of the mainlander power elite. The change of the ethnic composition of the power structure, therefore, has the most far-reaching implications for the issue of national identity and policy orientation. Generally speaking, the mainlander elites tend to maintain a "great China complex" and are more inclined to preserve the constitutional framework created in China in 1947. In contrast, most Taiwanese are more likely to look inward for Taiwan's own national identity. The concept of "Taiwan first," as opposed to "unification first," greatly influences their articulation and perception of national priorities for foreign and domestic policy. Thus, the dramatic shift in the ethnic balance of power is bound to have a crucial impact on Taiwan's future development (Feldman 1991).

III. The Rise of the DPP

The third critical aspect of the structural transformation of Taiwan politics in recent years is revealed in the dramatic rise of the opposition party, the DPP, since 1986. The functionalist approach to the causes of Taiwan's democratization stresses the thesis that the emergence of socioeconomic pluralism as a result of the KMT's "developmental authoritarianism" caused the erosion of the party state, and this in turn paved the way for Taiwan's democratization. However, the statist theorist emphasizes the critical role played by the opposition movements. What has made the difference is the determined struggles, purposeful strategies, and farsighted leadership of the opposition party (Cheng and Haggard 1992; and Winkler and Greenhalgh 1988).

Before the 1970s, there were practically no organized opposition or dissident movements in Taiwan. The effective execution of the "three controls" and "white terror" made it extremely difficult for any antigovernment activities to grow. Even isolated cases of individual challenges to the KMT autocracy were carefully suppressed. However, the expansion of national elections by filling the "supplementary seats" allocated to the "Taiwan region" after 1969 significantly enlarged both the scope and intensity of electoral politics. As elections became the only acceptable and legal channel of political participation by activists outside the KMT, electoral politics was quickly seized by political dissidents and counter-elites as a method of political agitation and mass mobilization (Yang 1989).

In the 1970s, various ad hoc campaign support groups or committees mushroomed during elections to help non-KMT candidates organize campaigns or mobilize voters. As activities of these various groups expanded and intensified throughout the island, their leaders converged to form loose networks of coordination and mutual assistance, commonly known as the *"tang-wai"* (outside the party) forces (Sutter 1988).

TABLE 7
Ethnic Distribution of Seats in the Legislative Yuan, 1988 and 1993

Year	Constituency	Taiwanese No.	%	Mainlander No.	%	Total No.
1988		78	25.0	234	75.0	312
1993	Regional	83	82.1	18	17.8	101
	Nationwide	43	71.7	17	28.3	60
	Combined	126	78.3	35	21.7	161

Sources: Kau 1989; Huang Teh-fu 1994; and
Chung-kuo shih-pao, December 4, 1989.

Organizationally, the *tang-wai* coalitions were deliberately vague and amorphous in order to avoid government persecution. From time to time, dissident magazines, such as *Mei-li-tao* (Formosa) in 1978-79, or scholarly institutions, such as Kung-kung Cheng-tse Yen-chiu-hui (Association for the Study of Public Policy) in 1984-86, were organized as cover for political activities of the *tang-wai* movements. Although the government continued to carry out sweeping repression against the dissidents (as in the cases of the Chung-li Incident of 1977 and the Kaohsiung Incident of 1979), as the opposition movements gathered momentum, such repressive actions became increasingly counter-productive. The *tang-wai* would exploit the violent suppression to step up agitations against the government and propagate the causes of political opposition at home and abroad (Huang Teh-fu 1992).

As political pressure mounted from without, Chiang Ching-kuo began to call for political reform from within. In September 1986, when the *tang-wai* alliance formally declared the formation of the DPP in clear defiance of the law, Chiang Ching-kuo decided not to prosecute and suppress it.

From its inception, the DPP made abundantly clear its political goals and platform. Calling the KMT an "alien regime" from China mainland, the DPP claimed to represent the true aspirations of the indigenous Taiwanese people. It articulated the political sufferings of the Taiwanese under the exploitation by the Manchu dynasty, Japanese Imperialism, and KMT dictatorship. The party vowed to build a free, democratic, and independent Taiwan based on the principle of self-determination. The DPP advocated the policy of "one China, one Taiwan," emphasizing that Taiwan's sovereignty does not extend over to the mainland and Outer Mongolia (as advocated by the KMT), nor does Beijing have sovereignty over Taiwan (as claimed by the PRC). The ultimate goal of the DPP is to establish a new Republic of Taiwan under a new constitution. The party pledged to achieve all these objectives through a peaceful and democratic process (Yang 1993; and Democratic Progressive Party 1994).

Since the mid-1980s, the *tang-wai* coalition and its successor, the DPP, have been making impressive progress in voting strength and political influence. In the last three elections of the Legislative Yuan in 1986, 1989, and 1992, as shown in Figures 1, the popular vote for DPP candidates expanded steadfastly from 25 percent to 29 percent and then to 31 percent, respectively. In contrast, the vote for the KMT dropped markedly from 69 percent to 59 percent and 53 percent, respectively, in the same period. While the DPP popular vote advanced close to one-third, that of the KMT declined to almost one-half.

The development of popular support for the DPP at the county and city levels was even more impressive (see Figure 2). For the last three local elections held in 1985, 1989, and 1994, the vote shares of the DPP leaped from 14 percent to 30 percent and 41 percent, respectively. KMT shares, however, dropped sharply from 61 percent to 56 percent and 47 percent. Since 1989, the DPP has captured one-third of Taiwan's twenty-one local chief executive posts. In other words, the DPP has been since 1989 the ruling party in one-third of Taiwan (Huang Teh-fu 1992). It should be further noted that in the latest local elections last spring, KMT popularity dropped below the 50 percent mark for the first time. Moreover, the DPP popular vote was only 6 percent behind that of the KMT (41 percent versus 47 percent). With only a 3 percent shift of the popular vote, the DPP would have surpassed the KMT in a contest of popular support at the local level.

The impressiveness of the DPP's rapid growth should be viewed against the historical background of the KMT as the unchallenged dominant force in Taiwan's political scene for more than forty years. The KMT not only claims an enormous membership of 2.5 million, but the party also owns a huge financial empire reportedly worth more than U.S.

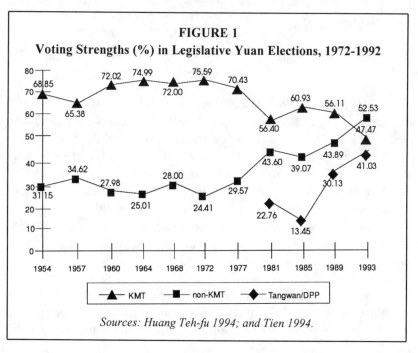

FIGURE 1

Voting Strengths (%) in Legislative Yuan Elections, 1972-1992

Sources: Huang Teh-fu 1994; and Tien 1994.

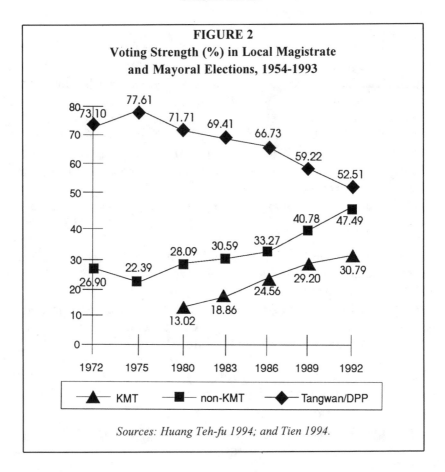

FIGURE 2
Voting Strength (%) in Local Magistrate
and Mayoral Elections, 1954-1993

Sources: Huang Teh-fu 1994; and Tien 1994.

$4 billion (Baum 1994). In contrast to the KMT's giant human and financial resources, the seven-year old DPP has a meager membership of about 70,000, and the party is constantly in financial destitution. The DPP is, therefore, often characterized as a "poverty-stricken, malnutritioned little kid" vis-à-vis the giant ruling party (Yang 1993). However, in the electoral arena, the DPP is indeed remarkably strong and competitive; it is catching up with its giant brother rapidly.

In fact, the DPP's political strength should be understood in more than simple statistical terms. Its contributions to Taiwan's democratization also rest on its determination and ability to challenge the traditional political "sacred cows," to raise the fundamental issues of political legitimacy and constitutional reform, and to break new ground for political imagination and innovation. As a matter of fact, many important and popular programs of constitutional and policy reform were originally initiated by the DPP, in the process of party competition for popular support, the KMT co-opted them as its own for political purposes. The KMT's change of position on such major issues as the direct popular election of the president and Taiwan's admission to the United Nations are clear examples (Feldman 1991).

In the Legislative Yuan, DPP membership is still relatively small numerically. Of the current 159 members, the DPP has only 51 as opposed to the KMT's 97. However, as DPP members maintain a high degree of solidarity and discipline while their KMT counterparts are highly factionalized and fragmented, the influence of the former is often greatly augmented through tactical maneuvers of forming ad hoc voting alliances with various factions within the KMT. The passage in 1993 of the Sunshine Law, under the leadership of the DPP and against the official stance of the KMT, was a case in point. The case demonstrated well the DPP's ability to exert influence and leadership beyond its minority status *(Chung-kuo shih-pao,* June 8-10, 1993; and Chu 1994).

Recent public opinion polls indicate that while the voters give high marks to the DPP's political leadership, personal integrity, and commitment to reform, they are rather unsure of the DPP leaders' administrative experience and policy constituency. The public is generally disenchanted with the KMT's internal factionalism, power struggles, corruption, self-complacency, and money politics. In response, the DPP has been trying to move away from the emotional and ideological questions of national identity and Taiwan independence and shift its emphasis to pragmatic public policy issues such as welfare reform, clean government, environmental protection, urban planning, and pensions for the elderly. Party members are attempting to project a positive image in which the DPP has outgrown the stage of the opposition movement and is advancing toward a new stage of maturity, responsibility, and policy leadership (Huang Teh-fu 1992).

On December 3rd this year, the governorship of Taiwan and the mayorship of Taipei and Kaohsiung will be open for popular elections. At the end of 1995, the Legislative Yuan will be due for reelection. And in the Spring of 1996, even the president of the Republic will be elected through direct popular vote for the first time in history. The DPP is confident that they can continue to do well. For the past decade, the party has managed to increase its share of the popular vote by 2 percent to 4 percent in each major election. If this trend can be maintained for the forthcoming gubernatorial and mayoral elections in December, the political future of the DPP could be even brighter. Certainly, the ruling

KMT still controls enormous amounts of organizational and financial resources far, far stronger than those of the DPP. Furthermore, Lee Teng-hui himself is immensely popular. However, the KMT is still seriously entrapped by its historical baggage and in its own organizational inertia of fragmentation and factionalism. How soon can it rescue itself through painful reform, and how long can it keep up with the growing challenge of the DPP? These are the most crucial questions that the voters will have to answer in the coming years.

Democratization and Its Impact on Mainland Policy

During the days of KMT authoritarianism, all public policies, especially those politically sensitive ones, belonged in the exclusive domain of the corporatist state. There was hardly any debate before the public; no dissent was allowed. As far as the KMT's basic policy toward mainland China was concerned, the position was simple and clear. The government insisted on "one China" doctrine, claiming that the ROC government remained the sole legal government of all of China and that Taiwan was part of China. The two sides of the Taiwan Strait (Taiwan and the mainland), it was argued, should be reunited ultimately.

Since no debate or challenge was permitted in the political arena on such a fictitious policy and claim, mainland policy was essentially a "non-issue" under the KMT authoritarian rule. Moreover, since the two sides of the Taiwan Strait were totally segregated during the Cold War era, the fiction and the realities simply did not meet. Consequently, there was no need even trying to wrestle and reconcile between fiction and reality.

During the second half of the 1980's, however, the process of democratization brought about competitive party politics and the freedom of speech in the political arena. The lifting of the ban on economic and social contacts across the Taiwan Strait in 1987 quickly intensified Taiwan's "indirect" trade, investment, and tourism with the mainland. As more and more people traveled across the Strait, they were inevitably led to question the fiction of "one China," and found the need to redefine for themselves their self-identity as well as political identity in light of the new realities—who they are and what they are in relation to the two societies competing for their political loyalty and social identity (Clough 1993; and Kau 1991).

Political democratization also offered a timely opportunity to air and debate the bigger and more sensitive political issues of national identity and the long-term future of Taiwan: Is Taiwan part of China? Are

Taiwanese Chinese? Should Taiwan be independent from China or be unified with China? Is there one China? Are there two Chinas? Or is there one China and one Taiwan? As the lid of authoritarian repression was lifted by the process of democratization, all these long-suppressed, sensitive issues quickly surfaced and moved to the center of the political stage. Moreover, they became closely intertwined with power struggle, factional politics, and policy debate, especially within the KMT (Kau 1992).

The past eight years witnessed constant debate and controversy over Taiwan's mainland policy among the major players of Taiwan politics. Three basic policy positions are now well articulated by the three major contending political forces in Taiwan.

On the right of the policy spectrum is the position advocated by the CNP and the non-mainstream faction of the KMT. They maintain essentially the traditional "one China" doctrine, insisting that Taiwan is part of China and should be reunited with the motherland as soon as possible. They are in favor of broadening and deepening the "three links" (trade, shipping, and communication) at a faster pace and especially want to change the current policy from allowing only "indirect" contacts to allowing "direct" links.

They believe that these functional activities will strengthen ties across the Taiwan Strait and lay down a strong socioeconomic foundation needed for political unification in the future. Because this position is about the same as that advocated by Beijing, its supporters are often identified as the "pro-unification faction," advancing the PRC's "united front" strategy in Taiwan. Also, as the policy is largely advocated by the mainlander old guards and the second-generation mainlander activists, the faction is also known as the "mainlander faction" (*Hsin hsin-wen*, November 20-26, 1994).

On the left of the policy spectrum is the DPP. As discussed earlier, the DPP leaders take a strong and clear stand for "one Taiwan, one China," advocating that Taiwan should seek complete and de jure independence from China. Arguing on historical, political, and economic grounds, they stress that Taiwan has its own national identity and is fully equipped with all the necessary conditions required for an independent state, not to mention its exceptional economic strength. So long as Beijing would respect this basic premise of national independence, Taiwan would open up direct interactions immediately with the mainland in all areas on an equal and friendly basis (Kau 1992).

Before the goal of Taiwan independence is reached, however, the DPP stresses extreme caution in dealing with the tricks and traps of both the Chinese Communist Party (CCP) and the KMT. They are absolutely against "party to party" negotiations between the CCP and the KMT, because they are fearful that the interest of the Taiwanese people might be sold out. To protect Taiwan against the threat of the giant China, the DPP emphasizes the strategy of "internationalizing" the issue of Taiwan in the world community. Taiwan's active international participation, especially its admission to the UN, they believe, is absolutely critical for the island's security and survival. Continuing domestic democratization and the expansion of the DPP's political role will make it impossible for the KMT, particularly its non-mainstream wing, to attempt any secret deal with the PRC (Yang 1993).

The mainland policy position of the mainstream KMT falls somewhere in the middle of the spectrum. The Guidelines for National Unification, officially adopted by the Presidential Commission on National Unification and endorsed by the Executive Yuan in March 1991, tries to steer a middle course between the policies advocated by the CNP and the DPP. Articulating a three-stage, gradualist approach, the Guidelines call for "indirect" and "unofficial" interactions to build confidence and mutual interest across the Taiwan Strait during the first stage. Beijing's "positive response" during this stage could be tested by three conditions: Its willingness to respect Taiwan as a separate, independent, and equal "political entity" in the international arena under the abstract principle of "one China," to stop obstructing Taiwan's international participation and formal diplomatic ties, and to renounce the use and threat of force against Taiwan (Huang Kun-huei 1991).

When these three conditions for confidence-building, mutual respect, and peaceful coexistence are met and verified, Taiwan would then move into the second stage of "direct" interactions and "official" contacts, including government-to-government negotiations on economic and other areas of cooperation. In the third and final stage, both sides would enter into negotiations on the framework and timing of ultimate unification. The KMT approach also emphasizes that there should be no fixed "timetable" for the progression of the stages; all depends on Beijing's behavior and good deeds.

The KMT rejects Beijing's "one country, two systems" formula, because it treats Taiwan as a "local government," and the "two systems" are unequal ones. Instead, the KMT advocates "one China, two [equal] political entities." In essence, the KMT's gradualist approach represents an attempt to strike a balance between the two extreme positions of unification and independence. While holding the hope of possible unification in the distant future under specified conditions, the KMT formula stresses the existing objective realities since 1949 of the separation and independence of the two sides. By insisting on no fixed timetable, the government will be able to control the pace and scope of interactions in accordance with internal sociopolitical developments on the two sides of the Taiwan Straits (Huang Kun-huei 1991).

It is significant to note that there appears to be an increasing convergence between the DPP and KMT approaches to mainland policy in recent years. DPP leaders seems to have come to realize that the high-pitch rhetoric of "declaring Taiwan independence" may be too provocative not only to Beijing but also to the voters in Taiwan who favor political stability, as Beijing threatened repeatedly that China would use force against the island under certain circumstances, including Taiwan's declaring independence (Kau and Marsh 1993, 333-407; and Chang 1993). In the 1989 National Assembly elections, the voters did not deliver strong support to the DPP (an exceptionally low 24 percent of popular vote), perhaps due to their concern over the DPP's strong campaigns for the establishment of a new Republic of Taiwan.

As pointed out earlier, the DPP has in recent years already toned down its rhetoric on Taiwan independence. They even co-opted some of Lee Teng-hui's argument that the ROC on Taiwan has been "independent" ever since 1949 and there is no need to "declare independence" redundantly. What Taiwan needs is simply more diplomatic recognition and international participation. To give Beijing's "one China" policy a humorous, yet serious, twist, the DDP argues that it, too, is in favor of "one China" policy. The DDP is perfectly happy to respect Beijing, and not the Nationalist government, as the "sole legal government of China." However, the DDP hastens to add that China does not include Taiwan, because the PRC, ever since its founding in 1949, has never exercised its sovereignty or jurisdiction over Taiwan for a single day. Therefore, Taiwan is not and never has been part of the PRC. Hence, unlike the KMT, the DPP would not challenge the PRC's "one China" policy at all (Yang and Hwang 1993).

On the other hand, the mainstream of the KMT is also moving closer to some aspects of DPP position concerning the Taiwan issue. For a long time before 1991, the KMT government was officially opposed to the idea of seeking UN admission or adopting the concept of "divided nation" and "dual recognition." However, as Taiwan's international isolation and diplomatic setbacks emerged as popular electoral campaigns issues for the DPP, the KMT was forced to reexamine and adjust its foreign policy stance. As the formula of "one China, two political entities" can not easily be understood and supported by the international community, the government has to shift to a less complicated, but much bolder, formula of the "two Chinas" policy, patterned after the former "two Germanys" and the current "two Koreas." Naturally, Beijing does not like it. Although the KMT is always very cautious about trying not to provoke Beijing, it will have to think of its own political survival in a highly competitive democratic contest where "voter sovereignty" is increasingly evident (Hu 1993).

There is now considerable discussion concerning the desirability and need to foster bipartisanship in the area of mainland and foreign policy. As the DPP fine-tunes its basic policy on Taiwan independence from the left to the center, and the KMT adjusts its strategy to mainland affairs from the center to the left, one could expect an increasing convergence of the two major parties on mainland and foreign policy in the future. In this regard, the moderating impact of democratization on the process of policy change should not be underestimated.

Conclusion

Following the success of its "economic miracle" in the previous decades, Taiwan has achieved another impressive feat in the past ten years. This time in the political arena. The corporatist party state of the KMT has been dramatically transformed into an open, competitive, dynamic democracy. This process manifests itself clearly in three crucial dimensions: the structural and functional erosion of the KMT party state; the Taiwanization of the power structure; and the dramatic rise of the opposition party, the DPP.

In the past decade, we have witnessed a most fascinating political phenomenon in Taiwan: the breakdown of a corporatist state and the emergence of a dynamic, pluralistic civil society. We have also seen how democratization has created a new "voter sovereignty" in Taiwan's competitive electoral market. Theoretically speaking, the traditional pattern of state dominance over society under KMT authoritarianism has been reversed. Now society is just as powerful as, if not more powerful than, the state. In a highly competitive democracy within a dynamic civil society, neither the KMT nor the DPP can dictate policy autocratically. They have to fight it out in the electoral market of voters and public opinion. As Lee Teng-hui put it, the concept that "sovereignty resides in the people" has taken root in Taiwan (Lee 1994).

In this regard, the impact of democratization on Taiwan's policy toward the mainland is most far-reaching. To begin with, democratization has set the stage for various political forces to bring out into the open the fundamental issues of Taiwan's national identity and its long-term implications for independence or unification. Although the issue has no immediate urgency, it is so powerful and charged with emotion that it has become highly politicized and intertwined with all other problems such as political reform, power struggles, and policy debate. There is no doubt that the issue of independence or unification will stay at the center of Taiwan's political arena for a long time.

Taiwan's democratization also has contributed to the opening of a new era of pragmatic economic and societal interactions with the mainland. Taiwan's business community wants to enter the market in China, and its residents demand to visit the mainland for reunions with relatives and friends. A democratizing government must respond to the demands and needs of its voters.

The continuous expansion of trade, investment, and social contacts of the last decade did relax some tension and advanced mutual interest across the Taiwan Strait. However, Beijing's unyielding position on Taiwan's international participation and its threat of force also imposed growing strain on the further development of functional socioeconomic interactions. Although Taiwan is willing to trade its economic chips for Beijing's political concessions, so far the PRC has not responded positively. Obviously, the trend of political interaction is running against the trend of economic exchange. If Beijing persists in its political intransigence, a political bottleneck is bound to emerge and inhibit the further deepening of economic interaction.

Continuing democratization and prosperity in Taiwan are increasing its people's self-confidence and national identity. A dynamic democratic society and its proud citizens are unlikely to bow easily to Beijing's political blackmail and military threats. Moreover, as the KMT and the DPP continue to converge on mainland policy ideas, the bipartisan cooperation and solidarity will certainly make Taiwan stronger in resisting Beijing's attempt to impose its "one China" doctrine. In the foreseeable future, both the KMT and the DPP may even be willing to work together to reconcile the differences between their formulas of "two political entities" and "one China, one Taiwan."

Democracy may behave chaotically at times, but it also has ways of generating order and unity during times of emergency and especially when national survival is at stake. In the dynamic democracy of Taiwan today, no single political party can arbitrarily superimpose its will on the people any longer. In the future, it will be even more difficult for Beijing to do that on Taiwan without incurring unacceptable costs and resistance.

DISCUSSION
The Politics
of Legitimacy

Lyman Miller, School of Advanced International Studies,
Johns Hopkins University

Professors Dittmer and Kao have given us able surveys of, respectively, the evolution of Beijing's approach to Taiwan reunification and the impact of Taiwan's domestic political evolution on Taipei's attitude toward the Chinese mainland. I will offer two broad observations to their analyses.

The first concerns the significance of the pattern of quasi-official political contacts, economic investment and trade, and popular exchanges that has developed across the Taiwan Strait since the late 1980s. Though the elaboration of contacts between the two sides may lay the foundation for eventual talks on reunification, there is nothing in the current process that necessarily brings reunification closer. Instead of momentum toward reunification, the pattern of contacts has brought stability to the long-standing competitive relationship between the two.

Above all, the Taiwan-Peoples Republic of China (PRC) reunification dynamic has always seemed intelligible as a struggle for legitimacy. In the domestic arena, it has been, from the beginning, a struggle to translate power won by military and other means into legitimate authority in the eyes of China's people. This has meant, in part, an effort to eliminate a rival claimant to national authority. Additionally, the struggle for domestic legitimacy has involved an attempt to defend against foreign encroachment. Internationally, the struggle for legitimacy has driven the effort to translate claimed sovereignty into international recognition.

The respective strategies of both the Nationalist Party (KMT) and the Communist Party (CPC) since the 1940s have always made sense in terms of this fundamental goal. Over the decades, there have been twists and turns in each side's approach to the other. Beijing has shifted tactics from armed struggle to peaceful liberation to peaceful reunification according to a "one country, two governments" formula. Similarly, Taipei has altered its approach, from the goal of recovering the mainland to variations on the "one country, two governments" formula. But all of these have been shaped by the fundamental goal of capturing and maintaining political legitimacy, both at home and abroad.

This has meant that the political stakes for both sides have remained extremely high. Because international recognition influences domestic perceptions of political legitimacy, each side has been extremely sensitive about the symbols of legitimacy. Internationally, each side has been careful about the nuances of diplomatic recognition. Domestically, symbolic questions remain, such as which side is the rightful inheritor of Sun Yatsen's legacy.

Similarly, bilateral contacts have been shaped by implications of legitimacy. For instance, Beijing proposes reunification negotiations with the Nationalist Party only as a wayward political party, never as a government that sits in Taipei. For its part, Taiwan persistently calls for government-to-government talks, seeking the legitimacy that such talks confer.

In looking at the recent pattern of informal contacts, economic relationships, and popular exchanges, little has changed in this quest for legitimacy. This constancy is clear as each side pursues contacts and exchanges across the Strait. The overall goal has remained the same— capturing and maintaining legitimacy. Beijing has sought to capitalize on its international standing and to use the lure of economic collaboration and popular contacts to win political accommodation from Taipei. Taipei seeks to translate its economic strength into international recognition while building economic relationships with the mainland.

Despite the interesting dynamic of contacts and exchanges, neither side has truly achieved significant progress on the unification issue. Beijing has not translated the dramatic expansion of contacts into political success. Here I differ from Professor Dittmer's judgment that Beijing's reunification pitch has been successful: it has, indeed, substantively achieved the *santong siliu*, but that has not brought reunification closer. Nor has Taipei achieved any significant success on the sensitive issue of international recognition, despite efforts to capitalize on its impressive economic and domestic political progress.

The reason for this is that the politics of legitimacy have created a zero-sum game. Economic and popular exchanges have not. Despite the dramatic increase in contacts, neither side gains on the fundamental goal of domestic and international legitimacy, except at the expense of the other.

Paradoxically, what we have is a dynamic but increasingly stable equilibrium. Exchanges and interactions have grown with impressive vigor. But they grown within a framework with boundaries dictated by considerations of political legitimacy and international standing. All else being equal, both Taiwan and Beijing benefit from collaboration on purely economic grounds and the stability that routine popular and cultural exchanges bring. But there is nothing in that dynamic that necessarily leads either side to concede significant ground on the fundamental issues of political legitimacy. Yet, the various exchanges have reduced cross-Straits tensions from their previously highly polarized state, frozen for decades by the Cold War.

Within this equilibrium, Beijing has declared its readiness to use force against Taiwan only if the "one China" principle is threatened by a declaration of independence by Taipei or by foreign intervention. To reject the use of force within territory over which it claims sovereignty is to limit and, ultimately, deny sovereignty. Consequently, the right to use force entails a question of legitimacy. Short of extreme threats to its legitimacy, however, Beijing has no real interest in using force. Besides, the cost of using force to Beijing's international standing and regional relationships would be astronomical. As the conclusion of Professor Kao's paper suggests, the impact of Beijing's statements on Taiwan is to moderate political agitation for independence. Taipei, with a growing economic stake on the mainland, has no interest in provoking Beijing into using force.

Nor is there a real international interest that compels intervention in the equilibrium across the Strait. Quite the opposite. Within the framework imposed by the politics of legitimacy, all foreign states—the United States included—can expand substantive relationships in the economic, cultural, and other arenas. Also, a certain amount of tinkering with the substantive representation of Taiwan in foreign capitals and in international organizations seems possible, as long as the issue of "official" standing is not raised explicitly. Here the labels remain important because the connotations of legitimacy attached to names like "Taipei, China" bring immediate political consequences. Despite the traditional value attached to "rectification of names" by Confucius, it is ambiguity, not precision, that permits latitude. Foreign capitals that ignore the politics of legitimacy in relations with Taipei run the severe risk of upsetting the stability of today's cross-Strait consolidation.

What can dissolve this dynamic equilibrium built on the politics of legitimacy? This question brings me to my second observation, which regards culture. It is frequently useful to assess the motivations of human interactions according to three categories: remunerative factors—things that people do because they will be rewarded for doing them; coercive factors—things that people do because something bad will happen to them if they don't; and normative factors—things that people do because they believe they should do them. Amitai Etzioni delineated these categories, as far as I know, for the narrower purposes of the sociology of organizations. But I am trained as a historian, and historians are notoriously insensitive to the niceties of theory. And so I appropriate them without guilt.

Applying these categories to the dynamic of Taiwan-mainland relations, it would seem that remunerative and coercive factors—the politics of money and guns—have resulted in no foreseeable change in overall equilibrium. Legitimacy, meanwhile, is fundamentally an issue of belief, associated ultimately with questions of national and cultural identity. It is in the arena of culture—all those mental frameworks and associations that bind people together into communities—that we see the greatest changes underway. Specifically, it seems that what promises to upset the prevailing equilibrium of legitimacy is the evolution of domestic politics and the accompanying transformation of culture on each side. In all societies, culture is never static. Culture may reinforce political authority and integration, and it may undermine it; but it is never politically neutral. In China and in Taiwan today, culture is a powerful engine of change with potentially subversive consequences.

Professor Kao's paper shows clearly how thirty years of economic and social change, the resultant fragmentation of the KMT, the Taiwanization of politics, and democratization have begun to challenge the environment of legitimacy within which Taipei and Beijing have previously competed. As he points out, the issue for Taipei is no longer which is the legitimate government of China. Rather it is whether Taiwan is part of China. This is ultimately a question of cultural and national identity.

On the other side of the Strait, the Deng Xiaoping regime has since 1978, sought to reestablish the legitimacy lost in the disasters of the Mao era through appeals to nationalism and policies of economic reform. The consequences of these policies have been profound. They have produced impressive economic growth and renewed national strength. But they have also produced challenges to domestic legitimacy. These include: the debilitation of the CPC apparatus with its shift in organizational mission from social revolution to economic performance; the relativization of Marxism-Leninism as "socialism with Chinese characteristics; the rise of new social and economic elites; the retreat of the state from large areas of private life; and the relative autonomy of some social and professional groups.

These changes have, in turn, brought an enormous flux of values and ideals, some cosmopolitan, some traditional, and some new. They have all called into question the politics of iconoclastic nationalism on which the communist regime was built. As a result, there is considerable turmoil over the meaning of the cultural symbols that unite the Chinese polity accompanying the collapse of Marxism-Leninism. An overall direction is difficult to discern. One can assess economic trends by studying trade volumes and investment patterns across the Taiwan Strait. One can also count the number of F16s on one side and SU-27s on the other, and come to some sense of the military balance across the Strait. But cultural trends are more difficult to survey and assess.

Nevertheless, my sense is that there is movement on the mainland to embrace a tradition that is in some measure more cosmopolitan. It would accommodate regional variation and reinterpret values and ideals to adapt to modern sensibilities more constructively than did earlier cultural iconoclasm after the May Fourth era. One sees this trend in debates among mainland scholars about the May Fourth era itself. Similarly, the anthropologist Helen Siu has shown has the revival of traditional rituals and practices in rural Guangdong has not simply meant the restoration of static traditions. Rather it reflects their rehabilitation with new meanings and association consistent with an increasingly modern rural setting.[1] In both academic historiography and in popular culture on the mainland, one sees a massive effort to recover a past previously rejected by Maoist obscurantism and the longer ultramodernist iconoclasm of the May Fourth tradition.

All these developments have the potential to scramble in unpredictable ways the politics of legitimacy that have structured cross-Strait relations. It may be that cultural changes in both Taiwan and the PRC will only reinforce the separation that has existed so far. If so, they may solidify separate identifies that may some day provide the foundations for independent nation-states.

But it is also possible, and I expect more likely, that the reverse will occur. Cultural changes and contacts will underscore the Chinese identities of the people on both sides of the Straits, aiding the establishment of some encompassing political framework.

As Tu Weiming has argued, the periphery of Hong Kong, Taiwan, and overseas Chinese communities is playing—consciously or not—a leading, catalytic role in the transformation of the cultural core on the Chinese mainland. There the Chinese are grasping for the cultural resources to redefine and construct their identity and meaning.[2] More dramatic, as Thomas Gold has shown recently, is the spread of Taiwan and Hong Kong popular culture on the mainland. There it is acquiring uses and meanings that subvert the official culture of the communist regime while building communities of cultural association and symbolism that abet integration.[3]

If there is reunification, it will come about, at least in part, because of the emergence of a revised Chinese nationalism built on a more unified cultural outlook on both sides of the Taiwan Strait. It will provide new meanings to traditional symbols of authority and unity, and become acceptable to enough people to transcend the politics of legitimacy that has divided them up to now. Prediction, again, is hazardous. But I expect it will require a long time. If Deng Xiaoping is ready to wait 40, 50, or even 1,000 years for reunification, I suspect his wait will be closer to the longer end of that span.

SECTION III
Economic Dimensions
of Cross-Strait Interaction

CHAPTER 4
Taiwan and the Mainland: Can Economic Interaction Mute the Conflict?

J.W. Wheeler,
Hudson Institute

The 1990s have witnessed remarkable transformations in the economies of China and Taiwan, in cross-Strait economic relations and in their respective economic relations with the rest of the world. Building upon the opening of China in the late 1970s and the extraordinary economic success of Taiwan, both societies have evolved, economically and politically, along lines making them nearly unrecognizable to the original protagonists of the conflict that has simmered since 1949 across the Strait. New forms of interaction and cooperation have become a reality—from Taiwan's tourists on the Great Wall, to formal talks in Singapore and Taipei, to billions of dollars of Taiwan investment on the mainland, to simultaneous involvement in the ADB, APEC, and possibly the GATT(WTO).

In light of altered international circumstances and the increasing web of commercial and other relations between Taiwan and the mainland, fundamental questions emerge regarding the impact of economic exchange on the tensions across the Taiwan Strait. Will economics become a new frontier of conflict and tension or does it offer opportunities for constructive conflict resolution?

This chapter will examine the broad economic dimensions of the current cross-Strait relationship, the reasons for and elements of progress, the potential stumbling blocks, and the key emerging opportunities. It will attempt to deal with all the major dimensions of the evolving economic relationship, presenting the costs and benefits of the growing interdependence as perceived by both sides, and speculating about how these various trends and conflicting pressures might play out.

Dimensions of the Cross-Strait Economic Relationship

Background

Until the opening of China in the late 1970s economic exchange was minimal. It consisted of smuggling and the indirect import through Hong Kong of Chinese medicines by an agency of the ROC government. With the adoption of its open-door policies in 1978, China also launched efforts to build closer links to Taiwan (and Hong Kong).[1] As part of its reunification strategy, China has granted a variety of special concessions to Taiwanese businesses.[3] For example, in 1980, China dropped all tariffs on Taiwan products, a policy that had to be changed in 1981 because of a flood of goods with fake certificates of origin. Nonetheless, the adjustment taxes subsequently levied on Taiwan goods remain less than prevailing tariffs, and Taiwan products face less stringent import controls than goods from other offshore sources. In 1988, a China State Council decree granted preferential treatment to Taiwan investments. In addition, city and provincial authorities usually give special treatment to firms from Taiwan. There have been important gaps in these various preferences and the consistency of implementation seem to wax and wane relative to the current state of cross-Strait discussions in ways interpreted on the ROC side as manipulative. Nevertheless, these preferences have helped to attract a growing flood of Taiwanese trade and investment. On December 20, 1993, a draft law was submitted to the PRC legislature to increase the protections and codify the treatment of Taiwanese investments.[3] While the new legislation incorporates the 1988 rules that many businessmen felt were seriously inadequate, it also contains some important new protections for property rights on assets and profits, assures repatriation of profits to Taiwan, and offers guarantees against expropriation. In general, Taiwan businessmen have reacted favorably, if somewhat cynically, to the proposed changes.

Though initially resistant, Taipei has over time permitted growing indirect economic exchanges, supported by gradual trade liberalization.

Not only was a rigid application of the "three-noes" [4] inappropriate under prevailing circumstances, but Taiwan authorities came to recognize that renewed contacts could allow them to influence internal changes on the mainland.[5] In 1984, import controls on some items from Hong Kong were eased—legitimizing indirect trade. Subsequently, a modified "three noes" policy was issued with regard to indirect commerce—no official contact, no encouragement, and no intervention.[6] Beginning in 1987, the ROC government permitted limited visitation among relatives across the Strait by traveling indirectly through third jurisdictions and explicitly allowed the indirect import of a short list of items, a list that has lengthened considerably over time. In 1988, the 13th Plenum of the KMT endorsed this policy shift by adopting a new Mainland Commerce Policy. Under the new policy, a whole series of additional restrictive laws governing cross-Strait travel, communications, and commerce have been replaced by permissive laws and regulations. The liberalization process culminated with the historic decision to terminate the "period of mobilization and rebellion suppression" by May 1, 1991 and the landmark 1992 *Statute for Relations across the Taiwan Straits*, which authorized the elimination of a wide range of controls on cross-Strait activities. The 1992 Statute also codified how the legal system would begin to deal with a complex array of special issues and problems that emerged from growing contact and commerce across the Strait. Recently Taiwan has begun to draft legislation that will govern commercial ties with Hong Kong after its reversion to PRC rule in 1997.[7] Cross-Strait commerce was a major beneficiary of emerging Taiwanese democracy and the evolution of the island's "Pragmatic Diplomacy."

Still, serious concerns about the potential political and security vulnerabilities that would be created by economic dependency have resulted in the continuation of an array of controls on interaction with the mainland. So far, direct commercial contact remains forbidden, forcing trade and investment through third parties—usually Hong Kong. Goods imports remain controlled by an approval list. Investment is permitted only in designated areas (though these now comprise a very long list) and large investments require case-by-case approval. Mainland investment on and travel to Taiwan is strictly limited. As the economic interchange between Taiwan and the mainland has grown, these controls have weakened, both through liberalization and through declining ability to contain indirect trade and investment, raising concerns about important gaps in legal protections for Taiwan individuals and firms on the mainland and about the potential for political manipulation.

Commercial Challenges

Taiwan businesses face a number of unique challenges in doing business with the mainland. All private firms going into China are in a very unequal bargaining position relative to mainland enterprises, with their close ties to various levels of government. The unique risks facing Taiwan firms emerge from the explicit goal of mainland official policy to exploit economic ties to advance their unification goals (i.e., firms can be caught up in political manipulation) and the lack of recourse to international commercial code and diplomatic channels to guide behavior, support business entry, and assist in dispute resolution. Just the simple lack of access to normal consular services can add significant transactions costs. More important is the lack of fundamental legal protection. The deficiencies of mainland China's commercial code are a critical matter facing all firms, but Taiwan firms do not have the protection offered by various international conventions and treaties to constrain the mainland's tendency to use law as a political tool. Moreover, the battle over sovereignty makes it difficult for the two governments to negotiate arrangements that are mutually beneficial.

Economic complementarity, proximity, reform and growth on the mainland, rapid escalation of land prices and wage rates in Taiwan, and communal and kinship ties combined to create a virtual explosion of trade and investment in the past decade. Trends point to continued expansion of economic ties at a rapid rate. This commercial explosion has induced the two sides to begin a pragmatic process of dealing with day-to-day issues and problems of business, even as most of the big issues of the cross-Strait relationship remain in deliberate studied ambiguity.

Trade

Data on trade flows is highly inaccurate both due to the use of third parties for transshipment and processing, and to the high volume of illegal commerce (under Taiwan law). Still, it appears that by the end of 1993, two-way trade exceeded US $14 billion, up from some $5 billion in 1990 and virtually nothing in 1980.[8] This flow is highly unbalanced, with Taiwan running huge bilateral surpluses. In part, this reflects Taiwan's restrictions on imports from the mainland in order to limit vulnerability to embargo. It also reflects the huge mainland demand for the mix of consumer and producer goods produced in Taiwan. Further, many of the Taiwanese funded enterprises on the mainland use capital goods and intermediate inputs brought in from Taiwan, but only sell product locally or in third markets. The trade imbalance, a desire to protect local industry, and an apparent effort to induce more Taiwan firms to move across the Strait, combined with political desires to expand Taiwan's economic dependency, have led Beijing, over the past several years, towards centralizing and imposing a variety of mechanisms to control trade with Taiwan, even as general preferential treatment was maintained.

Most of Taiwan's imports from the mainland are medicines, selected raw materials, and semi-finished goods (e.g. lumber). Taiwan's exports on the other hand are mostly manufactured goods, initially dominated by cotton fabrics and consumer goods. Over time, the range and sophistication of exports expanded markedly. Some two-thirds of exports are now machinery, electronic components, plastics, and textiles needed as inputs for mainland production and exports.

Foreign Direct Investment

Cross-Strait direct investment is essentially one-way, with Taiwan blocking all but a few relatively small-scale, illegal mainland efforts. As with trade, the available data are suspect. All Taiwan investments on the mainland before 1991 were illegal, so the values captured in the Hong Kong and Chinese data are almost certainly underestimates. Even after 1991, the requirement to seek approval for large investments (over US $1 million) and register all other investments with the authorities undoubtedly led to underreporting. Nevertheless, the available data demonstrate a dramatic expansion in investment growth to the mainland, from a cumulative US $1 billion in 1979-89, to some $3.7 billion in early 1991, to perhaps US $13 billion by the end of 1993 (of which only about US $4 billion has been officially approved). In the first half of 1994 alone, the ROC Investment Commission approved 587 projects involving US $467 million in Taiwan capital, with another 83 projects valued at US $118 million reported as being approved in early August.[9]

Taiwan investments are spread across the country, but most are concentrated in Guangdong and Fujian provinces, and secondly in the large coastal cities. Initial investments were predominantly in labor intensive and other "high cost" industries that have been losing competitiveness on Taiwan (e.g., food, electronic components, shoes, toys, agricultural machinery, ship salvage, and scrap). These early investments were made by small and medium-sized firms, and had short payback periods. More recent investments have been rising in capital and technology intensity, as well as size. Large firms are more strongly represented, and projects have much longer planning horizons.[10] For example, Taiwan's

Evergreen Group is seeking approval to indirectly invest US $80 million on the mainland in various port and container handling facilities.[11] Growing numbers of investments also have gone into services and real estate, along with speculative investments in the emerging stock markets. Today, Taiwan is the mainland's second largest investor after Hong Kong, substantially ahead of both Japan and the United States.

Travel and Communications

By the end of 1993, Taiwan residents were logging more that a million visits a year to the mainland, mostly via Hong Kong (in 1990, of the 950,000 Taiwan tourists entering China, 920,000 entered through Hong Kong).[12] The restrictions on who may visit the mainland have been steadily eased. Even government officials dealing with mainland affairs (below section chief) can now make "private" visits.[13] Mainland visitors to Taiwan, however are highly restricted. Besides the security concerns, officials worry about unleashing a flood of illegal immigrants. In 1992, there were already perhaps 36,000 mainlanders working illegally on Taiwan—some 500 per month were being deported.[14]

Direct transportation and communication links across the Strait continue to be forbidden, but indirect links have expanded dramatically. From March 1988 to July 1992 Taiwan residents mailed over 22 million items to the mainland and received almost 31 million in return. Between June 1989 and February 1992, over 1.6 million hours of cross-Strait phone calls were logged, along with 1,125 hours of telex messages.[15]

ROC Transportation and Communications Ministry announced on August 16, 1994 that cross-Strait telephone links will be upgraded by routing many calls through an international satellite rather than via the U.S. and other countries. The cable links through Hong Kong also will be improved. This preserves the principle of having only indirect communication. Since indirect communications began in 1990, the ROC has paid US $53 million in transmission fees to the U.S., Japan, Singapore, and Hong Kong.[16] Even some government representatives are admitting that the status quo is too costly, triggering speculation that certain direct links eventually will be allowed.

The Dynamics of Bilateral Relations

Mainland China has aggressively encouraged the growth of economic links with Taiwan. There are several clear objectives in this strategy. First, Taiwanese trade and investment offer significant contributions to Chinese economic growth, which has been among the highest national priorities since 1978. Second, the communist leaders believe that closer economic ties will reduce internal pressures for Taiwanese independence and improve the longer-term prospects for unification. Third, some of these leaders may also expect a more cooperative approach to cross-Strait relations to ease fears and tensions in Hong Kong about the 1997 takeover. Finally, growing interdependence seems to offer disproportionately greater political leverage to the PRC than to the ROC.

In recent years, the PRC has maintained a consistent "one country, two systems" policy toward negotiations over unification—the Hong Kong (1997) and Macao (1999) model. They have systematically rejected any compromise that might be seen as diluting Beijing's sovereignty, even as they have begun to deal across the straits in an increasingly pragmatic matter.

Since the late 1980s, Taiwan has progressively relaxed it's posture towards the mainland, including approval of the expanding economic ties. In part, this reflects growing self-confidence. The island's economic progress, the successful moves toward Taiwan democracy, and the greatly weakened domestic legitimacy of the communist leadership on the mainland have eased remaining KMT and ROC military fears of ideological contamination from across the Strait. Indeed, Taiwanese leaders now increasingly believe that greater interaction across the Strait will only demonstrate the superiority of Taiwan's path. Moreover, Taiwan's leadership also recognize that a China embedded in a complex, growing network of complementary economic exchanges may be a more stable, predictable, and pragmatic China—lowering the risk of armed conflict and increasing the odds for the longer-term emergence of a more pluralist form of government on the mainland. Enhanced economic relations also promised real economic benefits as well. Not only did China offer a huge market for Taiwanese goods, but the economic complementarity presented great benefits to Taiwanese industry. Many resources could be acquired more cheaply from China than anywhere else. Since Taiwan's labor-intensive and other high-cost industries were under great pressure to shut down or move offshore to lower cost locations, expanded cross-Strait economic ties provided an important response to Taiwan's changing economic context.

Yet, the rapid rise in the share of Taiwan's exports going to the mainland has raised concerns in official Taipei circles about the possible risks presented by too great a dependence on the huge mainland economy. Trade dependency (mainland trade as a share of total trade) has already passed the 10 percent mark that used to be viewed as the safe threshold.

In 1992, trade dependency on the mainland reached some 9-11 percent of two way trade and 13-18 percent of exports.[17] The existing series of restrictions on commerce, designed to reduce the political risk of economic interchange, are clearly inadequate to stop the current mainland surge. As a result, there is a split over future economic policy towards the mainland. Some Taiwanese leaders believe permissiveness has already gone too far and policy needs to slowdown and even pull back on cross-Strait trade and investment, while others favor immediately lifting the remaining restrictions to permit direct travel and trade. For now, this balance tends to temper any abrupt trade and investment policy changes from the status quo. Therefore, cautious, if erratic, opening towards the mainland will continue to be the most likely ROC cross-Strait economic policy for the foreseeable future—of course barring confrontational policies from the PRC.

Growing economic interaction has created a complex array of "governmental issues" that must be dealt with. Both sides have established "unofficial agencies" to negotiate the many practical details of the evolving relationship—the Beijing-based Association for Relations Across the Taiwan Strait (ARATS) and the Taipei-based Straits Exchange Foundation (SEF). The mainlanders have moved slowly in these practical negotiations. Indeed, one of the major problems has been the unwillingness of ARATS to build up a set of operational rules and precedents, preferring to treat every issue as a unique case. The mainlanders appear to be afraid that anything else would be seen as a concession of sovereign rights. Nonetheless, working level meetings have produced agreements on official document authentication and on registered mail, as well as dealing with a wide variety of specific issues and problems on an *ad hoc* basis.

The major breakthrough came with the agreement for an historic first meeting of the two sides on neutral ground in Singapore during April 1993. Although little specific progress was made, this meeting was widely perceived as the beginning of a new era in cross-Strait relations. The reality, of course, was quite a bit more restrained, but it did represent an opportunity for pragmatism that was just beginning to be utilized before being derailed by the unfortunate incident at Lake Qiandao on March 31, 1994, in which 24 Taiwan tourists were murdered, followed by incredibly bad management of the aftermath by Beijing authorities. This triggered a sharp increase in animosity and suspicion towards the mainland among Taiwanese.

The July 31-Aug. 7, 1994 talks in Taiwan between China's Tang Shubei (vice-chairman and general secretary for the Association for

Relations Across the Taiwan Strait) and his Taiwan counterpart, Chiao Jen-ho, appeared to signal a turnaround by making important, incremental progress on a number of bilateral issues. To some degree the constructive "Spirit-of-Singapore" (referring to the optimistic mood following the April 1993 meetings) was reignited. Both sides refrained from attacking one another and the meetings were held in a general spirit of conciliation and pragmatism.[19]

Areas of progress included: China's acknowledgment of Taiwan's right to try mainland hijackers and other alleged criminals before sending them back; agreement to allow mediators to collect evidence an assist in resolving disputes over fishing catches; agreement to allow coast guard vessels to intervene in disputes and perform rescue missions across territorial lines; as well as other agreements relating to stowaways; cultural, youth, scientific, and academic exchanges; and the establishment of a speed post. This agreement would suggest either an expansion of ARATS authority, or greater mainland interest in actually cutting deals.

However, several important issues were not resolved. For the purposes of this paper, the most important was the lack of significant progress on investment rights for Taiwanese businessmen. The mainland negotiators saw their new law submitted for approval at the end of 1993 to codify the treatment of Taiwanese investments as eliminating the need to establish the cross-Strait investment protection agreement sought after by the ROC negotiators.

Cooperation in International and Regional Affairs

Despite the progress in cross-Strait relations, little gain has been made on cooperation at the international level. The PRC automatically opposes any initiative by Taiwan or a third country that might raise the stature or official position of Taiwan, and aggressively pressures states to reduce official contact or relations.[19] Despite the steps that have led to joint membership in the ADB, APEC, and perhaps the GATT (WTO), China has shown remarkably little flexibility on a more pragmatic approach to Taiwan's involvement in multilateral organizations.

Because of Taiwan's economic stature, issues emerge with trading partners that require government action. At present, these are largely managed through "unofficial" bilateral channels that are little more than fictions established to play a complex political pasquinade in response to PRC pressures. Over the past several years, many states have quietly upgraded these unofficial bilateral ties. Unfortunately, such an unofficial approach has proven more difficult to use for participation in multilateral organizations.

Bringing both China and Taiwan into the WTO (GATT's successor organization) is an important step. As with their entry into APEC, it would create an umbrella for regular discussion and cooperation that is outside current political debate. Moreover, it locks both into internationally accepted conditions of behavior that will help integrate the mainland into the world economy. Taiwan is easy to bring in. It is a capitalist economy that has already gone through a variety of liberalizations. Only a few markets would face significant entry adjustment. The mainland is more problematic, and negotiations have been ongoing since 1988. Since the mainland would like to be a founding member of the WTO and participate in the development of its policies and procedures, Beijing has demonstrated some degree of accommodation, except on ROC membership. So far however, the industrial GATT/WTO signatories have yet to find mutually acceptable terms of accession.

Looking to the Future

Any attempt to assess economic dimensions of the future cross-Strait relationship must take into consideration how a number of critical trends and conditions are likely to interact with political and economic decision making. Some of these trends and conditions are briefly discussed, with the goal of identifying key questions.

Economic relations across the Strait is increasingly vital to economic progress on both sides. As long as economic progress has high political priority, both sides will consider alternatives and costs before seriously disrupting such mutually beneficial ties. This points to three key questions for consideration. How does economic interaction affect the relative political power of both sides over time? How does it interact with the perceived trade-off between economic and other goals as economic growth continues? And perhaps more fundamentally, what circumstances might lead to a dramatic change in the priority given to economic progress relative to other political, security, or nationalist goals?

Economic Interaction and Political Power

In terms of simple measures of political leverage (e.g., trade and investment shares), growing interaction across the Strait, combined with longer-term economic progress benefits the mainland more than Taiwan. Large economic entities simply have more options than smaller entities. Simple economic measures are rarely adequate to explain the political leverage inherent in complex commercial relationships—a key explanation of the repeated failure of so many efforts to use economic "sanctions" in pursuit of political and security goals. Nonetheless, these measures clearly point to a continuation of some aspects of the current policy mix on both sides of the Strait. In order to take advantage of disproportionate gains, the mainland has an incentive to induce as great an economic dependency on the part of Taiwan as possible, while seeking to assure that Taiwan firms do not gain control of "critical" goods or industries. At the same time, Taiwan has even stronger incentives to diversify its markets and investments as much as possible away from the mainland, while seeking to gain or keep at home the production of key goods, services, and technologies that the mainland would find difficult to replace. Intensified efforts to redirect foreign investment and trade towards ASEAN, which offers many of the same advantages as the PRC, partly reflect the desire to limit dependency on mainland markets.

More complex aspects of the political leverage inherent in commercial relations include individual, family, business, and institutional ties upon which commerce takes place, along with the perceptions of third parties about their indirect stake in the cross-Strait relationship. As noted above, a key aspect of the mainland's strategy was to use business ties to develop support for unification on its terms, both by reducing fear and by creating a strongly motivated pressure group to help influence policymaking on Taiwan. Similarly, Taiwan's leadership saw an opportunity to use people-to-people contact as a viable means of contrasting the two systems to as wide a mainland population as possible, thereby promoting Taiwan's policy positions. In addition, with the devolution of considerable power to the provinces and the great uncertainties inherent in the looming transition of power in Beijing, great potential advantages could accrue to establishing as wide as possible a network of contacts, influence, and perceived mutual benefit among the regional political and economic elites on the mainland.

Both strategies are working to some extent and, barring confrontation, almost certainly will continue. In the short-term, the mainland policy may have a stronger direct impact, since Taiwan is more democratic and trade dependent. In the longer term, Taiwan's policy builds on the fundamental dynamics of the emergence of a middle class and the pressures for political pluralism that inevitably result from economic progress. Whether either side can use the influence gained to affect outcomes of specific negotiations or disputes is uncertain, but the general impact will be to create broad pressures for non-confrontational approaches and outcomes. One unintended consequence of the openness strategy to both sides has been the unexpected sense of "difference" encountered by Taiwanese visitors to the mainland. Overall, this reduces support for unification and strengthens the independence movement.

The role of third parties can be extremely important. The mainland vehemently attacks third party commentary or intervention as interference in domestic affairs. Indeed, part of the reason for the PRC's continued staunch opposition to any direct or indirect role for Taiwan in international organizations and their aggressive response to all forms of official ties between Taiwan and third countries is their reluctance to grant any constraints on policy towards Taiwan to outside authority, such as that embedded in the United Nations Charter or even to commonly accepted norms of behavior among sovereign states. Likewise, seeking such constraints on mainland behavior is one of the factors driving ROC policy. Here mainland policy has had considerable success. With a handful of exceptions, Taiwan is excluded from international organizations and maintains diplomatic relations with only a small number of states.

Nevertheless, third party actions and positions can influence cross-Strait policy. The mainland desire to be accepted as a member of APEC clearly played an important role in their acquiescence to the joint entry of Hong Kong and Taiwan (of course after the *de rigueur,* vitriolic fight over Taiwan's name). Similarly, over the past several years, partly to avoid actions that might disrupt international ties vital to economic progress, the PRC has chosen not to go to the mat over the various upgrades in unofficial relations between Taiwan and third states— though aggressive efforts to further reduce Taiwan's diplomatic ties continue unabated.[20]

For the immediate future, declining international support for mainland intransigence combined with the logic of improving the effectiveness of Taiwan's participation in bilateral, regional, and global affairs suggests growing third party pressures on the mainland to extend its enhanced cross-Strait pragmatism to global relations. For example, Jakarta worked hard, though ultimately unsuccessfully, to prevent China from objecting to and blocking an invitation to President Lee Teng-hui to attend Asia-Pacific Economic Cooperation forum, scheduled for November 15, 1994.[21] Further, a relatively new direction in Taiwan's economic development strategy, as a regional operations center, has the dual benefit of developing stronger ties to major multinational corporations and through them their home governments, and building upon core strengths as the economy adapts to changing competitive conditions.[22] Although few countries will be willing to confront the PRC on what it sees as issues of sovereignty, trends point to a significant increase in third party pressures for greater flexibility.

Economic vs. Other Goals

For now, economic goals have high priority on both sides of the Taiwan Strait. Barring a fundamental change in political conditions (see below), economic growth will remain among the top objectives of the PRC government. It is the only viable means of rebuilding domestic legitimacy and leadership credibility, following the general discrediting of communist ideology, it is also the only way that China can establish its self-anointed role as the leader of Asia and its goal to be seen as a global power. This suggests that China will have strong incentives to avoid actions that threaten economic progress. However, it also is important to emphasize the strong nationalism and historically based resentment of foreign intervention in domestic affairs that pervades Chinese society. On issues related to Taiwan, there will remain strong tensions and an often unstable balance between nationalism and economics. As a result, logic and mutual benefit will often be less important than perception and form in the resolution of cross-Strait issues. This will be a special concern over the next several years, since whatever post-Deng government emerges will rely more heavily for political support on the PLA than the existing regime, and the core leadership of the military retains among the most inflexible positions regarding relations with Taiwan.[23]

On the Taiwan side, economic progress will remain a vital priority, but increasingly only one goal among others. We have already seen environmental concerns become a high enough priority to lead to the imposition of high costs on several important industries. Similarly, we have seen a clear willingness to accept the economic costs of greater policy instability resulting from democratization. Greater democratization also has forced strong consideration of domestic politics in the foreign policy decision process. In particular, the importance of unification has fallen relative to domestic policy concerns. Indeed, even the goal of unification is under challenge. This is perhaps most strongly reflected in the effects of the pro-independence position of the main opposition party, the DPP, on the government policy. It forces pursuit of policies that can demonstrate relatively near-term economic *and* political gains *vis-à-vis* the mainland in both cross-Strait and international arenas.

Dramatic Reordering of Priorities

There are only a few plausible, though very low probability, circumstances under which a dramatic reordering of priorities might occur, virtually all would increase political, security concerns relative to economics. Perhaps the most significant is a military confrontation between China and Taiwan. This has low probability, but cannot be dismissed in the near-term. The Taiwan issue could become embroiled in a contentious domestic PRC power transition. The power struggle for succession, of course, has already started, but Deng's eventual death will unlock the constraints. One issue agreed upon across the Chinese political spectrum is that Taiwan is part of China. Should Taiwan seek, or be perceived to seek independence during a PRC power struggle, it could become a nationalistic rallying point, around which the divided Chinese leadership could coalesce in support of military action. Because of the internal dynamics on both sides of the straits (the independence movement on Taiwan combined with the power transition on the mainland), we may be seeing an anomalous short-term increase in the risk of conflict even as the long-term trends are in favor of peaceful accommodation.

Another possibility is the risk of internal turmoil on the mainland. The details of any internal turmoil, of course, would be critical to the evolution of external policies, but is plausible only if the looming power transition somehow goes out of control. The reaction to foreigners could be xenophobic and potentially hostile. Taiwan could easily be drawn into the conflict, either as target or protagonist. This risk is reflected in the mainland government's past accusations of Taiwanese meddling in the events surrounding the Tiananmen Square confrontation, despite ROC efforts to maintain a low profile. Domestic affairs are almost certain to be very messy over the next several years, but the odds of severe internal turmoil are low.

A third possibility is a very bad outcome in the transfer of Hong Kong to PRC rule in 1997 (not the most likely outcome, but one increasingly that cannot be dismissed). Besides having the gravest economic consequences for Taiwan's indirect trade and investment with the mainland, it would confirm the deepest suspicions of the most conservative of the KMT/military leadership, while also reinforcing the independence platform of the DPP. At best, such an outcome would set back cross-Strait relations for years. The depth of Taiwanese suspicions about mainland intentions was revealed following the Lake Qiandao incident. Both governments were surprised at the magnitude of the public reaction, which undoubtedly was a factor in the greater flexibility of the ARATS leadership in the negotiations ending on August 6, 1994. At worst, such an event could trigger a willingness to challenge the PRC with a declaration of independence. With a visible Hong Kong catastrophe, the chances of Taiwan receiving international support for such a move would never be better.

Conclusions and Outlook

Economics has been an important element in the improved pragmatism of cross-Strait relations, an importance that is likely to remain high for the foreseeable future. However, important gains are likely only if the negotiations are kept largely over "low politics," generally taken to mean economic, technical, and bureaucratic actions that do not require senior political involvement. The progress made to date is mainly because both governments have been willing to devolve, at least rhetorically, some decisions out of the area of "high politics"—which in itself was a high politics decision. Although initiated by the mainland, Taiwan has gone the furthest in actions that reduce tensions and lay the foundation for pragmatism. The dynamic at work today in cross-Strait economic relations has shifted towards win-win from zero-sum, but continuation depends fundamentally upon mutual perception of trust—a trust that is demonstrably fragile today.

The next steps are threefold, and I believe politically feasible on both sides of the Strait. First, mutual accommodation needs to be made on a broader range of economic actions and agreements that can be treated as low politics. Second, some of this pragmatism needs to be brought to the international arena. Here compromise must come largely from the mainland. Without improved international access and stature, domestic politics in Taiwan almost certainly will evolve towards more radical initiatives. Third, the tit-for-tat propaganda rhetoric must continue to be reduced. Time has become the enemy on both sides of the Strait. The mainland leadership explicitly accelerated their unification objectives in the 1980s. Although reality has scaled back the goals, the leadership still demonstrates an unachievable impatience. In Taiwan, the DPP wants fast results and is willing to aggressively capitalize on any setback in the cross-Strait relationship. The fundamental reality is that until Hong Kong is successfully absorbed and the mainland leadership transition and its implications for policy are well understood, incremental gains are the best that can be expected.

Discussion
Can Economics
Mute the Conflict?

Harry Harding,
Brookings Institution

In principle, there are four general arguments regarding how economic trends and interaction can help mute the conflict across the Taiwan Strait. Unfortunately the theory and evidence for all four are at least partially flawed. The four can be called:

- Liberal
- Functional
- Cultural
- Economic modernization

The **liberal** argument suggests that countries with a strong stake in each other's economy do not go to war. It is a powerful argument, and one with strong suggestive historical evidence, but may be incorrect. Certainly a realist will argue that other factors will always dominate economic considerations in a crisis. Indeed, in this situation, the emerging asymmetry in economic leverage might well create behavior contrary to the liberal argument's predictions.

The **functionalist** argument is that growing economic interdependence requires growing interaction and the establishment of extensive interpersonal and organizational networks. These working relationships certainly will greatly enhance communication and reduce risk of inadvertent conflict, but they do not eliminate the basis for conflict nor will they necessarily evolve towards unification. Indeed, closer interaction may only serve to emphasize the differences in approach between the two sides.

The **cultural** argument builds on the notion that ties to the mainland will tend to reaffirm views of self as Chinese and reduce the risk of conflict. In fact, evidence suggests that growing ties both increase the sense of being Chinese and the sense of separateness between Taiwan and the mainland. It is not at all clear which will dominate at any point in time.

The **economic** modernization argument is mainly a focus on changes occurring on the mainland. The logic is that modernization, over the long term, will produce social and political changes reducing differences across the Strait, and in turn reducing barriers to peaceful accommodation ,even unification. This case is usually supported by the observation that small scale capitalism is sweeping the country from its introduction from Taiwan and Hong Kong. A key question is whether this is producing a civil society less inclined to conflict, or a bureaucratic capitalism (e.g. prewar Germany or Japan) that could well support conflictual policies.

Another economic trend that participants felt deserved special consideration as we continue to monitor the cross-Strait relationship is the impact of "hollowing out" of Taiwanese industry over time, as costs and other factors force many parts of Taiwan industry to move offshore. Increasingly Taiwan investment on the mainland must compete with investment at home and elsewhere in Asia. This open-ended trend may create more problems than it moderates. Certainly, some are increasingly concerned that Taiwan policy may become more vulnerable to being held hostage to economic leverage. At the same time economic interaction does not always imply economic vulnerability to the state. For example, much of the Taiwan investment on the mainland is in real estate, resorts, hotels, etc. A mainland policy that affects these assets will clearly impact the wealth of the Taiwan owners, with potential economic consequences for their operations elsewhere, but, in fact, is not a critical vulnerability to Taiwan's economy. Not surprisingly, "the devil is in the details," and serious analysis of economic vulnerability needs to drop well below the crude aggregate measures commonly used.

This economic leverage concern is both raised and muted by Taiwan's plan to develop into a regional multinational corporation operations center. This could well require direct transportation linkages with the mainland— and potential for even greater dependence—in order to support the type of business development sought by the ROC government. At the same time, expanding the regional focus will also help diversify the Taiwan economy among customers, and into higher value-added products and services that could be less vulnerable to crude leverage.

The participants also felt that any discussion of long term effects of economic interaction across the Strait must pay attention to the discontinuity caused by the post-1997 Hong Kong transition. Even though all of players are deep into preparation for this event, many of the consequences remain unclear. Focus is most often on the impact of a failed transition. But success has its own uncertainties. For example, one of those the most unclear consequences of a successful transition can be stated in the question: If this "one country, two systems" approach works for Hong Kong, why not elsewhere across China?

Essentially, the participants supported the notion that growing economic interaction across the Strait has a significant positive impact on improving cross-Strait relations, especially over the longer-term. The discussion also demonstrated a clear concern that the unique characteristics of the mainland-Taiwan conflict tended to raise uncertainty about the power of economics to restrain conflict in a crisis.

SECTION IV
Bilateral Interaction with the U.S., Japan, and Southeast Asia, and the Evolving Cross-Strait Relationship

CHAPTER 5
U.S. Policy Toward Evolving Taiwan-Mainland China Relations

Ralph N. Clough,
School of Advanced International Studies,
Johns Hopkins University

Historically, the U.S. interest in Taiwan was not based on the value of the resources on the island or even the use of the island as a base for the projection of U.S. power. In the latter half of the 19th century, during the heyday of territorial expansion by imperialist powers, the U.S. government rejected several proposals to acquire the island as a colonial possession. At the end of World War II Americans viewed Taiwan as a small, distant island with a population of 6 million, that would as a matter of course be taken from Japan and returned to China. No thought was given to making it a U.S. territory.

Americans became interested in Taiwan only when it began to be seen as an element in a broad U.S. global strategy. In 1948-49, when the conquest of the China mainland by the Chinese Communist Party appeared inevitable, the Truman administration and Congressional leaders became increasingly concerned that seizure of Taiwan by Chinese Communist forces would threaten U.S. interests in the western Pacific. The U.S. government explored various methods of denying Taiwan to the Communists: defending the island with U.S. forces, giving large-scale military and economic aid to the Nationalist government, backing the Taiwan independence movement, or placing Taiwan under United Nations trusteeship. None of these stratagems seemed feasible.[1] In January 1950, President Truman announced that the United States would not provide military aid or advice to the Nationalist government nor become involved in the Chinese civil conflict. Only after the signing of the Sino-Soviet alliance and the North Korean attack on South Korea in June 1950 did Truman reverse himself and decide that U.S. force must be used to prevent the People's Republic of China (PRC) from taking over Taiwan. Taiwan became part of a U.S.-sponsored bulwark to contain Sino-Soviet expansionism.

For more than 20 years the United States maintained diplomatic relations with the Republic of China (ROC) on Taiwan, continued to recognize it as the legitimate government of China, and refused recognition to the PRC. Gradually, however, it became evident that the PRC was firmly in control of the China mainland and that the rift between Moscow and Beijing was serious and deep. Moreover, international support for the continued recognition of the ROC as the representative of China in the United Nations was rapidly eroding. Established U.S. policy toward the PRC and Taiwan was too far out of line with the reality of the international situation.

In 1971 President Richard Nixon recognized that opening a diplomatic relationship with the PRC would strengthen Washington's position relative to Moscow and would facilitate the withdrawal of U.S. forces from Vietnam. In 1979 President Jimmy Carter completed the shift of relationships begun by Nixon. He recognized the PRC as the sole legal government of China, broke diplomatic relations with the ROC, and terminated the mutual security treaty with that government. Once again the United States drastically altered its relationship with Taiwan, not because of a change in U.S. bilateral interests in Taiwan, but as part of a broader regional and global strategy.

In 1979, as in 1950, there was a broad consensus among U.S. decision makers on the desirable goal of U.S. policy toward Taiwan, but deep differences on the tactics to be adopted and the price that the United States should be willing to pay to achieve that goal. In 1950 political and military leaders endorsed the desirability of keeping Taiwan free of Beijing's control, but shrank from intervening with U.S. military force to achieve that end. They differed sharply on whether large-scale military and economic aid to the Nationalists would prevent the military conquest of Taiwan by the PRC or would simply pad the pockets of Nationalist officials, add to the military booty Beijing would gain through a successful takeover, and deepen and prolong the confrontation between the PRC and the United States to the benefit of the USSR.

In 1979 there was a general agreement on the desirability of having full diplomatic relations with the PRC at a time when most Americans perceived the need for cooperation between the two governments in resisting Soviet and Vietnamese expansionism. But again sharp differences existed concerning the price to be paid in terms of U.S. relations with Taiwan. Many, particularly those in the Congress disgruntled at the failure of the Carter administration to consult them adequately before reaching agreement with the PRC, criticized the deal as not effectively protecting U.S. interests in Taiwan. Consequently, they wrote into the Taiwan Relations Act strong provisions designed to help protect Taiwan against hostile takeover by the mainland regime.

By 1979 the United States had developed an array of interests in Taiwan itself that had not existed in 1950. U.S. companies had substantial investments in Taiwan and the island had become one of the principal trading partners of the United States. Taiwan was a leading recipient of loans from the U.S. Export-Import Bank. The ROC relied on the United States for the weapons needed by its armed forces and coproduced F5-E fighter aircraft. Tens of thousands of students from Taiwan held advanced degrees from American universities. Most of them remained in the United States, many becoming American citizens, but they kept in close touch with family members in Taiwan. A multifarious web of personal, family, and institutional relationships linked the two societies, creating a widely-felt American concern with Taiwan's future. Hence, it would have been impossible in 1979 for any U.S. president to write off Taiwan as Truman had done in January 1950. Because he was aware of these U.S. interests, Carter rejected the PRC's demand that arms sales to Taiwan be halted and the Congress included in the TRA a provision binding the administration to continue to supply weapons needed for Taiwan's defense.

The U.S. decision in 1979 to shift diplomatic relations from Taipei to Beijing was based on broad strategic considerations as was the U.S. agreement in 1982 to limit arms sales to Taiwan. By the early 1990s, however, the strategic equation governing U.S. relations with the PRC and Taiwan had changed radically. The Soviet Union had crumbled and a rapidly growing network of economic and other relations had defused the hostile confrontation between Taiwan and the PRC. Moreover, Taiwan had become the fifth largest trading partner of the United States and other U.S. interests in Taiwan had continued to grow. Taiwan was the

15th largest trading nation in the world with over $90 billion in foreign exchange reserves and large and growing investments in the United States, Southeast Asia and mainland China.

In addition, Taiwan had made the transformation from an authoritarian to a democratic society at a time when communist regimes in Europe were collapsing and being replaced by democratic systems. The three remaining communist regimes in Asia: the PRC, Vietnam, and North Korea, appeared to be vestiges of a vanishing political order. Already the PRC and Vietnam were well advanced in changing from command economies to free market economies increasingly integrated into the global economy. In North Korea Kim Il Sung was desperately trying to shore up a declining economy and keep a nuclear weapons program as insurance against outside efforts to bring down his regime. Taiwan, along with South Korea and countries in Southeast Asia, seemed to be on the cutting edge of economic and political reform that was sweeping the world.

Formulating U.S. Policy in a Changed World

The disappearance of cold war alignments and policies left in its wake a confused picture in which long submerged ethnic rivalries broke into the open in the form of bloody civil conflicts. The world is less stable and predictable. The interests of the big powers are adversely affected by disorder in the world, but where, how, and to what extent to intervene to restore order has become difficult to determine.

With the decline in the military component of coalition politics that predominated during the cold war, economic interests have become dominant. The predominance of economics would appear to improve the international influence of the United States, which has the world's largest economy. Yet, economic instruments are often difficult to use, especially in a democratic system, where interest groups may succeed in getting the government to act in support of their particular interest, rather than the overall national interest. The relatively low American savings rate limits the resources available to the U.S. government for attaining objectives abroad and makes it dependent on a continuing influx of capital from foreign individuals, corporations, and governments. The growing role of transnational corporations, the instantaneous shifting of funds around the world through international capital markets, and the impact of the international media all place constraints on the ability of governments to manage their own economies and to anticipate and cope with international crises.

The unaccustomed fluidity that has replaced cold war rigidities has made a popular consensus on the organizing principles of U.S. foreign policy difficult to achieve. In the absence of an agreed framework or vision of how the United States should respond to crises in this changed world order, each new policy proposal is likely to provoke virulent controversy.

Policies Toward the PRC and Taiwan

It is in this new and confusing environment in which the United States is called upon to review its policies toward the PRC and Taiwan. Obviously, the cold war certainties that determined the principal foreign policy objectives of the United States have disappeared. U.S. policies toward the PRC and Taiwan must be based on our bilateral interests in each and on how each fits into U.S. global and regional strategy. U.S. policies will also be affected by the state of relations between the PRC and Taiwan, which have grown increasingly complex since 1987.

For many reasons, U.S. policy toward the PRC must be an important component of U.S. global and regional policy.[2] It is the most populous country in the world, with the third largest economy, an economy that has grown more rapidly over the past decade than any other large economy. It is engaged in a military modernization program which, in time, will provide it with a powerful nuclear and conventional power projection capability. It is one of the five permanent members of the UN Security Council, with veto power over any action that body may wish to take. It played an indispensable role in the international effort to resolve the Cambodian problem. As a producer of nuclear weapons, missiles and conventional weapons, it must be involved in measures by the world community to prevent the spread of nuclear weapons and missiles and to limit sales of conventional arms.

Given the dominance of economic issues in today's world, the United States must pay particular attention to U.S.-China economic relations. U.S. direct investment in China has grown rapidly, the cumulative pledged total reaching $10.8 billion in 1993, with at least $4 billion delivered. U.S. trade in 1993 was $40.3 billion, of which $31.5 billion was imports by the United States, creating a trade deficit of $22.8 billion. In line with U.S. efforts to create a more congenial global economic environment for the United States, the U.S. government has engaged vigorously in negotiations with the PRC aimed at improving market access for U.S. exports and service industries, improving the protection of intellectual property, and persuading the Chinese government to make extensive changes in its financial and trade regimes in order to qualify for membership in GATT.

In strategic terms, Taiwan is far less important to the United States than the PRC. It is not a UN member. It does not possess nuclear weapons and its military potential for becoming either a disruptive or cooperative factor in the region is much less than that of the PRC. In economic terms, the disparity between the two is smaller. Although the PRC's total foreign trade in 1993 of $196 billion substantially exceeded Taiwan's $162 billion, each had the same amount of two-way trade with the United States: $40 billion. U.S. exports to Taiwan, however, at $16.7 billion were nearly double the $8.8 billion in U.S. exports to the PRC. Cumulative U.S. direct investments in Taiwan of $3.1 billion were somewhat less than the U.S. direct investment of $4 billion in mainland China and the gap will increase rapidly as the rest of the $10.8 billion contracted for by the end of 1993 arrives on the scene.

In many ways, U.S. bilateral negotiations with Taiwan on economic issues paralleled those with the PRC. We thought the opening of Taiwan's market to U.S. exports and service industries, improved protection of American-owned intellectual property, and the removal of restrictions required to qualify Taiwan for membership in the GATT. We were concerned about the growing trade deficit in U.S. trade with both places. Up to the present, negotiations with Taiwan have achieved greater results than negotiations with the PRC, particularly in getting better enforcement of the laws protecting intellectural property. Moreover, Taiwan's trade surplus with the United States has been declining for several years, while the PRC's surplus has grown rapidly, in part because of the transfer from Taiwan to mainland China of labor-intensive factories exporting to the United States.

Academic, scientific and family ties between mainland China and the United States began to develop on a large scale in the 1980s, after the establishment of diplomatic relations between Washington and Beijing. By 1989 40,000 students from the PRC were in the United States, compared to 26,000 from Taiwan. As had happened earlier with Taiwan's students, a large proportion of the mainland students remained in the United States, a trend intensified after the suppression of the student movement at Tiananmen in 1989. Business, institutional, and family connections with China have multiplied, adding steadily to the pool of Americans who have a stake in the maintenance of friendly relations between the United States and the PRC.

Thus, the United States has important interests in maintaining good relations with both the PRC and Taiwan. In the past, it has successfully pursued a dual-track policy, dealing separately with Beijing and Taipei and refusing to become involved in mediating the differences between them or in exerting pressure on either party to negotiate with the other. It has maintained the position taken in the communiqués signed with the PRC that it will recognize only the PRC as the legal government of China, that it does not challenge the view taken on both sides of the Taiwan Strait that Taiwan is part of China, that it will maintain only nongovernmental relations with the people of Taiwan, and that differences between Beijing and Taipei should be settled by the Chinese people themselves.

Growing Links Between Taiwan and Mainland China

Since 1987 when President Chiang Ching-kuo lifted the ban on travel from Taiwan to mainland China, travel, trade and investment between the two sides of the Taiwan Strait have boomed, despite the ROC's prohibition of direct travel, trade, or investment.[3] By the end of 1993 residents of Taiwan were making more than a million visits a year to mainland China. Taiwan's entrepreneurs had invested some $13 billion in the mainland and two-way trade had exceeded $13 billion.[4]

The PRC vigorously encouraged the expansion of these economic links, both because of their contribution to economic growth on the mainland and in order to create as dense a network of connections as possible to improve prospects for unification and to weaken pressures for Taiwan independence. The ROC also approved the trend, as a means of easing tension with the PRC and to make possible the transfer to the mainland of Taiwan's labor-intensive industries. ROC authorities were concerned, however, lest Taiwan's economy become too dependent on the huge PRC economy and they imposed various restrictions on the economic interaction in order to minimize that risk. They hoped that in the long run mainland China's interaction with the outside world would result in the replacement of the communist regime by a government responsive to the people.

Negotiations Between Beijing and Taipei

The PRC pressed for the opening of negotiations on the unification of Taiwan with mainland China under the "one country, two systems" formula to be applied to Hong Kong and Macao in 1997 and 1999. The ROC authorities, however, rejected the PRC's demand that they accept

Beijing's sovereignty and negotiate in the capacity of KMT party officials or provincial officials. They declared that they would negotiate only if the PRC recognized the government of Taiwan as an equal political entity, dropped its threat to use force, and stopped interfering with the ROC's efforts to improve its international status. Since the PRC rejected these conditions as an attempt to create the proscribed "two Chinas" or "one China, one Taiwan," negotiations have not occurred.

Burgeoning people-to-people relations have given rise to many problems that require government intervention to resolve. In order to negotiate on such practical problems, the two sides have established nominally unofficial agencies, the Straits Exchange Foundation (SEF) in Taipei and the Association for Relations across the Taiwan Strait (ARATS) in Beijing. In a series of working level meetings the SEF and the ARATS reached agreement on the authentication of official documents and the handling of registered mail. A meeting in Singapore in April 1993 of Koo Chen-fu and Wang Daohan, the chairmen of the two agencies, agreed on an agenda and schedules for subsequent meetings. The two sides have had difficulty, however, in reaching agreement on the repatriation of Chinese illegally sneaking into Taiwan from the mainland, the punishment of hijackers, and the resolution of fishing disputes. These negotiations involved an acknowledgment of the Taiwan government's legal jurisdiction in such matters, which the PRC was reluctant to concede. SEF/ARATS negotiations were further delayed by the Thousand Island Lake tragedy in March 1994 in which 24 tourists from Taiwan were murdered. Despite the difficulties, both sides appear determined to maintain the dialogue in order to facilitate the continuation and expansion of people-to-people relations and to hold open the prospect of eventual unification.

Taiwan's International Status

While the opening of travel and trade across the Taiwan Strait have elicited a degree of arms-length cooperation on the part of the two governments, no similar cooperation is evident in the international arena. On the contrary, the PRC opposes any action by Taiwan that raises its unofficial relationships with foreign countries closer to the official level. Given Taiwan's important role in the world economy, states have found it necessary to engage in a wide range of governmental actions to expand economic relationships with Taiwan. The more important the economic relationships, the more difficult it is to avoid taking governmental actions to promote them. Thus, an elaborate charade has developed in which governments pretend that their relations with Taiwan are purely unofficial,

Taipei works hard to give these relations an official aura, and Beijing protests any action by a foreign state that seems to raise the degree of officiality with which it treats Taiwan. For Beijing, the contest with Taipei in the international arena is a zero-sum game, in which any gain by the ROC is a loss to itself.

President Lee Teng-hui has taken advantage of Taiwan's economic clout with the predominance of economic issues in the world to pursue a "pragmatic diplomacy" that has substantially improved Taiwan's international status, despite the PRC's efforts to interfere. His gains rest on the reality that Taiwan has function for decades as a de facto sovereign state and continues to do so, while the PRC case rests on the myth that Taiwan is a province of the PRC and that the PRC therefore has the right to control its international relations.

Incremental gains in Taiwan's relations with foreign countries have failed, however, to satisfy the people of Taiwan, who feel that the island's economic and political progress entitles it to equal treatment with other states. Hence, the KMT and the opposition party have joined forces in a campaign for Taiwan's admission to the United Nations. Although the PRC can block its entry, the campaign serves to draw world attention to Taiwan's situation and to the unjustness of the PRC's denial to the 22 million people in Taiwan of representation in the UN and other intergovernmental bodies.

Taiwan's Domestic Politics and Mainland Policy

As the political system in Taiwan has evolved from the authoritarian structure under Chiang Kei-shek and Chiang Ching-kuo to the increasingly pluralistic and democratic system presided over by Lee Teng-hui, Taiwan's international position and policy toward the mainland have become prominent political issues. The Democratic Progressive Party (DPP), which won nearly one-third of the seats in the Legislative Yuan in the December 1992 election, opposes the unification of Taiwan with mainland China and would establish an independent Republic of Taiwan. DPP members favor restraint in developing economic and other links with the mainland.[5] The Chinese New Party, consisting of a small number of prominent mainlander politicians who left the KMT in 1993, is prounification and advocates the early establishment of direct travel and trade across the Strait. Some senior mainlander members of the KMT hold similar views. The mainstream of the KMT, however, who back Lee Teng-hui, while in principle supporting unification and opposing Taiwan independence, tend to favor the status quo, de facto independence. They see little prospect of early unification, but they would refrain from declaring formal independence, for fear that it would not win the international recognition and support the independence advocates hope for, and might provoke a military reaction from Beijing.

Beijing's threat of force is a powerful deterrent to a formal declaration of independence by the people of Taiwan, but it also stimulates antagonism among them toward the government in Beijing. The PRC's interference with the improvement of Taiwan's international status strengthens that antagonism. The Tiananmen affair, the continued repression of political opponents by the Communist leadership, and suspicions of military complicity in the Thousand Island Lake murders make it very difficult for Beijing to create support in Taiwan for early unification under the "one country, two systems" concept. The people of Taiwan, observing Beijing's adamant opposition to Hong Kong Governor Chris Patten's modest effort to make the colony's political system somewhat more democratic prior to 1997, have little confidence in the promise of autonomy for Taiwan under PRC sovereignty. Thus, most of the basically conservative people of Taiwan favor the current state of peaceful coexistence between Taiwan and mainland China rather than efforts to move quickly toward either unification or independence.

Controversy in Taiwan over mainland policy has focused recently not on the broad issues of unification or independence, but on the pace and extent of Taiwan's economic integration with the mainland. One group, represented by Huang Kun-huei, chairman of the Mainland Affairs Commission, would maintain the ban on direct trade, travel, and investment and expresses concern that Taiwan might become too dependent on the mainland economy and therefore subject to political pressure from Beijing. The other group, represented by the minister of economic affairs, Chiang Ping-kun, while accepting the necessity of some restrictions on trade and investment in the mainland, favors opening direct trade and travel across the Strait. Chiang argues that if Taiwan is to attain its goal of becoming a regional operations center for transnational corporations, it must offer direct connections with the largest and most dynamic economy in the region.

Even though the unification or independence controversy has been somewhat muted during 1994, it remains the most divisive and potentially explosive issue in Taiwan politics. It could significantly influence the result of Taiwan's first popular presidential election scheduled for 1996. The DPP has maintained its commitment to independence, but the new party chairman, Shih Ming-te, elected in May 1994, declared that if the DPP should gain power it would not abruptly declare independence without consulting the wishes of the people of Taiwan.[6] Whether the people of Taiwan would be more inclined to vote for independence than they have been in the past would depend on a variety of variables:[7]

- the credibility of the PRC's threat to respond with military force;
- the perceived reliability of the US commitment to Taiwan's security in the Taiwan Relations Act;
- the extent of the conviction that only by dropping the one-China policy and embracing independence could Taiwan gain international recognition and respect;
- the value attached to the further development of economic and other relations with mainland China.

Taiwan-PRC Relations and U.S. Policy

In formulating policies toward the PRC and Taiwan, the United States must take account of the two principal strands comprising PRC-Taiwan relations: the growing interaction across the Taiwan Strait and the contest between Beijing and Taipei in the international arena.[8] The United States cannot avoid becoming involved at some degree in both these aspects of PRC-Taiwan relations.

Interaction across the Strait: The primary benefit gained by the United States from the growing interaction between Taiwan and mainland China is in the decline in hostility and the risk of conflict between the two. The military clash in the Taiwan Strait would shatter regional peace and stability, and force on the United States extremely difficult and unwelcome policy choices. Consequently, encouragement of peaceful coexistence between Beijing and Taipei should be a principal purpose of U.S. policy toward the two.

In concrete terms, what should the United States do to promote peaceful interaction across the Taiwan Strait? For the most part, the interaction rests on the complementarity of the two economies and the attraction of the China mainland for tourists from Taiwan. In these areas, whether interaction proceeds successfully depends on the decisions of individuals and the policies of the two governments. The United States can do little to promote it other than to commend the governments in Beijing and Taipei for the success attained. It would be undesirable for the U.S. government to take positions on the tactics being pursued by each side, as, for example, in respect to direct travel and trade. Becoming involved in issues best handled by the two governments themselves would unnecessarily complicate U.S. relations with both governments.

The United States could indirectly encourage the expansion of cross-Strait relations by supporting the evolution of Taiwan into a regional operations center. U.S. transnational corporations with activities on both sides of the Strait would benefit from the removal of restrictions needed to further the internationalization of Taiwan's economy. To some extent the United States has been exerting pressure in this direction through its negotiations with Taipei on its admission to GATT.

Bilateral Relations with Beijing and Taipei: In its bilateral relations with Taiwan the United States has had to walk a delicate line imposed by its commitments to the PRC to have only nongovernmental relations with the people of Taiwan and to recognize the PRC as the sole legal government of China. In September 1994 the State Department announced the results of a review of U.S. policy toward Taiwan initiated early in the Clinton administration. Basic policy was left unchanged, but several small adjustments were made in the conduct of policy, including easing restrictions on high-level visits and on meetings in government offices. The name of Taiwan's office in the United States was changed from the Coordination Council for North American Affairs to the Taipei Economic and Cultural Office in the United States, a more readily identifiable name that conforms to that used in Japan and various other countries. Beijing protested the action as interference in its domestic affairs, while Taipei expressed disappointment that it did not go further in upgrading the relationship.[9]

The increasing participation in mainland China's economy by Taiwan entrepreneurs can make them vulnerable to U.S. economic sanctions imposed by the United States against the PRC. For example, if President Clinton had withdrawn most-favored-nation treatment of PRC exports to the United States, hundreds of Taiwan-owned factories on the China mainland would have suffered losses. To the extent that economies on both sides of the Strait become more integrated, U.S. economic decision-makers will have to assess the implications of U.S. policies for both economies. Such considerations influenced the Congress in its rejection of the so-called "Pelosi bill," put forward by some lawmakers as a means of exerting pressure on the PRC to curb its violations of human rights. The bill sought to avoid damage to enterprises owned by Hong Kong, Taiwan, or mainland Chinese private entrepreneurs by limiting U.S. economic sanctions to the products of factories operated by the People's

Liberation Army or other state agencies, but the administration viewed such a law as impossible to administer.

The United States is affected not only by the legal cooperation between persons on the two sides of the Strait, but also by cooperation to violate U.S. law. A recent example was the use of Taiwan-owned fishing vessels with captains and crews from Taiwan to smuggle mainland Chinese into the United States. The U.S. government had to contact Taipei for permission to board the vessels on the high seas and get approval from Beijing to repatriate the intended illegal immigrants. The government in Taipei agreed, reluctantly, to reimburse the United States for the cost of intercepting and repatriating them.[10] Increased interaction between Taiwan and mainland China will provide other opportunities for criminals on the two sides of the Strait to collude in violating U.S. laws. Consequently, the United States has an interest in improving its intelligence capabilities on such activities and encouraging Beijing and Taipei to cooperate with the U.S. government in suppressing them.

Taiwan's International Position: The implications for U.S. policy of the growing interaction across the Taiwan Strait as discussed above suggest that relatively minor adjustments in policies toward Beijing and Taipei will protect U.S. interests. It is in respect to Taiwan's international position that the United States may be confronted with more difficult decisions. Increasing discontent among the people of Taiwan with their lack of official status in the world community have impelled Lee Teng-hui's administration to seek more innovative ways to enhance Taiwan's international relationships and to join with the DPP in a campaign to bring it into the United Nations. Prolonged failure to improve Taiwan's international status could strengthen popular support for the DPP and for Taiwan independence.

The U.S. interests in East Asian stability and in relations with the PRC would appear to be best served by holding firmly to the policy of recognizing the PRC as the only legal government of China, avoiding comment on the status of Taiwan, and discouraging independence advocates from expecting U.S. recognition of an independent state of Taiwan or U.S. military intervention to forestall PRC use of force against it. Yet, such an exercise of realpolitik might be opposed by many Americans strongly attached to the principle of self-determination and impressed with the contrast between the politically repressive communist regime in Beijing and the democratic system in Taiwan. Americans also prefer clarity over ambiguity and might well ask if Taiwan has function as a de facto independent state for so many years, why not acknowledge that reality by extending de jure recognition? The ambiguity in U.S. policy that has served U.S. interests well for the past 15 years may become more difficult to maintain. Indeed, members of Congress have recently submitted draft resolutions calling for the U.S. government to come out in support of the admission of Taiwan to the United Nations General Assembly, a move that would be a significant step toward the formal acceptance of Taiwan as a separate sovereign state.

In light of the fluidity and uncertainties in the international system referred to earlier in this chapter, as well as the difficulty of predicting political change in the PRC and Taiwan over the next few years, the U.S. government would be well advised to avoid any abrupt new departures in its policies toward the PRC and Taiwan. It is certainly in the U.S. interest for the U.S. government to do what little it can to further the development of a sustainable state of peaceful coexistence between Beijing and Taipei. Quiet support for Taiwan's activities in the Asian Development Bank and APEC and for its admission to GATT can readily be justified by Taiwan's economic importance. Consultations with other leading World Bank members, as well as with the PRC and Taiwan, should be undertaken in order to develop a formula for Taiwan's participation in the World Bank and the IMF. Similar consultations are desirable in regard to Taiwan's participation in certain technical intergovernmental organizations affiliated with the United Nations, but it would not be productive at present for the U.S. government to confront the PRC on the issue of Taiwan's admission to the UNGA.

Conclusion

The Taiwan Strait is peaceful today, but it may not remain so indefinitely because it rests on two clashing views of reality jostling with each other for dominance. Only if the leaders on each side can work out a lasting accommodation of the two views can rising tension and possibly even a military confrontation be avoided.

The reality subscribed to by the leadership and people of Taiwan is that the island has functioned in the world community for decades as a de facto independent sovereign state and that it deserves broader recognition and greater scope to carry on international activities. Pressure on the leadership to show progress in expanding Taiwan's international role can only grow stronger as the 1996 date for the first popular election of the president approaches. The conviction of the people of Taiwan that their view of reality should govern Taiwan's future will be held even more firmly as increasing numbers of people elsewhere in the world express sympathy with their objective.

The other reality is that Taiwan lies within mainland China's magnetic field, from which it cannot escape. It is bound to China by history, geography, economic complementarity, and cultural affinity. China's size and power are so great relative to Taiwan that other governments hesitate to challenge the PRC's interference with Taiwan's efforts to win formal acceptance as an international actor. Hence, the people of Taiwan have little choice but to try to work out their destiny primarily through accommodation with the PRC.

PRC leaders, who are not popularly elected, have a broader range of choices than Taiwan's leaders. They can totally reject Taiwan's view of reality, strive to limit as much as possible Taiwan's freedom of action in the international arena, and brandish the threat of force to deter the people of Taiwan from moving toward independence and to compel them eventually to accept unification on PRC terms. Such a policy would breed hostility toward the PRC among the people of Taiwan and would encourage the emergence of extremists, who might take desperate and dangerous courses of action.

The opposite policy for the PRC, which would produce a healthier relationship between the peoples on either side of the Taiwan Strait, would be to bind Taiwan to the mainland by loosening Beijing's grip. Instead of placing a high priority on restricting Taiwan's international role, the PRC would look for ways in which allowing Taiwan more freedom of action would result in international cooperation between Beijing and Taipei to the benefit of both. A friendlier posture toward Taiwan's efforts to improve its international status would pay off in reduced restrictions imposed by the government in Taiwan on cross-Strait interaction and a resulting acceleration in the growth of the web of relationships favored by the PRC and beneficial to both parties.

An accommodation between Beijing and Taipei would not finally resolve the question of Taiwan's status, but would make the relationship between the two sides of the Strait easier to manage and would prevent a decline toward a hostile confrontation. Each side would make concessions to the other's perception of reality. The current leadership in Taipei through its commitment to the National Unification Guidelines and in other ways already acknowledges that Taiwan's future lies in a close association with mainland China.

The PRC leadership, however, declines to acknowledge the reality of Taiwan's status as an international actor. It also fails to take sufficient account of the political dynamics in Taiwan, which compel the ruling party to demonstrate to the voters that it is working energetically to improve Taiwan's international status. It is in the PRC's own interest to make concessions in this area, otherwise it risks contributing to the rise of power of leaders who reject the long-term goal of unification with the China mainland and would slow the expansion of links across the Strait. As the "big brother," the PRC is in the better position to make the concessions required to nourish the bonds between the island and the mainland.

It is in the U.S. interest to promote better understanding of the realities on the two sides of the Strait, so that the governments can reach agreements that make the cross-Strait relationship more stable. Americans, through official and unofficial channels, have access to decision-makers and other influential individuals in mainland China and Taiwan. As outsiders, Americans can take a more objective view of the differences between Beijing and Taipei than those directly involved. Without becoming enmeshed in mediating between the two sides, Americans can, primarily through private conversations, help each side to better understand the other. They can help to strengthen the influence of moderate officials and politicians in Beijing and Taipei who recognize the importance of tenaciously pursuing the arduous task of fashioning a long-lasting state of peaceful coexistence between the two sides of the Strait.

CHAPTER 6
Japanese Policies Toward the PRC and Taiwan

Robert A. Scalapino,
University of California at Berkeley

In mid-1994, foreign policy was not Japan's highest priority. Not since the chaotic years shortly after World War II, had the domestic political situation been so unstable and uncertain. The one and one-half party system, having insured stability for nearly four decades, appeared to have ended in the midst of corruption, mediocrity, and the weariness of veteran politicians too long in office. The decline of the Liberal Democratic Party (although it is too early to proclaim its death) came at a time when the entire generation of prewar educated politicians were passing from the political stage, and a new generation, the so-called "aging baby-boomers," was coming to the fore.

The restructuring of the political parties is proving to be a complex, multifaceted task not likely to be consummated quickly. The splits within the LDP have resulted in the emergence of a multiplicity of new parties and a series of highly unstable coalitions. The current Murayama Tomiichi cabinet, composed as it is, of the Social Democratic Party (SDPJ) and the LDP, verges on the bizarre, although it has been clear for some time that the Socialists were hopelessly out of touch with times, and would have to fundamentally reconstruct their policies if they wished to play a role in governance.

Few observers, however, believe that the present government can have a lengthy tenure despite its survival through its initial period, or that the highly unstable party structure currently in existence will long survive.

The next Diet elections will be based upon a new electoral system involving a combination of single member constituencies and seats allocated to parties on the basis of their percentage of the vote. It seems inevitable that party restructuring and coalescence will take place prior to that election, probably in 1995, possibly earlier.

Meanwhile, the new policies set forth by recent governments have related almost wholly to domestic issues. In line with widespread demands both abroad and at home, deregulation in the economic arena has been pledged. Promises to seek the reduction of bureaucratic power have also been repeatedly issued. Past corruption in the political system has been acknowledged, and new legislation to tackle this problem has been forwarded. On a broader front, greater political openness has been championed.

Yet most of these pledges have been unfulfilled as yet. Scanty deregulation has actually taken place. The bureaucracy remains at the helm of governance, and given the fragility of current parties and political leadership, it could scarcely be otherwise. The most egregious cases of corruption have been prosecuted, but it remains to be seen whether the pattern of Japanese politics, with an exchange of funds for favors, will be changed. Money politics here as elsewhere is a prominent feature of the political landscape, and the source of much public cynicism about politics in general. In sum, while there are signs that a process of basic change in the Japanese political system may be underway—from closed to more open politics, from bureaucratic to political dominance, from limited to more diversified interest groups, from relatively tame to more assertive media—the path is likely to be long and tortuous. Up to date, the time and energy of Japanese politicians have been taken up largely in maneuvering for position and power.

Thus, it is not surprising that foreign policy has not been featured recently, with such matters handled by the bureaucracy, and with few if any signals of major change in past positions. Earlier, a serious debate about Japan's role in Asia and in the world was unfolding, but temporarily that discussion has been largely muted. Unquestionably, it will resume at some point. Meanwhile, the only change of consequence is that a portion of the Japanese Left, namely, the Left wing of the SDPJ, has at least nominally moved to the center—with Prime Minister Murayama pledged to firmly uphold the U.S.-Japan Security Treaty, and proclaiming the Self-Defense Forces as constitutional. For the moment at least, only the Communists are outside the fold. The movement toward greater consensus could prove to be highly important. But large, divisive issues lie ahead—among them, the question of Constitutional revision and Japan's obligations in connection with peacemaking and peacekeeping, especially should it become a permanent member of the United Nations Security Council, as is the hope of many leaders.

It is in this context that Japanese policies with respect to China and Taiwan should be viewed. Diplomatic relations with China were reestablished by Premier Tanaka Kakuei in 1972, in the aftermath of the Nixon visit to China, an event that made clear that U.S.-PRC relations were in the process of a major alteration.[1]

Taken by surprise (there was no prior consultation), Japan rushed to catch up. Long before that time, however, Japan's economic relations with China had been steadily growing, and despite the fact that the PRC attempted to put stringent conditions on Japanese firms wishing to enter China with respect to their economic relations with Taiwan, those restrictions were relaxed in practice, especially after 1972.

In the years that followed diplomatic recognition, the most prominent aspect of the Japan-PRC relationship has continued to be in the economic realm. In 1993, Japan-China trade totaled US $37.8 billion, with a relatively equal balance, due in part to the exports from China to Japan of the products of Japan-connected joint ventures. China has been importing large amounts of industrial equipment, advanced electronic goods, and similar items to service its rapid economic expansion. Three large yen-denominated loan packages had been advanced with a fourth promised. Earlier, Japanese investment had lagged well behind that of the United States as well as Hong Kong, reflective of the fact that Japanese business community had been cautious since being burned in a previous period by political and economic policy shifts. By 1993, however, optimism with respect to investment in China was growing in Japan, and a surge upward was to be seen. In mid-1994, the president of Toyota Motor Corporation announced that his company hoped to begin producing cars in China after 1996 when the PRC allows new assembly plants to be constructed, although lengthy negotiations to bring Toyota into a joint venture with a Tianjin factory now at this point ended in failure.[2] Japan's largest supermarket chain, Daiei, has applied to the Chinese government to establish an outlet in Shanghai, and has stated that it eventually planned to expand throughout the Shanghai-Beijing region.[3]

Thus, despite the economic and political uncertainties that becloud the PRC future, some of the major Japanese companies that have previously held back now appear to be undertaking or considering long-term investment in China. One issue, however, has not yet been resolved. PRC authorities have long complained that Japanese companies have been very reluctant to transfer technology, concentrating primarily upon the China market, but being unwilling to risk the competition that might eventually come from sharing advanced technology—the so-called boomerang effect. The American record in this respect has been considerably better according to Chinese accounts. Will that now change?

Meanwhile, the economic relationship with China has not interfered with Japan's extensive economic relations with Taiwan. Trade with this society of some twenty million people with a per capita annual income over $10,000 is virtually equal to that with China, and with a varying but sizable trade balance in favor of Japan.[4] Investment in Taiwan, moreover, continues to be substantial. Japanese entrepreneurs, for example, were the leading foreign investors in Taiwan during the first half of 1994, with new investments totaling US $153.3 million.[5]

In economic terms, Japan pursues a de facto "one China, one Taiwan" policy, and it a policy that has come to be acceptable if not welcomed by all parties concerned. To facilitate such a policy, Japan earlier made certain concessions beyond those proffered by others. For instance, arrangements were made for commercial aircraft from Taiwan to use Haneda airport, not Narita where PRC commercial airlines were accommodated. Moreover, a separate name was put on Japanese commercial aircraft serving Taiwan. Even without such concessions, however, Japan had an historic reach, that with its debits and assets, was unequaled by others. It is not surprising that Manchuria has been a region favored by some recent Japanese investors, and that in Taiwan, it was easy to continue old ties in certain instances.

When one surveys the economic aspect of the picture, Japan has very little reason to want to see a change in the status-quo. Grievances on the part of both China and Taiwan exist, to be sure, relating to a range of issues from technology transfer to trade balances and even working conditions in foreign-funded factories in China, but they are not as serious as Japan's problems with the United States over the massive trade imbalance.[6]

When one turns to the broader strategic and political issues surrounding Japan's relations with the two Chinese societies, however, the picture become considerably more complex.[7] Since Japanese interaction with both China and Taiwan is closely related to the perception of these two governments regarding the contemporary world and the proper course for their foreign policies, these matters should be briefly explored. Needless to say, no full consensus either in China or Taiwan exists on the former matter, nor full agreement on the latter. The official positions, however, can be outlined with reasonable accuracy, and other views can be cited where important.

In recent years, PRC spokesmen have generally agreed upon three cardinal facts regarding the changing world. First, the triumph of the West in general, and the United States specifically in the cold war is temporary.[8] The U.S. is indeed the only global superpower today but it is beset with serious internal problems, and will undergo progressive weakening. Even now, its ability to exert its will on others has declined. Further, Europe is in the throes of multiple economic and political difficulties that are systemic in nature; hence, it will never again exercise its previous influence on the world.

Second, Asia will be the most dynamic region of the coming century, with its economic growth continuing, its domestic problems contained, and its subregional and regional controversies settled or set aside in the interests of an intra-regional harmony enabling rapid domestic development. Moreover, Asia is becoming increasingly self-confident and self-reliant, less dependent upon the West. Thus, the Asianization of Asia will progress at an ever more rapid pace. Taken as a whole, these views reflect a remarkably optimistic view of Asia's future, perhaps considerably more optimistic than that held by many Chinese in private.

Third, economics will be the critical factor in international relations. Ideological differences, while continuing, will be of little importance in determining relations between and among nation-states. Strategic considerations will play a significant role, but with the old alliance system based upon balance of power irreparably gone, all relationships will have elements within them of cooperation and contention. Yet, by pursuing the Five Principles of Peaceful Coexistence, conflict can be averted. Among these principles, none is more important than the upholding of the sovereignty of the nation-state, hence, noninterference in the domestic affairs of another state. This, together with the acceptance of all nations as equals and pursuit of negotiations over differences, with a willingness to set aside differences when they cannot be resolved in favor of a concentration upon points of agreement, will assure harmony. One can dispute the degree to which this official framework has been, or will be applied in the execution of its foreign policies, but it has been repeatedly voiced through diverse channels.

Authorities in Taiwan, namely, officials of the Republic of China on Taiwan, have aspired to less grandiose conceptualizations of the global environment, being content with effecting certain important changes in their policies both toward the PRC and toward others. Step by step, the ROC has dismantled the old position of insisting that war against the Communist "bandits" continues, of contending with the PRC for the sole right to be considered China, and of pursuing the "Three Noes with Beijing, namely, no contact, no compromise, and no negotiations.[9]

Today, the government in Taipei accepts negotiations with Beijing through two quasi-governmental agencies, its Straits Exchange Foundation (SEF) and the PRC Association for Relations Across the Taiwan Straits (ARATS). It asserts that Taiwan and the mainland are both parts of China, and that the two "political entities" should treat each other as equals and participate alongside each other in the international community. It states that the existence of the Republic of China is an undeniable fact, that the Beijing government has never had jurisdiction over the territory encompassed in the ROC, and that sovereignty in the ROC is exercised by the whole people on Taiwan. The division of China, it maintains, is a temporary phenomena, but peaceful unification can only come when the mainland has undergone a process of democratization, and is prepared to operate under the Three People's Principles enunciated by Sun Yat-sen. Underlying the latter theme is the conviction in Taipei that Marxism-Leninism cannot survive on the mainland, and that the broad trend will be toward political openness.

Coupled with these pronouncements have been the accelerating efforts of Taiwan to achieve greater visibility both in Asia and in the world at large—diplomatic recognition where possible, higher level official and quasi-official interaction where full recognition is not feasible. This has included the drive for membership in the United Nations. Meanwhile, President Lee Teng-hui has engaged in "vacation diplomacy," making trips to various countries and soliciting other invitations. To forward these policies, Taiwan has heralded the fact that it is the 13th largest trading country in the world, the 7th largest investor, having a GNP per capita that ranks 20th, and possessing either the largest or next largest foreign exchange reserves—in mid-1994, over $85 billion. Taiwan's official position and the policies that now accompany it straddle the one China, one Taiwan issue, and enable competition with the Kuomintang's leading political competitor, the Democratic Progressive Party (DPP) which formally advocates Taiwan's independence.

As might be expected, the PRC government and a large number of institute commentators in China have vehemently denounced the propositions set forth in recent official pronouncements including a White Paper issued in the spring of 1994, as well as the actions and statements of President Lee. The repudiation of the PRC's "one country, two systems" formula is in fact an effort to achieve "two Chinas" or "one China, one Taiwan" through devious means, it is asserted. And Lee has revealed himself as a separatist, whatever his convoluted arguments.[10]

With new weapons being employed in the political contest between the ROC and the PRC, and growing evidence that the confrontation may become more serious in the future, a troublesome, potentially dangerous problem is posed for other nations, and most especially, for the United States and Japan. Under various names and conditions, Taiwan has been admitted to certain international agencies, notably in the economic and financial realm, such as APEC and the Asian Development Bank. It is seeking admission to other major international organizations—the World Bank, the International Monetary Fund, the GATT, and the United Nations. Deeply alarmed by trends, Beijing has placed numerous obstacles in Taiwan's path with respect to these efforts. It has indicated that it is against Taiwan's admission to the GATT (soon to be the World Trade Organization (WTO) until it has obtained membership, that it will resolutely oppose the admission of Taiwan into the United Nations under any conditions, that it will regard high level official treatment of ROC officials as a serious affront to its sovereignty, that it will view very negatively the furnishing of Taiwan with sophisticated military equipment, and that it will not tolerate diplomatic efforts to officially recognize two Chinas or "one China, one Taiwan" in any form. It has even refused to attend nonofficial conferences dealing with political and security matters where Taiwan representatives were in attendance. This confronts nations contemplating changes in policy toward Taiwan yet wishing to maintain good relations with China with a dilemma. How far can they go without risking retaliation?

At present, Japan gives every indication of continuing its commitment to the status quo in all important aspects of its foreign policy with modest, incremental changes at most. The focus will be upon relations with the United States, partly because of the importance of that relationship, partly because of pressure from Washington. Despite its economic problems with the U.S. and the growth of resentment within the Japanese public against what are perceived to be U.S. "strong-arm methods" in seeking its ends, the Japanese public, and even more, the Japanese government sees Japan's interests best served in preserving the U.S.-Japan Mutual Security Treaty, and working closely with Washington on the complex issues confronting the region. Even the Socialists in their September 1994 convention somewhat begrudgingly approved the U.S.-Japan security pact, noting that its military components "will fade," and it should gradually serve as the foundation for cooperation in other matters, with the party working to incorporate the treaty into a broader security framework supported by the UN and the Asia-Pacific region as a whole.[11]

Behind the desire to maintain the security relationship with the U.S. is the fact that most Japanese officials and scholars view the Asian-Pacific region in more complex, and less optimistic terms than the official PRC position. Russia—either prostrate or neonationalist—presents a worrisome possibility, with little immediate likelihood that the specific issues separating the two countries can be resolved. The Korean peninsula constitutes another worrisome uncertainty. Can a post-Kim Il Song North Korea move down the path signaled by the Great Leader in his final days, with or without Kim Jong Il? Or will far less attractive possibilities come to pass: a collapsed DPRK, with the huge economic and political costs for the South—and others—that this would entail?; a nuclear North Korea, defiant of its neighbors, and making nuclear proliferation a greater likelihood? And is China destined to be the economic giant that most observers expect, hence, a major competitor—and not merely in economic terms?

Given these views, and the uncertainties on the domestic front, it is not surprising that Japan shrinks back from asserting leadership at this point, content with trying to hold intact its two principal bilateral ties, the first with the United States, the second and somewhat lesser, with the People's Republic of China. Thus, it becomes nervous when one of these two major states puts pressure upon it to join in disciplining or chastising the other. In the Kaifu era, it formally incorporated four principles that were supposed to govern its Overseas Development Assistance (ODA), including the extent of a recipient's military spending, progress in democratization and advances toward a market economy,[12] but strict adherence to these principles has—to put it mildly—been sporadic. There is no evidence, for example, that any of these principles has been applied to China. More recently, it has stipulated that a minimum of 10 percent of its aid must be devoted to tackling the pollution problem, and given Japan's deep concern about acid rain from China, this stipulation may be enforced.

On occasion, Japan has served as a middleman between the U.S. and China, particularly in conveying to Washington the views—and desires—of Beijing. It has also been anxious to have China fully consulted on matters pertaining to the Korea peninsula, and seen the cooperation of the concerned states with regard to that matter as highly important. On its own count, Tokyo was not eager to apply sanctions to the DPRK, at least until the diplomatic route had been exhausted, but the PRC stance no doubt strengthened that position. Now that U.S.-DPRK negotiations are ongoing, Japan hopes they will result in an agreement with long-range potentials, and if the signs are favorable, it will move toward a two-Koreas policy.

Meanwhile, in the broadest sense, Japan-PRC relations are more extensive and more positive than at any time in this century. In addition to the far-reaching economic interaction, high-level visitations, including the trip of Emperor Akihito in the fall of 1992, symbolize the desire of both parties to eliminate past memories. Even in the military realm, exchanges have taken place between academic researchers and other contacts have been made.[13]

At a time when there are numerous subregions crises, some of them close at hand, Japan views the China connection as critical to its interests— strategic as well as economic. Consequently, Tokyo is certain to be very cautious in giving support to the new thrust of the ROC policies. It should be pointed out that Japan has long been a haven for Taiwanese who support independence, and some of them have had access to important Japanese politicians. Indeed, various semiofficial "friendship" groups have existed, connecting both the old Liberal Democratic and Social Democratic parties with counterparts on Taiwan, and visits have been frequent at that level and slightly higher. Moreover, in Japan as in the United States, there is a growing sentiment that Taiwan warrants greater international recognition. In only a few quarters, however, does that translate itself into support for an independent Taiwan, at least in de jure terms. Most Japanese are satisfied with the fact that Taiwan is independent in de facto terms. Tokyo recognizes, moreover, that the fact that Japan and the U.S. hold to a "one China" policy is one of the strongest restraints on the Taiwan independence movement. Without recognition from these two sources, the risks would far outweigh any possible gains in so far as a majority of the Taiwanese are concerned.

Nevertheless, both major states will be required to face a much more nuanced set of issues: Lee Teng-hui's travels, including the desire to visit the U.S.; higher official contacts in general; attitudes toward Taiwan's admission to the GATT (WTO), and other international bodies including the UN; and the ROC (Taiwan)'s participation in international conferences on a wide range of subjects. As yet, neither nation has formulated a fixed, broadly gauged set of policies on these matters. Thus, issues will be determined in an ad hoc fashion for the time being, with caution the byword in Japan.

One such issue seemed about to be placed on Tokyo's lap in mid-1994. ROC President Lee Teng-hui was invited to attend the October 2-16 Asian games in Hiroshima by the president of the Olympic Council of Asia. Beijing immediately protested, and implied that if Lee attended, it would withdraw from the games. In response, Taiwan's representative to Japan, Lin Chin-ching, asserted that the Japanese government had agreed to abide by the Olympic Council's constitution which states that politics should not influence the games.[14] A debate opened in Japan over the government's response. The Foreign Ministry's initial response was that the Council should negotiate between Beijing and Taipei as to whether Lee should be allowed to attend, but *Mainichi Shimbun* reported that if no agreement could be reached, Tokyo would have to make a "political decision," one unlikely to be favorable to Taiwan.[15]

Perhaps fortunately for the Murayama government, the Olympic Council of Asia decreed in early September that non-Japanese politicians would not be "invited or accommodated" to the Hiroshima games, in effect rescinding the invitation. What type of pressure or "influence" was applied, and by whom, on this matter—from beginning to end—is presently unclear, but a potential crisis seemed at least temporarily averted.[16]

Meanwhile, Tokyo undoubtedly viewed with great interest the result of a review by the U.S. government of its policies toward Taiwan. The U.S. decision was to promote somewhat higher-level visitations between the American and Taiwan officials (but not to authorize a visit by President Lee to the U.S.) and to allow a change of name for Taiwan's representative offices in the U.S., with the designation "Taipei" permitted. While the PRC protested these actions, as expected, Taiwan was disappointed in the limited extent of the changes.[16]

Almost certainly, Japan will join the United States in creeping forward along the path marked "one China, one Taiwan," measuring its steps by an assessment of their impact upon Sino-Japanese relations. Economic advances will be the most visible. In September 1994, for example, it was announced that Japan and Taiwan had agreed to revise their civil aviation pact to permit one additional company from each country to operate between the two countries.[17]

It remains, however, to deal with the complex psychological factors as well as the subterranean concerns that are not set forth in official pronouncements, either in Tokyo or Beijing. Beneath the surface, there are deep, abiding suspicions on both sides. The millennium with respect to Japanese-Chinese friendship and trust has not arrived, notwithstanding all of the fine words that have been uttered and written.

China intends to be the paramount power in East Asia, a position that it considers its right by virtue of its size, its capacities, and its history. The Chinese have never been overly troubled with an inferiority complex, and whatever trauma befalls this vast land, the belief in the ultimate triumph of the Chinese people is likely to remain undaunted. Toward those around it who "behave properly," it will respond benevolently. But to those who challenge Beijing's policies, either frigidity or a show of imperial power—if the adversary is small—may ensue. Vietnam provides an example, not merely in 1979 but in 1994—despite the "friendly relations" that prevailed.

Japan is seen by many Chinese as the principal contender for regional influence, a nation more compact than China, more developed, and with a latent nationalism that could take a virulent form. It is difficult for China's leaders to believe that a nation possessed of such enormous economic power will not sooner or later translate this into military power, especially under the conditions envisaged with respect to the future of the Asian-Pacific region.

Hence, despite its periodic anger at the United States, Beijing does not really desire an end to the U.S.-Japan Mutual Security Treaty at this point, thereby forcing an independent strategic stance. Nor does it want developments on the Korean peninsula—or elsewhere—that might encourage Japan to adopt a more high-posture military course. Its opposition to Japan's activities in peacekeeping in Cambodia and elsewhere has softened—but not by much. It expects—and fears—that Japan will sooner or later amend its Constitution to permit greater "normalcy" in its activities as a major power. And periodically, it finds Japanese revisionists speaking out on their version of conflicts of the 1930s and 1940s, promoting deep misgivings. If the past is rewritten, what about the future?

For its part, Japan wants a tranquil China, and one that continues to make economic progress while being interwoven ever more solidly into the Asia-Pacific region. But it does not want China to acquire power too rapidly. Privately, many Japanese are troubled by what they see as a Chinese military modernization program that aims at extending the PRC's reach by air and sea to other areas. China is a nuclear power with an extensive missile capacity. It is acquiring modern aircraft and naval vessels. *And* it is a nation not fully satisfied with the territorial status quo. Japan's own territorial dispute with China is relatively minor (the Senkaku or Diayutai islands), but when China insists that sovereignty belongs to it, Japan strenuously objects. The truly critical issues, however, relate to Taiwan and to the South China Sea. In the former instance, most Japanese leaders believe, China's threats of a resort to force are credible should a Republic of Taiwan be formally inaugurated; in the latter case, force—even recently—has been used.

As the immediate post-1945 pattern of international relations, with its tight alliances and balance of power politics, recedes, the prospect of a renewed contest for regional authority between China and Japan is one of the scenarios with which one must conjure. Certainly, conditions do not permit the type of singular dominance sometimes exercised in the past. The small and medium Asian countries are too strong, too assertive, and too independent to permit that, and there are other parties in the scene, including the United States and Russia. But throughout the region, China and Japan are moving forward in a myriad of ways, economically first and foremost, but with political and strategic implications following. Mongolia, Siberia, Southeast Asia, including the ASEAN members, Myanmar and the states of the former Indochina, are all recipients of this trends in varying degree. In every case, there is a consciousness of a more meaningful presence of Japan and China, or at least one of these.

This does not necessarily presage some type of overt conflict or all-encompassing bilateral confrontation. China and Japan both have weaknesses, material and institutional in nature, and in the case of Japan, a weakness of will. In the case of China, rationality would dictate a continuing priority on its further internal development—and cohesion—perhaps for decades. On the part of Japan, a greater world role, but one in concert with the United States and others, would seem to be the best way to fend off suspicions lingering from the past.

Yet only one aspect of the future appears certain. The Sino-Japanese relationship will continue to be complex and many faceted, as indeed, will be all bilateral relations between major states in the coming decades. Internal trends in both countries will of course be of major importance in determining the trends, as will the general climate within the region. And here, the most critical wild card is likely to be Taiwan—its future course, domestic and international.

On this issue as on others—and notably those involving the Korean peninsula—close consultation is essential, not only between Japan and the U.S., militarily allied nations, but also with all of the Northeast Asian states, including China and Russia. Nor should ASEAN be ignored. However difficult and troublesome, collective action in pacemaking and keeping is the only rational course. Unilateralism is no longer a viable option in this part of the world, and any nation that forgets this fact will pay a heavy price, be it Asian or Western.

CHAPTER 7
ASEAN, Vietnam, and the Taiwan-Mainland China Relationship

*Dr. Sarasin Viraphol, Ministry of Foreign Affairs, Thailand,
and Umphon Phanachet, Chulalongkorn University*

Introduction

The objectives of this chapter are to:

- assess the economic impacts of the quadrangle relationship of ASEAN, Vietnam, Taiwan, and mainland China, and the role of Hong Kong in the relationship;
- study the rapidly changing scenes in the areas of geopolitics, security and trade and investment;
- project some possible developments in the four entities in the next decade, taking into consideration the possible changes in the leadership, especially in the mainland, and
- finally, some conclusions are drawn from the findings in the previous paragraphs.

The dramatic change in mainland China's economic policy took place in 1979 when it adopted a more liberal, open economic, especially trade and investment policy. Not only the indirect economic relationship between Taiwan and mainland China has grown by leaps and bounds, a process of economic integration involving South China, Hong Kong, and

Taiwan has been set in motion. Mainland China has since become an important market for Taiwanese manufactured products, and 2 million Taiwanese tourists had visited China in 1993. In addition, some 3,000 Taiwanese firms have made investments in China, which will have far reaching implications for both the Chinese and Taiwanese economies. At the same time, China has also exported an increasing quantity of goods to Taiwan. All these dynamic economic activities were carried out through Hong Kong. The role of Hong Kong as a middleman has greatly enhanced since 1979.

The creation of the Special Economic Zones and the structural transformation of the Hong Kong economy together with the phenomenal growth in the Hong Kong's entrepot activities have precipitated the economic integration between the Pearl River Delta and Hong Kong. The process of the integration has been going on for more than a decade, but in recent years, its pace has significantly quickened.

Furthermore, in view of the close economic contacts between mainland China, especially Fujian province, and Taiwan, and the role which Hong Kong plays in it, the economic nexus among South China, Taiwan, and Hong Kong has become very strong and unseparable. Some economists have even gone so far as to propose the formation of a trading bloc consisting of these three trading entities plus Macau.[1] Whether or not some sort of organization will eventually emerge out of this movement remains to be seen. But a de facto economic integration among these three economic entities seems inevitable and Hong Kong has played a pivotal role in this process, which is bound to have significant economic implications not only regionally (especially ASEAN and Vietnam) but also globally.

Policy Changes as Prima Facie Factor
for Economic Contacts: A Historical Perspective

In retrospect, in the history of the past 45 years since 1949, the relationship between Beijing and Taipei can be subdivided into three periods:[2]

1949-1978: This period lasted for 29 years, during which mainland China and Taiwan were in the state of mutual hostility. There were military confrontations and virtually all the contact avenues were severed.

1979-Oct. 1987: In this period Beijing's Taiwan policy was characterized by "Peaceful Unification," while Taipei's policy on mainland China was by "Unification of China through the Three Principles of the People." The military confrontation and the tension on both sides had largely eased.

Nov. 2, 1987 - Present: The Taiwanese government lifted the ban on visits to China imposed since 1949. This was followed by the announcement of any new measures aimed at making economic and human contact between the two sides easier. In this period, the economic relationship, in terms of trade, direct foreign investments, capital flows, and tourism has tremendously expanded. Since all the economic relationships are basically indirect in nature, Hong Kong, as their middleman, has played a vital role in it and indeed benefited economically out of it.

Economic Relationships between Mainland China and Taiwan

In 1979, mainland China proposed the "Three Linkages" policy, namely, direct mail, direct air and seas links, and direct trade. In addition, a variety of preferential treatments were offered to Taiwanese businessmen to attract their investments. Among others, the incentives included the opening up of domestic markets and minimum tariffs for importation of manufactured products from Taiwan. In 1987, the Taiwanese government lifted the exchange control and allowed its people to visit mainland China. As a result, millions of Taiwanese have visited mainland China each year, and some 3000 Taiwanese enterprises, mostly small to medium size, have set up shop in China. The "China fever" culminated in the announcement in the late 1980s that the number one industrial tycoon in Taiwan, Y.C. Wong (Wong Yung Ching), had visited Fujian province, which lies just across the Taiwan Straits, and planned to build a huge petrochemical complex in Hai-Tseng county. This news has deeply stirred both the public and government in Taiwan, as it would single the speeding up of the hollowing-out process in the manufacturing industries in Taiwan.[3] In 1991, the Ministry of Economic Affairs in Taipei conducted a survey on the firms investing in China, in which some 2,750 firms voluntarily responded. With this move, the indirect trade and other economic relations between China and Taiwan have been formally sanctioned. The close economic relationships between two sides are most vividly demonstrated in the phenomenal growth in the trade volumes through Hong Kong. In 1980, the total trade between them was only US $210 million. (China's exports amounting to US $56 million and Taiwan's exports at US $154 million). By 1991, the total trade rose to US $5,793 million. (Taiwan's exports to China were US $4,667 million while China's exports to Taiwan were US $1,126 million). In a decade's time, the trade volume has augmented by more than 27-fold. The growth pattern is less smooth for Taiwan's exports to China than that for the trade flows in the reverse direction. This implies that Taiwan's exports to China have been more vulnerable to the general economic situation and policy changes in China. From 1980 to 1991, the exports from Taiwan to China grew on the average at 130 percent per annum, while the exports from China to Taiwan increased at 36 percent each year.

The future course of development depends firstly on economic situations both in mainland China and Taiwan in the years to come, and secondly on Taiwan's mainland China policy. Given the fact that mainland China's current open door policy will likely continue, a strong economic performance on both sides will lead to a stronger demand for each other's commodities, and consequently their indirect trade via Hong Kong, will rise. As far as Taiwan's mainland China policy is concerned, the pressure from the private sector for establishing direct links with mainland China has been mounting. In the event that one day the direct links are allowed, the present indirect trade and investment arrangements are bound to be reduced and the Hong Kong economy will inevitably be most affected.

Mainland China's Investments in Hong Kong

Ever since 1949, China's investments in Hong Kong have been increasing steadily. Before the economic reform of 1979, Hong Kong had served as China's exclusive window to the outside world. The bulk of mainland China's foreign trade was conducted through Hong Kong, which was also a major market for Chinese products in addition to being an entrepot for reexports from and to mainland China. It was estimated that Hong Kong contributed more than 60 percent of mainland China's foreign reserves during this period. In connection with the reexport activities, mainland China's interests in Hong Kong then were mainly in banking, retail business, warehousing, tourism, and shipping. After 1979, her investments in Hong Kong have been diversified into other sectors, especially construction and building, shipping, and above all manufacturing. The importance of Hong Kong to mainland China has not been reduced by the latter's open-door policy because Hong Kong has continued to serve as mainland China's main avenue to attract foreign capital and investments and conduct foreign trade. Even now some 40 percent of mainland China's foreign reserves are attributed to Hong Kong. It has been estimated that since 1949 mainland China has invested a total of US $10 billion in Hong Kong and about US $3 billion[4] in manufacturing industries. According to official records, some 400 state-owned companies have been approved by Beijing to operate in Hong Kong. This figure appears to be grossly understated when one considers that each state enterprise has set up a host of subsidiaries to conduct a variety of business here. The actual number of the firms controlled by Chinese capital may be as high as 5,000!

In terms of organizational structure, pre-1980 Chinese enterprises may be classified into four categories; namely,[5]

- Bank of China and its affiliated banks: This group is under the jurisdiction of the Ministry of Finance. The group is responsible for all of China's foreign currencies transactions, including remittances, currency dealings, and all the usual business conducted by local commercial banks.
- China Resource (Holding) Group: This group is under the Ministry of Foreign Trade and Economic Cooperation and is responsible for foreign trade in Hong Kong.
- The "Shipping Bureau" Group: This group belongs to the Ministry of Transport; it is responsible for shipping Chinese commodities as well as cargo handling.
- "China Travel Agency" Group: This group is under China's National Tourism Bureau, and is handling all the business relating to China's tourism.

After 1980, because of the new economic policies, there has been a substantial transformation in the structure of the Chinese companies in Hong Kong. The following events are most relevant.

- The two provinces adjacent to Hong Kong, namely Guangdong and Fujian, were granted a special status to attract foreign capital, skills, and investments by Beijing in the early 1980's. East province had subsequently set up its own conglomerate Yuen-Hai and Hua-Min to conduct business in Hong Kong.
- In August and October 1980, four Special Economic Zones, namely Shenzen, Chu-Hai, Shan-Tou, and Xia-Men were created, and each has established a company in Hong Kong. Besides, practically each ministry and CITIC, etc. have set up companies to do business in Hong Kong.

- In 1984 14 coastal port cities were opened up and at the same time, the Pearl River Delta, Hsia Chang Delta in South Fujian, and Chang Jiang Delta were also designated economic development regions.
- In 1988 Hai-Nan Island was upgraded to a province and made a special economic area.

In order to attract foreign capital, skills, and investments (especially from Hong Kong), all the local authorities in these special economic regions have set up companies in Hong Kong.

Because of all these recent developments, Chinese institutions in Hong Kong have vastly multiplied. Not only has each ministry in Beijing established companies in Hong Kong, provincial and even county governments have also set up representative offices here to promote exports of goods produced in their region. But most of the firms or representative offices set up by the provincial (with exception of Guangdong and Fujian province) or county governments are relatively small in size. Business is still controlled by the major Chinese companies belonging to the various ministries. These include Bank of China group, CITIC (which controls business in the field of telecommunication and aviation), China Travel Agency and China Resources group, whose business volume in 1989 amounted to HK $50 billion (which has surpassed the amount of HK $46.8 billion achieved by the British trading giant Jardine Matheson group in 1990).

Since the Sino-British Joint Declaration announced in 1984, British capital has been dwindling. In its place, capital from other nations such as China, Japan, USA, Taiwan, etc. has increased. As the year 1997 draws nearer, it is expected that mainland China will step up her investments in Hong Kong. This will serve a dual purpose: increase Chinese influence in the economy, and ensure the stability and prosperity of Hong Kong. (A stable and prosperous Hong Kong economy will be most beneficial and essential to mainland China's current economic modernization endeavor).

As far as Chinese investments in Hong Kong are concerned, the following may be expected.

- "The Bank of China" group will become a major player in the banking and financial sector. The Bank of China has recently joined the Hong Kong Bank and the Chartered Bank in issuing the local currency.
- More investments will be made by China in the manufacturing

industries, especially in the electronics, textiles and clothing as well as toys industries. They will prefer to form joint ventures with local industrialists so that they can learn and obtain production technologies and management skills, which are critical to industrial development in mainland China.

- Mainland China's investments in the construction and building industries will also increase. Among others, their companies will try to participate in the new Hong Kong airport and its related transport infrastructure projects, which were estimated to cost about HK $127 billion.
- Mainland China's investments in the tourist sector will also increase. Since 1987 Taiwanese people have been allowed to visit mainland China. Last year about 2 million Taiwanese visited Hong Kong and 90 percent of them went to mainland China. The China Travel Agency and its subsidiaries will be expected to expand to cope with the development.

Taiwan's Investment in Hong Kong

In addition to trade, there have been substantial two-way flows of direct foreign investments between Taiwan and Hong Kong. For example, in 1991, Taiwan invested a total of some US $199.6 million in Hong Kong (about 43 percent of its investments in the region, US $461 million, while the reverse flows from Hong Kong to Taiwan amounted to US $128 million (101 million by foreigners, and 27 million by overseas Chinese in Hong Kong), which is equal to 13.2 percent of the total investments in Taiwan from the entire Asian region of US $965 million.[6]

Taiwan's investments in Hong Kong were quite trivial before 1991, with most of the DFI from Taiwan going to Southeast Asian countries. The dramatic upsurge of Taiwan's investments in Hong Kong since 1991 can be attributed to several political and economic factors. It is obvious that many of these investments were related to the burgeoning indirect trade and investments between mainland China and Taiwan. The majority of the 2,750 firms which have been registered with the Ministry of Economic Affairs in Taipei to do business with mainland China have also set up a branch office in Hong Kong. These firms have not only facilitated the indirect trade and investments from Taiwan, they also made bona fide direct investment in Hong Kong. The main investments were made in the service industries. Their investments in the manufacturing industries were also significant.

On the other hand, direct foreign investments in Taiwan from Asian region have been far above the Taiwanese investments in this region. Between 1952 and 1991, some US $6,958 million from the Asian region have been invested in Taiwan, while only US $2,0004 million (1959-1991) worth of investments from Taiwan in this region were officially reported. Even after taking that into account, due to exchange control, the DFI from Taiwan were grossly understated. The DFI in Taiwan from the Asian region is many times that of the reverse flows of the DFI from Taiwan. As far as Asian Pacific region is concerned, Taiwan was until recently clearly a net receiving country of the DFI. However, in the last few years, there has been an exodus of labor intensive factories from Taiwan to mainland China and the situation has started to change. Although official figure on Taiwanese investments in China stand at US $700 million, unofficial sources have estimated it to be in the order of US $2 billion. Furthermore, with the Taiwan's banking sector liberalized now, it is expected that the DFI in this sector will greatly increase in the years to come.

Taiwanese Investments in Mainland China

For economic, geographical, ethical, and language reasons, mainland China has attracted a large amount of investments from Taiwan. At the beginning, the scale and magnitude were rather modest. For example, between 1979-1987, the accumulated amount of Taiwanese investments was only US $100 million, mostly in Fijian province. In 1988 alone, the amount jumped to US $300 million, in 1989 to US $600 million. The accumulated amount for the entire period 1979-1989 is estimated at US $1 billion.[7]

By April 1991, there were more than 2700 Taiwanese firms operating in China, with a total investments of US $3.7 billion.[8]

The following observations are worth noting. Firstly, most of the investments were made in those industries which were well developed in Taiwan in the past but which had in the meantime lost their competitiveness due to high wage rate, high rental cost, currency appreciation, and environmental reasons. They include electronic, vehicles, footwear, services (mainly entertainment setups, transport and tourism), plastic, as well as port items and textiles. Secondly, the bulk of the investments have been concentrated in the areas close to Taiwan, namely Guangdong and Fujian provinces; more specifically, Shenzhen Special Economic Zone, Xiamen, Shanghai, Guangzho, Fuzhou, have gained importance recently. Thirdly, Taiwanese investments had started with Fujian province, especially Xiamen, and have quickly spread to the Pearl River Delta, and further to the 14 coastal cities, especially Shanghai and Tianjin. Some have even moved inland. In other words, the investments started at a point, quickly extended to a line, and gradually spread out into the inland provinces.

Until last year, the indirect investments from mainland China were banned in Taiwan. But last year, Taipei formally sanctioned this kind of activity and officially asked those firms which had made investments in China to register themselves with the Ministry of Economic Affairs. About 2,750 firms registered then. Since then the indirect investments by Taiwanese firms in mainland China have been legalized. On August 20, 1994, the Ministry of Economic Affairs announced an addition of 633 items for investment in the mainland.

The economic relations between mainland China and Taiwan began with the indirect trade. But since 1988, when mainland China launched a new strategy in the coastal areas to promote exports, incentives were provided to attract capital and skills from abroad, especially from Hong Kong. In order to attract investments from Taiwan, special preferential treatments were offered to them. As a result, in the last few years, besides the rapidly growing indirect trade relations, there have been rapidly increasing indirect investments from Taiwan. These indirect trade and indirect investments relations will have far reaching implications both for the economics of mainland China and Taiwan.[9] The rapid shifting of the production facilities by the Taiwanese firms, mostly small-to-medium size labor intensive firms, are attributable to the following factors:

- The declining investment climate in Taiwan. The bulk of firms in Taiwan are relatively small in size. Their products such as sport shoes, electronics, toys, clothing, and textiles, etc. are labor-intensive. The skill level is low and they did not pursue original research and development; for these reasons, they can hardly survive in the changing environment.
- Since 1988 mainland China started to actively attract capital from overseas. More incentives were offered to investments from Taiwan. The indirect economic relations between mainland China and Taiwan have upgraded from indirect trade to indirect trade to indirect investments. But the indirect investments have in fact become and important sources for indirect trade. Investments and trade are mutually supporting.

- In the last ten years, China has experienced a double-digit annual growth rate. People living in the coastal areas have become relatively affluent. The market potential for manufactured consumer goods is great. This vast market potential has also become an important factor to attract investment from Taiwan.[10]

Economic Cooperation and Integration: Implications for the Taiwanese Economy

The massive relocation of production facilities from Hong Kong[11] and Taiwan to mainland China are bound to have far reaching implications. While these firms will help mainland China develop her labor-intensive industries, which are largely compatible with her comparative advantages, in addition to capital and equipment, they also introduce new management skills, technologies, and marketing techniques. Both hardware and software knowledge is vital for mainland China's industrialization. At present the direct investments are still concentrated in the southern provinces of Guangdong and Fijian and other coastal areas, but there are noticeable trends that direct foreign investments are spreading toward the North and inland as wages there are considerably lower.

The outward processing arrangements of the firms from Hong Kong and Taiwan are to use mainland China as their overseas production base. The manufactured goods are aimed at overseas markets. In the early 1980's, mainland China's imports from Taiwan mainly consisted of consumer goods, capital equipments, as well as intermediate inputs; while China's exports to Taiwan were confined to primary goods, chemicals, and raw materials. The indirect two-way trade had therefore a high degree of complementarity which was beneficial to both parties. But owning to her rapid industrialization in recent years, mainland China has increasingly exported more manufactured consumer goods, which are in direct competition with Taiwanese products on international markets. For example, in a recent study, in the U.S. market alone, some 45 percent of the 382 commodities surveyed are simultaneously exported from mainland China and Taiwan. Especially, textiles, fabrics, and garments are manufactured on both sides of the Taiwan Strait and compete for market shares in the U.S. Although no similar study was carried out for Hong Kong, judged by the commodity mix, there is reason to believe that a similar situation should prevail.[12] It is therefore evident that the two-way commodity flows between mainland China and Hong Kong, as well as Taiwan, have rapidly transformed its interindustry into intraindustry trade.

As a result, the degree of complementarity has been reduced and the degree of competition has increased. Under the circumstances, the future of Taiwanese economy depends on the successful industrial restructuring and technological upgrading, lest her industrial products soon lose their competitiveness in the international market.

The endeavor in Taiwan to develop new high-tech industries has scored initial successes. The Shin-Chu Science Park has in this regard played a catalytic role. Through the incentives of excellent infrastructure, subsidized rental cost, and provision of cheap venture capital, the Park was able to lure back hundreds of well-trained scientists and engineers from the Silicon Valley in California and elsewhere to set up new firms there, which aimed at producing technology intensive products. As a result, all the available factory space in the Park has already been taken up, and the authorities are now busy with creating a second one in the vicinity. Their products are export-oriented and they have in effect made a dent in the trade pattern. The export share of the conventional labor-intensive goods such as textiles, clothing, sport wears, shoes, machinery, etc. has gone down, while that of high-tech manufacturers has gone up. But looking ahead, one wonders whether the current industrial restructuring will be a success and the new high-tech industries will really take root in Taiwan so as to become their new engine of growth in the future. The research and development (R&D) investment in Taiwan is way below the western industrialization nations. Without massive investments in R&D, no country will be able to become a truly advanced industrialized one. Although it is important for Taiwan to develop, liberalize, and modernize her service industries, especially in the financial sector, Taiwan is in many respects different from Hong Kong. For obvious reasons, while Hong Kong can become China's New York and indeed thrive without having a strong manufacturing section, the Taiwanese economy cannot possibly survive without a strong manufacturing sector. The Taiwanese economy also cannot possibly survive without a strong industrial base. The shifting of labor-intensive sunset industries to mainland China is merely to prolong their life span. In fact, this has spawned the hollowed-out process in the manufacturing sector. If they are not replaced by new technology-intensive industries, the Taiwanese economy will increasingly depend on mainland China, which will make Taiwan vulnerable.

The industrial restructuring is now even more urgent than ever as Taiwan is about to become a full member of the GATT; and the U.S. is making trade more difficult by forcing the Special 301 on Taiwan. Both events will force Taiwan to observe more closely the principles of fair trade and further open domestic markets. In the end, the local business will be subjected to stronger international competition. Under the circumstances, only a massive R&D program can guarantee a success for the current industrial restructuring endeavor in Taiwan and ensure the ability to face the increasing competition, both domestically and internationally.

ASEAN, Mainland China, Taiwan, and the Vietnam Security Issue

Both mainland china and Taiwan see ASEAN and the Southeast Asian subregion as growing in importance politically, economically, and strategically. By the early 1990's, Beijing had normalized diplomatic relations with all the six ASEAN nations, and has resumed normal ties (after terminating the state of hostility) with Vietnam—following the latter's withdrawal from neighboring Cambodia. In addition, mainland China has formed a link with ASEAN by becoming an invited guest (along with Russia) at the annual ASEAN Ministerial Meeting (AMM). It will be a matter of time before ASEAN will consider accepting mainland China as full-fledged dialogue partner.

Mainland China's rapid economic expansion has spurred ASEAN's efforts in trade and investment in that country. This has added to the acknowledgment of China's role as being essential in the maintenance and enhancement of regional peace and stability—notwithstanding the wariness by some about the Chinese armed forces modernization currently under way, as well as Beijing's claims over the vast expanses of the South China Sea which conflict with claims by some ASEAN states.

Taiwan's interest in ASEAN and Southeast Asia picked up momentum in the late 1980's when the subregion started it economic boom. By the end of the decade, Taiwan's investment, partly driven by the need to relocate her own labor-intensive manufacturing facilities, peaked in the Philippines and Thailand. With the opening of Vietnam, Taiwanese trade and investment have come to figure most importantly there—with direct commercial flights between Taiwan and Vietnam launched in 1992. The absence of diplomatic ties with these states has not deterred Taipei to stake its "claim" in the rapidly growing subregion.

Nevertheless, as part of the emerging strategy to enhance its international political standing, and as part of the effort to diversify trade and investment, Taipei has initiated the "Southward Drive" (*Nan-Xiang*), a diplomatic offensive to cultivate political ties with Southeast Asian political leaders. Both Prime Minister Lian Chan and President Li Tenghui of Taiwan have taken turns to visit various ASEAN capitals, much to

Beijing's consternation. Although the visits have not led to any formal re-recognition of the Taipei regime, the "Southward Drive" strategy is at least an answer to Beijing's continued drive to diplomatically shut out Taiwan. The strategy in the post-cold war period (with the primacy of economics over politics and ideology) may prove to have a life of its own if properly nurtured.

Against the background of a triangle trade of Hong Kong, Taiwan-mainland, the role of ASEAN and, to a lesser extent, Vietnam could be viewed as both complementary as well as competitive, ASEAN and Vietnam seem to have a broad common ground. The recently concluded 27th AMM achieved a new horizon in the field of regional security in the form of the ASEAN Regional Forum (ARF)[13] which served as a unique platform for ASEAN's dialogue nations to collectively discuss regional political issues.

It should be noted that both mainland China and Vietnam are now dialogue partners in ARF. The AMM urged that ASEAN should work with its ARF partners to bring about a more predictable and constructive pattern of relations in the Asia-Pacific. A test case is perhaps the sensitive issues of sovereignty over the Spratley and the Paracel Islands in the South China Sea.

In this respect, while there is now an appropriate forum for all claimants to settle their conflicts, this development may equally complicate the search for a solution.

At this important AMM, ASEAN affirmed its readiness to provisionally accept Vietnam. Certainly, this is a major accomplishment for Vietnam for political and economic reasons.

Mainland China, on the other hand, may view this new development as Vietnam's attempt to forge itself with the rest of the ASEAN nations for a better leverage in dealing with China in security issues. Regardless, it cannot be denied that Southeast Asia has gone a step further to strengthen its geopolitical position in the regional scene. Further analysis may reveal that mainland China cannot help but attempting to pursue a more cautious security policy to avoid suspicion among its southern neighbors.

In the meantime, a recent calculation by the Bangkok-based International Institution for Strategic Studies of mainland China's total defense spending reveal it as the third largest in the world, while her 3 million strong armed forces remain the world's largest.

According to Beijing, official military spending, which declined during the 1980's, has risen sharply in the past three years. In 1994, it increased by 25 percent to RMB 52 billion Yuen (US $6 billion). It was estimated that actual military spending may be up to five times as high because the Chinese do not include research and development and pensions in their official figures.

The extra budget is spending on more sophisticated weapons, faster-moving troops and transforming the "brown-water" Chinese navy around coastlines to a longer-range "blue-water" navy. Concerns about this development are reflected in the considerable increase in military spending among mainland China's neighbors.

Furthermore, some of the gap between the official budget and the resources at the disposal of Beijing's People's Liberation Army (including the navy and air force as well) is filled by approximately 20,000 companies owned by the army. The army's annual profits are estimated to be about US $5 billion.

Increased diplomacy and more frequent face-to-face contact through organizations such as the AMM and ARF enable China to become better friends with Russia, India, and Vietnam. As a result, the Southeast Asian subregion looks less dangerous than a few years ago. In addition, mainland China's armed forces are probably preoccupied with modernization and profits.

Taiwan's involvement with the ARF thus far has been confined to its expressed interest in joining the security dialogue process. Furthermore, however, there was little possibility of Taiwanese participation owing to objection by Beijing. While Taiwan was allowed to join APEC as a major regional economy, in the security realm, only states maintaining association with ASEAN in some capacity are invited. At least such is the current arrangement.

Conclusion

Political and economic developments in the quadrangular entities in recent years amply demonstrate that economic gains through cooperation outweighed military tensions caused by ideological and geopolitical disputes. Hence, it is envisaged that economic interactions among the four parties concerned will move faster than any political initiatives, and East and Southeast Asia could form an association by formalizing a grouping.[14]

It is interesting to follow the prospective roles of Taiwan and mainland China by considering the nature of relationship between the two sides of the Strait which significantly altered in the late 1980s. Whether increasing economic interactions between Taiwan and mainland China will pave the way to reunification remains unanswered. However, in near terms, the possibility of the two sides of the Strait being unified remains distant. The most obvious barriers lie in marked differences in political ideologies and social systems. Despite significant progress Taiwan has made in accordance with its National Unification Guidelines throughout the late 1980s and early 1990s, there is no specific timetable for the eventual reunification of mainland China and Taiwan. Nevertheless, it is expected that bilateral economic exchanges will continue to strengthen in the absence of any political dialogue.

For Taiwan, a major remaining obstacle to advancing reunification is the threat of an armed invasion by mainland China. So far, the prime proposal from mainland China is to grant Taiwan autonomy after reunification (a formula dubbed "one country, two systems"), a deal which the Taipei government has found unacceptable. At the domestic level, rising challenges from the opposition party seeking independence for Taiwan, which the Kuo Min Tang (KMT) fears will provoke an attack from mainland China, may not easily subdued. Nevertheless, the KMT will pursue the one-China policy, with the expectation that increasing contact between the two sides will create mutual trust which will be a solid foundation for peaceful reunification.

One dilemma about Taiwan's booming trade and investment on mainland China is the fear of the island state becoming too economically dependent on mainland China and being gradually absorbed into the latter's social system. It has been proposed that Taiwan's mainland policy should be reviewed at this stage. It was suggested that Taiwan provide guidelines for Taiwanese entrepreneurs to cool off the overheating trade and investment on the other side of the Strait. By opening the island's door to mainland China, some fear costly security risks are possible in this liberalization.

To predict the reactions from mainland China in the years ahead, one may expect its continuing pressure on Taiwan, aiming at isolating the island from the world community, or downgrading the Taipei government to provincial-level authorities. Not to be intimidated by such pressure, Taiwan will earnestly strive towards her goal of internationalization. The adoption of pragmatic foreign policy by the Taipei government including the recent "Southward Drive" policy, and the emerging economic power of the island may be key factors which will enable Taiwan to figure importantly on the world stage. However, with many countries recognizing mainland China as the sovereign state of China, to what extent can Taiwan coexist with mainland China in the current global political setting remains to be seen, especially if Taiwan is perceived to proceed down the path of becoming a distinct and separate political entity.

In addition to the political conflicts with mainland China, Taiwan is being faced with various challenges in the process of restructuring its economy from labor to capital—and advanced technology. To help make possible Taiwan's transition to the status of a fully industrialized country by the end of the century, the government has put into effect a gigantic budget of US $300 billion for 779 projects in the Six-Year National Development Plan (*Economic Review*, 1991). Hopefully, Taiwan could, as a by-product, enhance her unofficial relations with major advanced countries through their participation of the Six-Year National Development projects.

Another scenario for Taiwan's future economic interactions is related to trade and investment with other counties in the East Asian Region. With the emergence of regionalism in Europe and North America, further economic cooperation between Taiwan and its East Asian counterparts is expected. Realizing that no single country can compete against an entire, well-organized region, Taiwan will have to make enormous efforts to overcome barriers established by regionalism. In fact, Taiwan's economic policy directions are being discussed towards recent and foreseeable regional integration. According to the island's Economic Minister, Taiwan should exert influence in favor of openness and multilaterlism rather than bloc protection.[15] This is signified by Taiwan's keenness in its role in the Asian and Pacific Economic Cooperation (APEC) which is also driven by political motives. Whichever directions Taiwan will take, it is clear that the island will continue to be a significant player in the growing regional economy.

DISCUSSION
Bilateral Interactions with the U.S., Japan, and Southeast Asia

Jonathan D. Pollack, RAND Corporation

The focus of this chapter was on how the bilateral relationships between some of the key players in Asia, and both Taiwan and the mainland, might interact in the cross-Strait relationship. Clearly the U.S., Japan, and the ASEAN states all face different constraints and concerns. However, given the importance the mainland now places on economic growth and on managing the relationships with its neighbors in a more-or-less cooperative fashion, participants believed that third parties had a potentially positive role to play in the evolution of cross-Strait relations. At the same time, that role must be indirect. Efforts to become directly engaged in cross-Strait issues, no matter how strong the short-term logic, generally appear to have counterproductive longer-term consequences.

Third parties have many common interests in the evolution of mainland-Taiwan relations—expanding trade, minimizing arms buildup, promoting dialogue and negotiation rather than confrontation and threat, increasing stability in favor of huge policy swings, etc. Each also has its own unique set of interests and concerns with both parties. In general, pragmatism has come to dominate ideology and rhetoric across many dimensions of the relationships. As a result, it is easy for outsiders to both underestimate and overestimate the continued importance of ideology and rhetoric in mainland-Taiwan relations.

Indeed, no third party has any incentive to destabilize the status quo. But the status quo is not stable. Regional and country-specific trends are altering interests and introducing new opportunities and risks.

Clearly, the growing importance of economic interaction between both sides of the Strait requires increasingly complex governmental and legal interaction. This inevitably runs afoul of the traditional mainland positions on third party interactions with Taiwan. Such tensions will clearly intensify.

A second inevitable source of concern is the myth vs. reality of the emerging Chinese threat. The mainland is and will continue to modernize its military forces. Some of the developments, particularly substantial enhancements of force projection capabilities—such as enhancing its "blue water" naval potential and attempting to introduce in-air refueling—are seen with great concern around the region. The mainland has done a poor job of assuaging the concerns of its neighbors, and the PRC government needs to be constantly reminded about these third-party concerns. Progress in making security policy and objectives more transparent would clearly help ease uncertainty on Taiwan as well. Regardless of external considerations, however, internal dynamics almost inevitably will accelerate military modernization.

Participants raised concerns that there is too much linear thinking regarding mainland-Taiwan relations. They argued for an increased effort among third parties to increasingly support discussion that allows for more diversity of outcomes in dealing with the mainland and Taiwan. This in turn should indirectly help both governments take such contingency analysis into consideration as they interact across the Strait. There are many topics that neither Taiwan nor the mainland could introduce on their own, but might be willing to discuss (internally, if not in cross-Strait discussions).

In a related vein, a number of participants raised concerns that the discussion in this session and in general focused to much on narrow bilateral issues. There was concern that not enough attention was being paid to large regional and global changes that might alter the way that third parties looked at the mainland-Taiwan issue.

In general, it was felt that the U.S. faced the greatest responsibility for policy action and guidance, especially regarding its role in Asia — not direct involvement in the cross-Strait dispute. It was argued that many dimensions of the evolving cross-Strait relationship will depend upon calculations of the role of the U.S. in the region by both sides.

It was felt that there was a critical need for a more nuanced and complex foreign policy on both sides of the Strait, moving away from the tendency to focus so unidimensionally on the cross-Strait issue in dealings with third countries.

SECTION V
Alternative Scenarios

CHAPTER 8
Probable Directions
in Cross-Strait Negotiations

Bob C. L. Li,
Cathay Finance and Economic Development Associates

A conference on this subject is very timely and the subject itself is very dear to me. As a native Taiwanese, my family, relatives, and friends live there, and I am concerned for the people's and the island's well-being. At the same time I have spent more than half of my twenty-two-year career in the World Bank as an international civil servant working in various capacities for mainland China, facilitating her opening up to the outside world. Particularly during the past couple years, I have been acting as an intermediary for the Wang-Kuo meeting in Singapore in April last year. So, on both sides of the Strait, I feel very close to them all, and I am hoping for a peaceful resolution to the conflicts. This is the first time I have spoken out in public on the issues. In the past while working for the World Bank, because of the rule of conduct, I would not be allowed to do so. I realize that this subject is very sensitive, but I'd like to speak to it from the bottom of my heart.

Before I start discussing probable directions in cross-Strait negotiations, I have to put the subject matter in proper perspective. We must know the key players in this game. We must try to find out what common interests they are pursuing and what threats and challenges exist. We must know what scenarios are available and what the impacts of these scenarios. Among the key players are: (1) those within mainland China; and (2) those within Taiwan.

Within mainland China are: (1) those who have been in the long march during the Civil War. For this group, the independence of Taiwan will be a taboo. For them that will not be acceptable; that will be the greatest failure in their revolutionary mission and they will not tolerate it. They will anything in their power to prevent it; (2) those who are now in the central government. The closer they are to the central government, the stronger they are about the issue of unification; (3) those who are far away from the central government and are enjoying the fruits of reform (i.e., coastal provinces). They are more interested in economic gain than in political integration; and (4) the younger generation. They are currently less concerned about the issue. However, cultivating this young generation seems to be an important vehicle to achieve goals in this game.

In Taiwan the two major groups are (1) KMT and (2) DPP. These two groups currently have divergent goals. The KMT are pursuing the definition of "ROC in Taiwan." The DPP is pursuing, "one China, one Taiwan." They are in complete opposition, and we must find some common interest to agree upon, if we expect to be able to propose any acceptable solution for them.

Between mainland China and Taiwan, the conflict seems to be that mainland China poses a serious threat, not only militarily, but also economically. In the long run, the economic threat to Taiwan could be even greater than the military threat. During the past several years, Taiwan's trade without China would be in the deficit column. Recently, large Taiwanese companies, such as Evergreen, which is the Sealand of Taiwan, or the President's group, which is the General Foods of Taiwan, have gone to mainland China. Why are they doing so? The reason is simple. If they don't land a beachhead at this time, they could be behind internationally very soon, or even lose the whole market forever. Because of the size of the national resources and the economic growth pace in China, even the World Bank estimated that the China's GNP by the year 2015 may surpass the total GNP of the U.S. With the abundance in natural resources and cheap labor, China's greatest threat to Taiwan could come economically rather than militarily. On the other hand, the mainland has threatened to use force if and when Taiwan declares independence.

On Taiwan's side the challenges to mainland China could be a progress in political reform and continuous growth. But more importantly the challenge could be continuous improvement in education, health care, the environment, etc. On the other hand, Taiwan has not been happy that

Taipei has not received coequal treatment by Beijing and has been blocked out from the international organizations.

Keeping the key players in mind, I will now describe what approaches are probable directions in cross-Strait negotiations in the future. In general, one's past experiences seem to have influence on what one could do in the future. Because of this, my past experiences with the UNDP and the World Bank have had major impact on my thinking; this includes the following: (1) my experience in establishing the TOKTEN (Transfer of Know-how Through Expatriate National) program under UNDP support has helped greatly in opening China up to the outside world since 1979. Under this program, overseas Chinese with special expertise have been recruited on a short-term basis to visit China, providing technical assistance from time to time. They have been recruited without compensation but out-of-pocket expenditures are to be reimbursed by UNDP. They spoke the language, knew the culture and traditions and the results of their assistance has been quite productive. Also the Chinese in China and those overseas have benefited very much from this program. Because of the success of the program, several thousand have contributed to the effort and the program is still continuing today. (2) As the program coordinator for the UNDP/ World Bank training program for China, I have seen more than 5,000 mid-level and senior officials received training in almost every economic sector under the program between 1986-1990. I had the opportunity to visit China in almost every province. I have come into contact with senior officials, discussed with them training needs, and have chatted for some time about cross-Strait issues.

Having experience with these programs in the past, I have come to realize the same approach can be used in proposing probable directions in the cross-Strait negotiations. Why can't the same spirit of TOKTEN also be applied in cross-Strait matters as a preparatory step, not for any political purpose or discussion, but for opening up contact and dialogue? Funding, instead of from UN systems which are already in financial difficulty, could come from Taiwan's public or private foundations. If one is fearful of political motivations for the program, then international organizations or nongovernmental organizations (NGO) could be entrusted to administer the program. The real purpose of the program is to provide assistance with one another's needs. One old Chinese saying is "seeing each other's face alone has already accomplished 30 percent good feeling toward each other." These contacts, instead of political discussions, could facilitate exchange of economic development experiences and policies. For example, the World Bank arranged for K.T. Li, former economic minister from

Taiwan, to attend a meeting in Dalian to discuss Taiwan's experience in controlling inflation. I would like to see more of these kind of meetings taking place in an organized program. Do they constitute official contact? Yes and no: In their individual capacity, the answer is yes; but in the subject of their discussion, no. There is no fear of corrupting each other, but only good intentions to help each other in almost every economic sector.

Currently, both Taiwan and mainland China try to lure diplomatic recognition among nations. They use monetary and economic bait, competing for recognition among nations. This is a waste of national effort and money and corrupts the world's morale allowing nations to play one against the other, not necessarily in the best interest of either mainland China or Taiwan. They should use these resources to pursue the spirit of TOKTEN. Taiwan should establish a World Bank trust fund, which could be used to recruit Taiwanese expertise to help China's economic reform, to promote training as well as economic development studies, and vice versa. At this stage any political discussions between Taiwan and mainland China will not get very far. The very reason why the Wang-Kuo meeting could be held was because they could agree on "one China, but not trying to define it." Otherwise, the meeting would bog down as soon as they started to meet, if they started with any political discussions, including the definition of "one nation, two countries" or "one China, two governments" or "one country, two systems" or "one China, two sovereign states" or "one China, one Taiwan" or "two Chinas" or "one country, two governing entities." These discussions will completely stop any meaningful dialogue. Therefore, in the foreseeable future, one must realize that they could start only from nonpolitical discussions if they expect to get any results from their meetings.

In the cross-Strait negotiations, one must give the other some sense of security feeling. Mainland China has threatened from time to time to use force if Taiwan declares independence; that means mainland China needs some assurance. On the other hand, Taiwan keeps talking about dignity, about coequal treatment as the other brother across the Strait, and about some room in the international community, particularly the international organizations. Taiwan has no intention nor ability to replace mainland China in the international arena. If Taipei can give Beijing the assurance, will mainland China accept the participation of Taiwan into the three Breedenwood institutions, such as GATT, IMF, and the World Bank? With Taiwan and mainland China both in the Breedenwood

Institutions, the nonpolitical cooperation mentioned earlier could take an even more active approach for financial and technical cooperation. Only with assurance given and some international room provided, could the nonpolitical cooperation start. Otherwise, each side is marching on its own spot with no chance to take a step forward. Taiwan could not cause any threat to mainland China militarily or economically. Given assurance, the big brother should have the courage to give his counterpart some room in the international financial organizations for nonpolitical cooperation.

At the current stage of Strait relationship, any probable directions in the negotiations must include, but not be limited to, low key, behind-the-scenes personal contact with the two brothers, particularly those who have the trust of the two. Chinese problems must be solved in a Chinese way by Chinese. One vehicle is through the nonpolitical cooperation mentioned earlier.

On the definition of one China, let's stay the course. Under the current agreement, in which I had personally acted as a go-between, the acceptable definition of one China is not to give a definition, i.e., "one China, but not trying to define it now." I do not see what is wrong with that definition as long as the two brothers could continue to cooperate and progress in all directions for the benefit of their people. Let's stay with that definition, keep on pursuing nonpolitical cooperation, and hope that one day both brothers can agree on a definition.

Having described the probable directions for Taiwan and mainland China in future cross-Strait negotiations, I am now turning to the international community, particularly for those military and economic superpowers, such as the U.S. and Japan. There has been some doubt in mainland China about the sincerity of international community to see a peaceful resolution on the conflict. The military superpowers would like to see the conflict continue, so that China will continuously be in check. The economic superpowers do not want to see capital and management expertise from Taiwan helping China's economic reform, eliminating China's need for their own expertise. With such doubt, it is in the interest of the international community to assure China that (1) they don't intend such conspiracy; and (2) that peaceful resolution will be to their own national interest as well. Only by convincing China that they don't have such a conspiracy, will their suggestions will be accepted and appreciated. Failing to do so will generate resistance among all Chinese, no matter how productive the suggestions may be. Nevertheless, Chinese problems

159

must be solved by the Chinese, and it is to our best interest that we solve our problems peacefully.

This chapter will be published in newspapers in Taiwan. I hope that once it is published, the article will also receive attention in mainland China, and that the news about my efforts in the past to promote the Wang-Kuo meeting in Singapore will receive proper attention for policy debates in both Taiwan and mainland China. I hope that these debates will produce comprehensive dialogue, generate compromises, and reach some sort of agreement to start nonpolitical cooperation. Both sides must compromise to reach where they are going. As a footnote, our organization, Cathay Finance and Economic Development Associates, whose members are all Chinese retirees from international organizations, including GATT, IMF, the World Bank, and UNDP, has established a center for economic development studies. The center invites senior officials from both sides of the Strait to share experiences in economic development. This is a very small way of providing opportunity for nonpolitical dialogue between the two sides. We hope it may produce a miracle some day. It is a Chinese way of solving Chinese problems.

CHAPTER 9
Alternative Scenarios of Interaction in the International Arena

Garret W. Gong,
Center for Strategic and International Studies

Introduction

This chapter is designed to consider, in a "creative, not necessarily linear manner," possible alternative scenarios of interaction for Taiwan and the mainland in the international arena.

I interpret "creative, not necessarily linear" as an invitation to consider current premises and issues, ongoing policies and prospects, and future possibilities with an eye to identifying key variables, trends, and uncertainties, and especially alternative scenarios which may link them in possibly different patterns.

In particular, I am asked to explore whether the current cross-Strait relationship based on direct political competition will continue to determine the interaction between Beijing and Taipei in the international arena, or whether Taipei and Beijing may discover or create a broader, convergent set of international arena interactions, which over time could even influence the core cross-Strait relationship. The question is timely: whether recent cross-Strait interactions simply stabilize the PRC-Taiwan relationship within the same framework, or whether current trends may signal a historic shift in Taiwan's approach to legitimacy.[1] This chapter is accordingly divided into three sections:

- Current Premises and Issues
- Ongoing Policies and Prospects
- Future Possibilities

In its conclusion, this exploration of alternative futures offers some policy suggestions.

Current Premises and Issues

Current developments (including Tang Shubei's August 3-7, 1994, Taipei visit) underscore the potential utility in making explicit for analysis the underlying premises and issues which set the intellectual and policy parameters governing the interaction in international arenas between Taiwan and mainland China. These current premises and issues may or may not be uniformly held or recognized within Taiwan, the PRC, or within other parts of the international community.

Nor are these basic operating assumptions necessarily uniformly or consistently held by the same groups, or even by the same persons, over time, or at a given time. Indeed, as is the case with policy generally, aspects of these operating perceptions may be shared by different generations, groups, or individuals across the Taiwan Strait, or within the various overseas Chinese or international communities.

Some may be so well known or obvious as to hardly necessitate articulation; others, taken together and made explicit, may merit analytical discussion.

These caveats and delineations of nuance recognized, some of the key premises or issues which set the framework for Taiwan-mainland relations in the international arena include the following.

1. As a matter of principle, as is clear from Taiwan Executive Yuan and PRC State Council documents, the cross-Strait relationship, including its manifestations in the international arena, has been respectively defined by competing assertions—Beijing's de jure assertion of a single, inviolable sovereignty and Taipei's de facto assertion of separate, coexisting political entities.

Taipei describes the "essence of and real reason for the division" as a "struggle between two contrasting political, economic, and social systems and two different ways of life," i.e., "between the China of the Three Principles of the People, which is founded on Chinese culture, and Communist China, rooted in Marxism."[2]

In contrast, Beijing declares "the sovereignty of each State is an integral whole which is indivisible and unsharable."[3] The PRC contends "the Government of the People's Republic of China, as the sole legal government of China, has the right and obligation to exercise state sovereignty and represent the whole of China in international organizations."[4] Further, "the Taiwan authorities' lobbying for a formula of 'one country, two seats' in international organizations whose membership is confined to sovereign states is a maneuver to create 'two Chinas.'"[5]

Taipei counters that President Lee Teng-hui's April 30, 1991, announcement terminating the period of mobilization for the suppression of communist rebellion as of midnight on May 1 "showed that the ROC government would no longer compete with Peking for the 'right to represent China' in the international arena. The government held that 'there is only one China,'" but prior to unification "these two parts of China should have the right to participate alongside each other in the international community."[6]

The concept of a "political entity" is advanced to serve as the basis of interaction between the two sides (which is of a "domestic" or "Chinese" nature), asserting that "only when we set aside the 'sovereignty dispute' will we untangle the knots that have bound us for the past forty years or more and progress smoothly toward unification."[7]

> **2.** As a matter of practice, as is clear from the mutual actions and reactions on both sides of the Taiwan Strait, the cross-Strait relationship (and thereby in the international arena) has been handled as part of an essentially political, dynamic interaction.

In fact, an essentially political, dynamic interaction implies a multiplicity of multilayered political interactions: *politics within Taiwan* and the PRC (succession politics, bureaucratic politics, popular and electoral politics, media politics, generational and regional politics, special interest politics including possibly counterpoised interests in economic integration and political competition); *cross-Strait politics* (touching on Asia-Pacific politics and regional and global positioning); the *politics of international diplomacy* (including the politics of bilateral and multilateral relations); and the *politics of international organizations*, which vary per organization.

As a practical example, this means that, as part of their targeted, practical political calculus, key decision-makers in Taiwan carefully scrutinized the personal ties between PRC Party General Secretary Jiang Zemin with both the Governor of Zhejiang and the head of the Zhejiang

Peoples Armed Police (PAP) in formulating Taiwan's public and private responses to the Thousand Lake (Qiandaohu) boating tragedy.

Clearly, no simple approach or strategy can cover all these political interactions; only political determination of prioritized interests can establish the degree of political salience (thereby determining resources and priority) respective parties attach to various aspects of their interaction within international fora. These political assessments are, of course, constantly shifting over time, according to perceptions and developments. For example, in addition to the core issue of sovereignty, bureaucratic processes integral to foreign policy formulation and implementation in (1) both the mainland and Taiwan (i.e., the embedding of the international organization function within foreign ministries beholden to higher political authorities), and (2) in the political world of international organizations, contribute to the politicization of perception and decision-making.

By their nature, issues involving international organizations bring the cross-Strait relationship into a broader, multilateral arena, which represents an aggregation of triangular relationships, namely PRC-Taiwan-other country relations; the respective bureaucracies of the various international organizations must also be dealt with.

Issues of competitive national pride are a natural and inescapable part of such bureaucratic structures, which may be accentuated by media coverage and competition (both international and domestic), and lead to the belief that timing of actions may be causal, as in Taipei's belief the PRC pressured South Korea to break diplomatic relations at the time and in the way it did as a response to Taiwan's other diplomatic successes.

3. Because both Beijing and Taipei have defined their cross-Strait relations, including in international fora, primarily in competitive, political terms, there has been some room for political compromise and maneuver, including within international fora.

One might logically expect the obverse, but the record to date, reflecting Chinese sensibilities and practical approaches, has been to find politically determined solutions where circumstances warrant. As within the ADB and APEC, these political compromises can be subtle and not, direct and not.

Changes in Taipei, Beijing, and the international society have contributed to ameliorating in practical ways the otherwise zero-sum confrontation on principle.

There is thus both some irony and political wisdom in the Mainland

Affairs Council's repeated assurance that its cross-Strait talks are functional, dealing with specific practical issues, not political.

Two caveats also apply:

To say the Taiwan-mainland interaction in the international arena is essentially a political, dynamic interaction is not to overlook the overlap of politics, economics, and society; the shift in emphasis toward economic relations in the post-Cold War period; or the broadening definition of power and influence to encompass traditional "hard" power and emerging sources of "soft" power, etc.

Nor is it to imply *ipso facto* that political interactions are necessarily competitive in a zero-sum fashion. Indeed, a purpose of this paper is to consider to what extent and where, within the parameters of a changing political relationship the cross-Strait Taiwan-mainland interaction in international arenas might be conducted in a broader, less directly zero-sum competitive fashion.

4. For both Taipei and Beijing, some cross-Strait contact in international fora may be necessary to demonstrate and advance their respective "one China" assertions, though no clear "one China" direction (unification) has yet definitively emerged from cross-Strait interaction in international fora.

This situation encompasses at least six, related dilemmas.

First is the dilemma between Beijing's refusal to renounce force for unification and sentiments within Taiwan to declare a more independent position.

Beijing's threats to use force no doubt give substance to its claims to sovereignty (its carrots cannot entice unity as well as its sticks); however, Beijing's actual demonstrations of force, whether at Tiananmen or Qiandaohu, seem to increase sympathy for a more independent Taiwan.

This is also why Taipei pointedly balances the counterpoised trends of integration and separatism, recognizing "in objective terms, the degree of acceptance which these two trends enjoy among the people of Taiwan will depend on the future development of relations between the two sides of the Taiwan Strait."[8]

Second and related is the dilemma of polarized leverage.

Because one way Beijing strongly asserts sovereignty is directly or indirectly to threaten Taiwan with force, e.g., multiple, large PRC combined forces exercises opposite Jinmen in Fujian province, popular interest in greater independence is one development in Taiwan which may remind Beijing of its limited ability to compel compliance with limited models of sovereignty.

165

Underscored is the possibility that perceived leverage on each side of the Taiwan Strait is not only counterpoised, but polarized. As each side seeks to maximize polarized lines of leverage, they may find themselves moving toward unintentioned greater risks of brinksmanship or even conflict.

Particularly if the DPP and KMT positions regarding Taiwan's international identity converge, it would be ironic if the dilemmas of polarized leverage pushed both sides of the Strait in directions toward which each threatened but neither particularly wanted to proceed.

Third is the dilemma between Taiwan's domestic electoral legitimacy and its international position.

Today's Taiwan continues to be reshaped by structural transformation, processes of "Taiwanization," the rise of the Democratic Progressive Party (DPP) as a political force, the ongoing stages of democratization. A political reality in Taiwan, not completely understood in Beijing, is that popularized, democratized local politics in Taiwan have linked frustration over international recognition and popular elective legitimacy.

This interaction is itself also double-edged. On the one hand, the DDP has made some political inroads by identifying international recognition as a potentially potent popular issue; on the other hand, political realists express concern that good local politics may create potentially volatile international misunderstandings.

For these and other reasons, Taiwan's constitutional reforms have encompassed the complex intersection of internal, cross-Strait, and international positions.[9] Even more fundamentally, while the broadening of political participation in Taiwan may have strengthened domestic legitimacy, it may also reflect (and possibly increase) demands for a separate Taiwan culture and identity,[10] further accentuating areas of divergence across the Strait.

And the conventional wisdom remains that the KMT must assiduously avoid party-to-party talks not only because it downgrades its status to a local party, but also because any perception in Taipei of a working through of "mainlander" interests across the straits would create a crisis of confidence in Taiwan.

Fourth is the dilemma between Taiwan's international position and its international legitimacy.

For Beijing not to allow or determine some "breathing space" for Taiwan may be to encourage a political desire for independence; to allow Taiwan expansive de facto international personality may be to erode any meaning or incentive to maintain "one China."

Beijing does not want frustrations about independence to create a negative self-fulfilling prophecy. Conversely, Beijing recognizes that granting legitimacy through international recognition to the ruling party in Taipei (whichever that might be) may also create a self-fulfilling trend toward, if not Taiwan independence (*tai-du*), than perhaps an independent Taiwan (*du-tai*).

Fifth is the dilemma between the name by which Taiwan chooses to identify itself and participate in the international arena and the acceptability of that involvement within the international community.

Not to determine which the name and conditions by which Taiwan would participate in the international arena (its objectives and motivations) is to leave unclear how outside powers such as Tokyo, Washington, Johannesburg should react. Indeed, it is unlikely the PRC (or other interested countries) can take definitive, formal positions on Taiwan's international participation within specific international organizations without a clear definition of the conditions under which Taiwan would seek membership.

In other words, a determination on the name issue (e.g., Republic of China on Taiwan, Republic of Taiwan) may be a prerequisite to the formulation of a consensus within the international community — even as its postponement may broaden political consensus within Taiwan's domestic political scene.

This juxtaposition of names and approaches was evident at the time of the APEC conference when op-ed pieces presented cases for Taiwan from two different angles.

In a *Seattle Times* editorial section commentary, Taipei's Government Information Office Director-General Dr. Jason Hu asserted that, "The ROC has adapted a pragmatic policy of recognizing that the PRC governs mainland China," while disputing the PRC claim that it governs the Republic of China. China "is now a divided nation and has been so since 1949," meaning that precedents for "parallel representation for divided nations" in the UN organization and other political and economic realities argue that "a realistic and fair appraisal of the international situation cannot fail to conclude that the Republic of China is fully qualified to become a member of the UN."[11]

Similarly in the *Seattle Times*, Mr. Juang Lu Lin of the Formosan Association for Public Affairs in Seattle contended, "Taiwan is a sovereign and independent state because it has control over its people, a defined territory, and a government capable of governing effectively in internal processes and of acting responsibly in external relations on the basis of the international legal requirements of statehood." Thus, Taiwan, "as an independent country should apply for admission as a new member of the United Nations in accordance with Article 4 of the UN Charter."[12]

Sixth is the dilemma between Beijing's potential (direct or indirect) involvement in Taiwan politics relating to international personality and its potentially counterproductive results.

At issue is the possibility that, as progress in international participation becomes necessary for political popularity (electoral legitimacy) in Taiwan, Beijing may in fact begin to exercise, through its willingness or not to allow such participation, increased leverage or influence over Taiwan elections than authorities in Taiwan might have otherwise intended or thought wise.

A related concern is that the existence or appearance of such PRC efforts to manipulate the situation in Taiwan, e.g., the accusation of seeming to favor the KMT in an international arena interaction, could create a backlash in Taiwan. These concerns increase in immediacy with reports by Taiwan's central bank that PRC entities may now hold 1 percent of Taiwan currency directly, and may be seeking through stock holdings and other direct and indirect investments, acquisitions, or other means to influence Taiwan's economy and politics.

5. It is important to ascertain the essential interest and purpose of participation in international organizations, for these intents set the parameters of the principles, resources, and standards of evaluation used to judge success or failure.

For example, interests in international participation discussed in Taiwan include:

- international status; sense of not being isolated, of belonging to, and being respected by, the international community as a full and contributing member;
- domestic political concerns;
- security; some in Taiwan have argued UN membership may ultimately enhance Taipei's self-defense; moral authority, and international stature undeniably attach to international organization membership which buttress claims to legal personality and political legitimacy;
- leverage with the PRC.

This analysis should also consider what international membership currently entails. A society of states (or international society) is measured in terms of certain fundamental commonalities; common interests, and values, commonly binding rules, and common institutions.[13] Historically, as codified in legal theory and customary international practice, international societies have designated criteria for full and partial membership. Though with initial reference to states, five are applicable to political entities and have been especially important and enduring:

1. the political entity guarantees basic rights, i.e., life, dignity, and property; freedom of travel, commerce, and religion, especially that of foreign nationals.
2. the political entity as an organized political bureaucracy with some efficiency in running the state machinery, and with some capacity for self-defense;
3. the political entity adheres to generally accepted international law, including the laws of war; it also maintains a domestic system of courts, codes, and published laws which guarantee legal justice for all within its jurisdiction;
4. the political entity fulfills the obligations of the international system by maintaining adequate and permanent avenues for diplomatic interchange and communication;
5. the political entity by and large conforms to the accepted norms and practices of the established international society.[14]

In this regard, Taipei contends its clear adherence to the first three criteria (those often associated with international recognition) qualify it as a political entity, part of a temporarily divided China. Much of the current focus has been on the fourth criteria, regarding diplomatic exchange and communication, including through international organizations. Also, Taipei's emphasis on domestic legitimacy, freedom, pluralistic politics, and market-oriented economics is intended to demonstrate consistency with the underlying values-orientation of the international system (the fifth criteria).

Taipei and Beijing will continue to assert their respective cases in terms of political pragmatics; international and economic realities; recognized indicators of international personality; and the moral case of global public opinion.

Ongoing Policies and Prospects

Consideration of ongoing policies and prospects from Taipei's and Beijing's perspectives suggests that, at the level of practice, some scope for positive interaction still exists.

Taipei

Taipei's basic argument contains several points:[15]

- by objective criteria related to control of territory, governance, established law, international participation, etc. Taiwan deserves more international position and recognition; by such objective criteria, Taiwan is more deserving of UN membership than two-thirds of current UN members;
- this is especially true if moral criteria are included, such as China's participation as a founding UN member, its maintenance of obligations and opportunities even following its leaving the UN;
- it should include recognition of Taipei's continued and expanding de facto and de jure involvement with the international community;
- it should reflect Taiwan's economic influence at a time when the international system is shifting from cold war configurations to ones in which both "hard" and "soft" power should increase Taiwan's stature.

Per the analysis in this paper's previous section, it is necessary for Taipei to determine its purposes and objectives in seeking international representation so as to determine its priorities and thereby to inform its tactical human and other resource allocation by a broader strategy.

To date, Taipei's four-pronged diplomatic approach has focused on:

1. strengthening substantive relations with countries with which the ROC lacks diplomatic relations;
2. press for admission to international organizations;
3. develop relations with communist countries for the first time;
4. challenge the PRC in countries with which the PRC had diplomatic relations.[16]

In this approach, admission to international organizations is embedded within a general competitive strategy wherein it is difficult to separate the willingness to challenge the PRC generally from a more specific interest in joining a particular international organization. There is thus a parallel complementarity in seeking to establish representative offices, upgrade their status or names, broaden their functions, and participate in more high-level visits and international conferences and in seeking to join more governmental and nongovernmental institutions, gain entry under flexible nomenclature if necessary to more institutions with the PRC, and in general to seek a broader international status.

Within the international organization category, there have been successes to date. These have come within the competitive paradigm, largely on substantive grounds, advanced through a working political context.[17]

Beijing

Beijing's current approach toward Taipei's participation in international organizations tries to temper a strong assertion of the sovereignty principle within the practical realities of a fluid cross-Strait and international situation.

For example, Beijing recognizes, "It should be affirmed that the desire of Taiwan compatriots to run the affairs of the island as masters of their own house is reasonable and justified. This should be no means be construed as advocating 'Taiwan independence.'"[18] The principle remains that, "As a part of China, Taiwan has no right to represent China in the international community, nor can it establish diplomatic ties or enter into relations of an official nature with foreign countries." However, "considering the needs of Taiwan's economic development and the practical interests of Taiwan compatriots, the Chinese government has not objected to nongovernmental economic or cultural exchanges between Taiwan and foreign countries."[19]

Perhaps most flexibly, Beijing notes, "Only on the premise of adhering to the principle of one China and in the light of the nature and statutes of the international organizations concerned as well as the specific circumstances, can the Chinese government consider the question of Taiwan's participation in the activities of such organizations and in a manner agreeable and acceptable to the Chinese government."[20]

Future Possibilities

Without a transformation of international politics, it is unrealistic to consider a complete, immediate separation of developments in international arenas from the fundamental political competition between Beijing and Taipei.

However, it is worth asking whether or not a positive feedback relationship might exist, or be created between changes at the core cross-Strait relationship and their subsequent international arena manifestations. In essence, political pragmatism may note an explicit or tacit recognition, negotiated or not, that greater international "breathing space" is in both Taipei's and Beijing's interests. Similarly, Beijing and Taipei may find issues of common interest in the international arena in which the political interests of both are not directly involved, or in which they are subsumed in other greater concerns.

It remains an open question whether the creation or discovery of mutual international interests may soften the otherwise harder political edges of the cross-Strait relationship; to date, the reverse has been true, i.e., the international arena interaction has been determined by the Beijing-Taipei relationship rather than the other way around.

The task of this chapter's third section is to combine the premises and issues of the first section with the Taipei and Beijing policies and prospects of the second section into a discussion of Taipei-Beijing international arena interactions according to a different paradigm.

The paradigm of international arena interaction discussed thus far derives from a dynamic, politically competitive interaction. Within this dynamic, politically competitive framework one does not necessarily have to assume either Kantian or Hobbesian outcomes. Beyond pure functionalism, a Grotian position can recognizing that, while any alternative approach will have to coexists within the realities of sometimes zero-sum political interactions, four propositions may nevertheless suggest a less confrontational approach:

1. In some cases, greater common ground can be formed by positive interaction within international arenas.
2. Carried out in a practical, nonzero-sum fashion, such interaction can perhaps modify the central juxtaposition of competing asserted principles.
3. Just as in domestic societies, so in international ones: common interests can be forged by joint efforts toward larger common objectives, sometimes indirect efforts are more efficacious in tension reduction and in confidence building than direct efforts to negotiate away bilateral differences.
4. The transnational, emerging issues may best lend themselves to such a joint agenda.

More specifically, the initial premises for such cooperation include recognition of the interplay between principle and legitimacy:

1. the efforts cannot be taken primarily as a way to jockey for political advantage, though such efforts (as similar efforts within some specialized UN institutions) take place within the political contours and constraints of the international system;
2. it is neither desirable nor practical to wait until political competition disappears before attempting such joint efforts; i.e., some political content will likely have to be overcome in their initial stages;

3. in some cases, virtue (i.e., the accomplishment of humanitarian purpose by joint efforts) will have to be its own best reward; if too much political or other credit is claimed, it must be claimed within the cooperative framework if such efforts are to succeed.
4. ideally, such joint efforts must go beyond the symbolic (the propaganda value) if they are to build maximum confidence on the human level across the Strait through genuine outreach to those in need.

Needless to say each case has its own particulars, though the broad framework and rationale for cooperation might be similar.

This approach takes the current cross-Strait approach and pro-actively expands it. The current *modus vivendi* for contact is to work on specific, pressing issues drawn from increasing contact: notaries, registered mail, regular meetings, and ongoing agenda. Recent cross-Strait meetings also reached agreement on specific problems, namely hijacking and fishing disputes.

Some of these issues are a natural and unavoidable consequence of opening ties across the Strait. Some are individual acts; others may be influenced, indirectly or directly, by a need to spur the process of cross-Strait communication. It may also be the case that some issues are used as political control rods to regulate the agenda and sense of immediacy of cross-Strait relations.

Beyond the current agenda, other largely transnational issues may offer a means to blur traditional boundaries and concerns for sovereignty; they may offer Taipei and Beijing a natural way to broaden their own cross-Strait interests within a wider international arena, including within appropriate international organizations.

Humanitarian Fora

Humanitarian issues may be considered within a cross-Strait, regional, or global context.

Some humanitarian assistance occurs in a cross-Strait context, often with a targeted eye to specific localities, "home villages," or other (sometimes commercial) ties. Beyond cross-Strait programs within the ARATS-SEF framework (where opportunities likewise exist), humanitarian efforts could be expanded to include possible joint, multilateral participation in UN organizations such as the UNHCR, the Global Information and Early Warning System and Food Security Assistance Scheme of the Food and Agriculture Organization (FAO), expanded participation in the International Red Cross (IRC), or in new regional humanitarian organizations. These efforts could be seen as a natural extension of Taiwan's International Disaster Relief Fund, established in 1990.

The recent devastation of Typhoon Fred could provide a case in point. Premier Lien Chan approved NT $10 billion for disaster relief in Taiwan; across the Strait, damage in coastal Zhejiang has been estimated at US $1.6 billion, with some 8 million people affected. Similarly, storms and floods this year have killed more than 1,400 persons in Zhejiang, Guangdong, Guangxi, Hunan, Jiangxi, and Fujian provinces. In July 1993, floods in China's northeast provinces and Inner Mongolia destroyed more than 522,000 houses and damaged more than 591,000 others, causing direct losses of US $942 million.[21]

Beyond or perhaps in parallel with joint cross-Strait humanitarian efforts, with a division of labor in which each side contributed supplies, labor, personnel, or financial assistance in an agreed-upon manner, humanitarian efforts may be usefully considered within a Northeast or East Asia regional context.

No doubt Tokyo, Seoul, Taipei, and Beijing, as well as others, may find an interest to work within a UN or specialized agency framework to mobilize humanitarian assistance within their home region. Such a mechanism may find multifaceted regional humanitarian applications, e.g., in the PRC and Taiwan, in the event of precipitous change on the Korean peninsula, in finding avenues for Japan's regional humanitarian participation, etc.

Over time, Taipei and Beijing may also consider joint humanitarian efforts on a more global basis.

Such efforts could possibly occur in Africa or other places where Taipei and Beijing have in the past been direct competitors. The approach and symbolism of such humanitarian efforts, e.g., in a Rwanda or Somalia, would be threefold: (1) the "one China policy" is shared by Taipei and Beijing in a practical way which benefits third countries in distress; (2) cross-Strait personnel and governmental systems, though distinct, need not operate in a competitive or politically zero-sum manner in certain humanitarian areas of the international arena; (3) though still developing politically and economically, China and the Chinese people share a concern for people elsewhere.

Cooperative humanitarian efforts might also be developed in three other areas of pressing concern: drugs; women's and children's issues; and disease control, particularly AIDS and other infectious diseases.

Drugs/Crime. Taipei and Beijing share an interest in limiting international crime including drug trafficking, particularly that which transits the mainland, Taiwan, and Hong Kong, as well as which involve overseas Chinese communities.

For logistical, political, and other reasons, such shared interests could be expanded within the international arena, possibly through the offices of the U.S. (DEA, Justice, etc.) In any case, the model would not want to repeat past unpleasantries associated with the Taiwan-mainland interaction in INTERPOL.

Instead of only bilateral drug enforcement efforts, Beijing (including Guangdong, etc.), Taipei and Hong Kong could meet in joint drug enforcement seminars, information exchange, etc. Expert-level personnel as well as senior officials in the appropriate law enforcement agencies of the PRC, Hong Kong, Taiwan, the U.S., and other concerned parties, could meet on a rotating basis in Hong Kong or the U.S. first, and then, as appropriate, elsewhere. To repeat, the thrust of such efforts must be understood not to internationalize sovereignty concerns, but to address more effectively the specific, transborder issues in question.

Such groups could interact at times in a symbolic, higher-profile fashion—to establish an international presence for such efforts. More likely, such groups would generally meet privately, even confidentially, to minimize political posturing and to maximize impact in their target areas of operation.

Beyond combatting crime or drugs, such joint efforts could include a needed element of public education. A positive, shared values approach could find resonance by building on an anti-drugs nationalism. Everyone could benefit: public antidrug awareness in the PRC, Taiwan, and Hong Kong should be increased; laws and jurisdictions, harmonized; gang activities, countered; and hopefully drug use and addiction, diminished.

Women's and children's issues. It is said that open windows bring in flies, and the more open the windows of marketized economic opportunity, the bigger the flies. On both sides of the Taiwan Strait, economic dynamism has opened new issues of how to protect traditional society and established values from unbridled economic Darwinism. In particular, the reduction of women and children to the marketized status of moveable property may be another area where Taipei and Beijing could find common cause within appropriate international institutions.

To the extent each is concerned with pornography, similar efforts within the crime/drug framework noted above may also be considered.

More broadly, international organizations such as the UN

Commission on the Status of Women seek to protect women from violence, foster good family health, and alleviate poverty. Scheduled to meet in Beijing in September 1995, this kind of commission within a UN framework should offer joint opportunity to pursue women's and children's issues. Beijing should be forthcoming with information and opportunities for full, constructive participation; Taipei should be forthcoming with a non-politicized willingness to help address the full range of concerns.

Likewise, enlarged scope for joint efforts regarding children may arise through the UN Convention on the Rights of the Child (1990), promoted by UNICEF.

Diseases. Often closely related to the issues of drugs and sexually transmitted diseases associated with prostitution, the issues of disease extend to other questions which affect Chinese citizens, e.g., smallpox, typhoid, and hepatitis.

Through the WHO and other organizations, Taiwan and Beijing may be able to widen common ground, perhaps by focusing on issues first within Taiwan that would allow PRC specialists a natural reason to visit Taiwan and share their expertise, and then rotating or sharing issues so concerns would be balanced. In this regard, through appropriate discussions, there is every reason for Taiwan to gain at least associate member status in the WHO, especially since WHO explicitly provides for such status.

Population, pollution, and other sustainable development issues may likewise provide opportunity for joint cross-Strait efforts, perhaps including international fora.

Developmental Fora

A similar approach may be taken in international developmental fora. Both Taipei and Beijing have an interest to contribute to and draw on multilateral efforts aimed at agricultural assistance, reforestation, population education, etc.

These are future-oriented efforts, which naturally encourage consideration of future generations in China. Some related commercial interests may be jointly pursued as well.

Beyond cross-Strait relations, Beijing and Taipei could create roles for joint efforts within international development fora. In this context a *modus vivendi* should be worked out for Taipei's participation in the World Bank, IMF, etc. Here the overt public focus is not so much on Taipei's economic power (though this is a necessary prerequisite) as on the common developmental interest.

Since Taipei and Beijing are already both ADB members, common opportunity also exists to coordinate funding for projects of mutual interest, perhaps including technology transfer, etc., in key areas of sustainable development, at least initially within the cross-Strait jurisdiction, but perhaps over time extending to other areas of interest (e.g., Chinese communities) in Asia.

A tacit compromise may be encompassed in such an approach: by letting actions speak, Taipei could quietly downplay claims to a superior development experience; Beijing could quietly benefit from Taipei's willingness to supply needed financial assistance through multilateral financial institutions or developmental institutions.

Economic Fora

Since a premise in Taipei's approach is to begin with the pragmatic substance of relations, it has been natural for Taipei to focus on potential enlargement of its role in the international economic arena.

Various strategies have been advanced for parallel participation in the GATT. Taipei's decision to apply on the basis of a customs territory seemed to emphasize its interest in reducing the political element and capturing a spot in the World Trade Organization. Nevertheless, coming to full GATT compliance has and will necessitate continued adjustment and reform within Taiwan. It also reflects an ongoing cost-benefit analysis within Taiwan over how to make Taiwan's GATT accession significant and beneficial in actual, not only symbolic terms.

Similarly, much attention has been focused on APEC as an emerging institution of Asia-Pacific regional prominence. The diplomatic efforts of South Korea and others to facilitate Beijing, Taipei, and Hong Kong joining the APEC at the time of the Seoul meeting underscores the political utility of international "honest-brokers" in finding necessary international arena accommodations.

APEC establishes another set of linkages across the Strait, including the ability of APEC trade and economic delegations to visit Taipei. In this regard, some interest has reportedly been expressed in joint Taipei and Beijing involvement in an APEC energy working group.

The broad APEC trend—to reduce barriers and open possibilities for trade and investment within the Asia-Pacific — will continue the process of structural change which forces continuing evaluation and shifts among the APEC countries. Taken in aggregate, these trends may increase opportunities for cross-Strait economic cooperation, particularly from Taipei's perspective, to develop economies of scale and natural alliance lines for markets and sourcing, in relations which will remain both competitive and cooperative in economic and political terms. More specifically, these are trends decision-makers in Taipei are considering with regard to Taiwan's long-term ability to function as a regional service center.

The PRC notes, "As to regional economic organizations such as the Asian Development Bank (ADB) and the Asia-Pacific Economic Cooperation (APEC), Taiwan's participation is subject to the terms of agreement or understanding reached between the Chinese Government and the parties concerned which explicitly prescribe that the People's Republic of China is a full member as a sovereign state whereas Taiwan may participate in the activities of those organizations only as a region of China under the designation of Taipei, China (in ADB) or Chinese Taipei (in APEC). This is only an *ad hoc* arrangement and cannot constitute a 'model' applicable to other intergovernmental organizations or international gatherings."[22]

In any case, within APEC, in an effective, practical way, Taiwan has "become one of the most active members in the most important institution[s] in the Asian Pacific Region."[23]

It likewise became a member of the Central American Bank for Economic Integration (CABEI, November 1992); South-East Asian Central Bank (SEACEN); International Seed Testing Association (ISTA); and Asian Vegetable Research and Development Center (AVRDC). It also sent observers to conferences of the International Commission for the Conservation of Atlantic Tuna (ICCAT) and the Inter-American Development Bank (IDB).[24]

It has already been suggested that ongoing efforts to find appropriate representation for Taiwan within the financial arms of appropriate international institutions, particularly the World Bank and IMF, should continue to move quietly forward.[25] The issue again is to reduce the element of direct political competition while emphasizing potential areas of common interest and enhanced ability to work cooperatively, as noted above.

Security

It is not premature to consider where and how Taipei and Beijing might consider mechanisms for addressing security concerns through appropriate involvement in international fora.

Three, in particular, come to mind.

First, both Taipei and Beijing should see the non- or quasi-governmental fora and regional security dialogues as a potentially useful, multilateral mechanisms for addressing common security concerns.

This is not the place to detail the conceptual and practical nuances of collective security organizations, regional security dialogue, regional security fora, regional security arrangements, etc. Needless to say, thus far Beijing has equated security questions with sovereignty and refused to "internationalize" the Hong Kong or Taiwan issues. The logic of political leverage is straightforward.

However, under a number of future scenarios, both Beijing and Taipei may find it useful, perhaps necessary, for cross-Strait communication channels in broad, multilateral fora. Such efforts may underpin confidence building, tension reduction, and ameliorated miscalculations.

It must be recognized that Beijing may already feel on the defensive given its neighbors' concerns over the PRC's growing but non-transparent, understated military budget; post-Gulf military modernization; nascent power projection capacities (including navy and naval air); and increasingly nationalistic (superseding ideological) rationale for its security policy. Given cross-Strait domestic economic imperatives, important elements in both Taipei and Beijing, perhaps by way of implicit compromise, may find it mutually useful to develop means to make regional military budgets, deployment, threat assumptions, and operational doctrines more transparent.

This would not eliminate the political or competitive element of changing balances of comprehensive national strength, but it may provide a longer term perspective on the mutual advantages of opening avenues for regional (and thereby indirectly cross-Strait) discussion in a way that could involve the Asia-Pacific militaries.

As a tactical matter, it is probably better to involve a range of research institutes in the PRC and Taiwan for any such regional dialogue. This would diffuse the pressure on a single institution whose position might be construed as nationalistic.

Second, a new international commission or institution might be formed to deal with specific dispute resolution in the Asia-Pacific which could include areas involving Taipei and Beijing. It might include, for example, the Northern territories, Diaoyutai Islands, Spratlys, etc. The idea here is that Taipei and Beijing may find common cause on Diaoyutai or the Spratlys by building on a shared political interest in the former case, or for a willingness to look at joint development in the latter. Again, Beijing cannot be expected to favor such an arrangement if it perceives that it undercuts its sovereign claims; on the other hand, a regional dispute resolution mechanism (perhaps including a hot-line, boundary fact-finding, etc.) may provide a necessary means for various authorities within the

PRC and Taiwan to communicate should it be difficult (for whatever reason) to do so within current cross-Strait channels.

Third, Taipei and Beijing could conceivably find it useful to have parallel participation in international peacekeeping fora. Through flexibility, each could find an appropriate formula and command structure to allow participation in UN peacekeeping operations. The symbolic utility of such an effort would be the visible joint contribution to peace through a parallel participation within a multilateral framework. Establishing such a mechanism may also provide an early channel whereby military officers across the Strait could cooperate in a larger cause.

As noted, underlying these potential avenues and scenarios of Taiwan-Mainland international arena interaction is the continuing reality that the international interaction will in many ways reflect, depend on, and be conditioned by the cross-Strait political relationship.

At the same time, within an international environment less focused on limited definitions of sovereignty and more concerned with transnational issues, largely influenced by economic and financial factors, common ground may be found or created through joint or parallel involvement by Taipei and Beijing in selected international institutions and arenas.

Conclusions

Some basic action suggestions may be worth considering.

1. Changing conditions in Taiwan, Beijing, and the international system may create nonzero sum opportunities for Taipei and Beijing to develop broader common interests and means for pursuing them in international fora.

Taipei will want to continue efforts to comply with the requirements of different international organizations, e.g., evidencing willingness to accept pacific settlement as a peace-loving country, appropriately modifying conflicting claims with other members of the international community (e.g., as it did regarding Mongolia).

2. Domestic education remains important in Taiwan to help ensure that the full spectrum of interests there have a clear picture of the strengths and limitations, costs and opportunities, of participation in the UN and other international organizations. Expectations must be realistic, both as to avenues for participation and the likely substance of participation.

Legislators, media, and other opinion-leaders should have as much direct experience with these organizations as possible, but they must also resist the natural inclination to politicize their perspectives, thereby potentially clouding the intricacies of Taiwan's domestic political situation and its larger, enduring interests across the Strait.

This also means delineating between symbolic objectives and actual interests as advanced through participation in international organizations.

3. In their common interests, both Taipei and Beijing may want to find a *modus vivendi* for taking lower-profile, less political and more substantive approaches to selected international organizations, in whichever arena. Perhaps a range of profiles would allow a segmented, more subtle approach to satisfying the cross-section of political and other concerns across the Strait and within their respective decision-making bureaucracies and broader publics.

In some cases, this means not asking too many questions in advance, since public positions, taken early, on either or both sides of the Strait may limit subsequent flexibility, even in cases where it is mutually desired and beneficial.

In some cases, sensitive diplomacy is best kept secret. This helps control rhetoric and expectation levels. Legitimacy requires a certain recognition of the need for openness in terms of Taiwan's domestic political dynamic, but such efforts cannot be counterproductive to Taiwan's overall international legitimacy.

4. There is no single solution to the dilemma posed by assertion of a single, indivisible sovereignty and the assertion of two coexisting political entities: in the reality of the dynamic tension between the absolute assertion of either position is the opportunity for broadened common interest as well as competition managed so as not to irrevocably disrupt a cross-Strait dynamic equilibrium.

In this regard, it is usefully remembered that, if viewed in a zero-sum or competitive framework, the incentives for Taiwan are roughly reversely proportional to the disincentives for the PRC in any change in status within international arenas. Thus, as this chapter suggests, a key focus is how to build new areas of convergent interests, thereby expanding the realm of common interaction.

DISCUSSION
Alternative Scenarios

Hungmao Tien,
University of Wisconsin

The key policy conclusion that emerges from this discussion is the tyranny of timing. In Taiwan, we must deal with a political evolution that is not just foreign policy related, but reflects the expression of democratic processes. On the mainland we must contend with a domestic power transition that by its very nature limits policy flexibility relative to Taiwan. Neither of these trends can be significantly influenced by third parties. For some observers, concern is growing that we may actually have to confront Taiwan independence before the political dynamics on the mainland have sorted out. Neither this discussion, nor the policy debate in general have dealt adequately with policy options for managing this contingency.

At the very least, the efforts of Taiwan to rock the boat regarding an expanded international role has mobilized internal bipartisan support. There is a strong effort to use this to leverage the PRC regarding international organizations. Any scenario analysis must start from here as the new baseline. The former status quo will not be reestablished. Policy discussions therefore need to be better informed about the zeronegative-sum game character of the debate on Taiwan's role in international organizations, and how this character might be changed to both parties best interest.

The general policy strategy of the past several years, both on Taiwan and among other key players has been to enhance information flow and interaction across the Strait, directly or via third parties. Essentially, the goal was to create a habit of discussion and cooperation across as broad a range of relatively non-confrontational issues as possible, in the hope that the habit would eventually carry over into managing crises whenever they might occur. One can point to clear successes in this strategy, but many feel that the progress made to date is adequate to deal with a real independence crisis.

The urgent issue is to develop a preventive policy to deal with growing contradiction between the external interest in not rocking the boat on the broadly accepted "one China" policy and the reality of new domestic politics within Taiwan. Unfortunately there is no silver bullet. Outside players, but especially the U.S. need an incrementalist policy to both the mainland and Taiwan. It is important to open new channels of communication, especially on the mainland—unofficial, semiofficial, and official. These new channels will help establish flexible fronts for creative policy discussion and change, but step by step with less rhetoric and more action.

Both sides need to clarify their real positions. Taiwan has perhaps moved the furthest on this score. The "name" issue with the PRC is now much less of a problem and some effort has been made to lay out concrete steps to long-term accommodation, even though these steps remain largely unacceptable to the PRC. Most participants tended to believe that third parties need to help persuade the PRC that its own interests are served by greater flexibility. Now the PRC actions and rhetoric help fuel the independence movement on Taiwan and force a more confrontational dynamic. There is no good evidence that official levels on the mainland recognize this negative result of their policy.

Scenario analysis also must examine the limits and conflicts inherent in the rapid growth in functional interaction across the Strait since the late 1980s. The PRC is highly resistant to the implications of creating formal structures that implicitly grant sovereignty to Taiwan. Moreover, from both Taiwan's and the mainland's perspectives the shift from indirect to direct interaction raises serious security concerns. The international community seriously under-appreciates the security issues at stake across the Taiwan Strait.

The consensus was that the only way to avoid more negative scenarios and to help strengthen the possibility of favorable outcome was to focus on recognizing that change is coming and adapting real policies to managing the inevitable frictions that result. More concrete proposals need to be put on the table and less rhetorical posturing. For example, is a Taiwan role in Bretton Woods feasible? At what price? Will this satisfy the domestic political demands emerging from the nation building search for identity that is part of the democratization of Taiwan. Is it possible for the PRC to come to see this as also supporting their interests?

BIOGRAPHIES

Ralph Clough is coordinator of the SAIS China Forum, Nitze School of Advanced International Studies at Johns Hopkins University. He specializes in East Asia and the problems of divided countries. He has also served as Fellow in the Woodrow Wilson Center, an instructor at American University, a Senior Fellow at the Brookings Institution, as a member of the U.S. Foreign Service, and as Director of the Office of Chinese Affairs with the U.S. State Department. His most recent book is *Reaching Across the Taiwan Strait: People to People Diplomacy* (1993).

Lowell Dittmer is a professor of political science at the University of California-Berkeley, specializing in China and its politics, relations with the former Soviet Union, and political culture. He has also taught at the University of Michigan-Ann Arbor, was a Fellow at the Social Sciences Research Council in Hong Kong, and taught at SUNY-Buffalo. He is the author of several books, including *China's Quest for National Identity*, edited with S. Kim (1993); *Chinese Politics Under Reform* (1993); and *Sino-Soviet Normalization* (1992). He has a Ph.D. in Political Science from the University of Chicago.

Gerrit W. Gong is Director of the Asian Studies Program at the Center for Strategic and International Studies. He previously served as Special Assistant to Ambassador James R. Lilley and Ambassador Winston Lord, U.S. Embassy to the People's Republic of China. In May 1994 he presented testimony before the Subcommittee on East Asian and Pacific Affairs, U.S. Senate Committee on Foreign Relations. He earned his Ph.D. in International Relations from Oxford University.

Harry Harding is a senior fellow in the Foreign Policy Studies Program at the Brookings Institution, and Dean of the Elliott School of International Affairs and professor of political science and international affairs at George Washington University. He is presently chairman of the Program on International Studies in Asia, a trustee of the Asia Foundation, a member of the Committee on Scholarly Communication with China, and a director of the U.S. Committee of the Council for Security Cooperation in the Asia Pacific. He is author of *A Fragile Relationship: The United States and China Since 1972* (1992). He earned his Ph.D. in political science from Stanford University.

Karl D. Jackson was a senior fellow and Associate Director of the Competitiveness Center of Hudson Institute at the time of the conference. He was also Senior Research Associate of the Gaston Sigur Center for East Asian Studies at George Washington University. Currently he is Managing Director of FX Concepts in Washington, D.C. He has also served as Assistant to the Vice President for National Security Affairs, Special Assistant to the President for National Security Affairs, and Senior Director of Asian Affairs. He earned his Ph.D. in political science from M.I.T.

Michael Ying-Mao Kau is a professor of political science and Director of the Mao's Writings Project and the East Asian Security Project at Brown University. He also serves as President of the 21st Century Foundation (Taipei) and editor of the quarterly journal *Chinese Law and Government* (New York), and is on the Advisory Boards of the Institute of International Relations (Taipei), the Taiwan Area Studies Program at Columbia University, the Center for East Asian Studies at Cornell University, and the National Committee on U.S.-China Relations. He earned his Ph.D. in Comparative Politics and International Relations from Cornell University.

Lyman Miller is Director of the China Studies Program at the Nitze School of Advanced International Studies at Johns Hopkins University, specializing in Chinese history from 14th century to the present, and in politics and foreign policy. He has served as Senior Analyst, Branch and Division Chief of Chinese Foreign Policy and Domestic Politics, East Asian Affairs, at the Foreign Broadcast Information Service. He is the author of numerous books and articles. He earned his Ph.D. in History from George Washington University.

Jonathan Pollack is Senior Advisor for International Policy at RAND in Santa Monica, California, which he joined in 1978. He has also served on the faculty of the RAND-UCLA Center for Soviet Studies and the RAND Graduate School of Policy Studies. He is a member of the International Institute for Strategic Studies, the National Council on U.S.-China Relations, the China Council of the Asia Society, and the Committee on International Security and Arms Control of the National Academy of Sciences. His most recent book is *India's Defense Modernization in the 1980s and Beyond-Ambitions and Realities* (1994). He earned his Ph.D. from the University of Michigan.

Umphon Phanachet is Lansam Professor of International Business at Chulalongkorn University in Bangkok, Thailand, and Director of the Chinese Studies Center, Institute of Asian Studies at Chulalongkorn University. He also serves as Senior Advisor and Chairman of the Advisory Board on International Business at SCB Holding Co., Ltd., and Senior Consultant at the Hong Kong Trade Development Council at the Consultant Office in Thailand. He is a Senior Fulbright Scholar at Stanford University and the University of California at Berkeley and a Visiting Scholar at the Australian National University in Canberra. He also has served for more than thirty-two years as a Senior Economist with the United Nations Economic and Social Commission for Asia and the Pacific. He is the author of the *Guidebook on Trading with the People's Republic of China,* the fourth edition of which was published in 1993 by the United Nations. He earned his M.A. in International Economics from Cornell University.

Viraphol Sarasin is Deputy Permanent Secretary at the Ministry of Foreign Affairs of Thailand. He entered the Ministry in 1976 after the normalization of relations between Thailand and the People's Republic of China, with the express purpose of joining the first Thai diplomatic mission in Beijing. He has also served as Director of Policy and Planning and Personal Assistant to the Foreign Minister of Thailand, Deputy Chief of Mission in the Thai embassy in Tokyo, Deputy Director-General of the Foreign Ministry's Political Department, and Ambassador Attached to the Ministry. His principal duties have included the diplomatic negotiations over the Cambodian problem at various international forums. He helped organize the workshop series on cooperation between ASEAN and the United Nations in preventive diplomacy. He earned his Ph.D. in East Asian languages and history from Harvard University.

Robert A. Scalapino is a fellow of the American Academy of Arts and Sciences. He was made a Berkeley Fellow in 1993. He serves on the Board of Directors of Pacific Forum-CSIS and the National Committee on U.S.-China Relations (of which he was a founder and first chairman), and on the Board of Trustees of the Asia Foundation. He was recently named Director Emeritus of the Council on Foreign Relations. He is Co-Chairman of the Asia Society's Asian Agenda Advisory Group. His most recent book is *The Last Leninists: The Uncertain Future of Asia's Communist States* (1992). He earned his Ph.D. from Harvard University.

Hung-Mao Tien is a professor of political science at the University of Wisconsin and a senior fellow at the East Asian Legal Studies Center at the University of Wisconsin Law School. He is also President of the Institute for National Policy Research at Taipei, member of the Asia Society President's Council in New York, and member of the National Unification Research Council, ROC President's Office in Taipei. His most recent book is *The Chinese Communist Party: Party Powers and Group Politics from the Third Plenum to the Twelfth Party Congress* (1984).

Jimmy W. Wheeler is Director of International and Asia-Pacific Studies at Hudson Institute. He joined Hudson Institute in 1977, specializing in Asian economic and security issues, international trade and finance, urban development, and enterprise zones, and defense conversion. He is Vice-President of the board of directors of the Japan-America Society of Indiana and is a member of the Society for Policy Modeling and the World Future Society. Prior to joining Hudson, he was an assistant professor of economics at Florida International University and an instructor at Rutgers University.

BIBLIOGRAPHY

Aberbach, Joil D., Dollar, David, and Sokoloff, Kenneth L., eds. 1994. *The Role of the State in Taiwan's Development.* Armonk, NY and London: M. E. Sharpe.

Baum, Julian. 1994. "The Money Machine." *Far Eastern Economic Review,* August 11: 62-67.

Chang, Parris H. and Lasater, Martin L. 1993. *If China Crosses the Taiwan Strait.* Lanham, NY and London: University Press of America.

Cheng, Tun-jen. 1989. "Democratizing the Quasi-Leninist Regime in Taiwan," *World Politics* 41 (July): 471-499.

Cheng, Tun-jen and Haggard, Stephan, eds. 1992. *Political Change in Taiwan.* Boulder, CO: Lynne Rienner.

Chu, Yun-han. 1994. "Electoral Competition, Social Cleavages, and the Evolving Party System." Paper presented at the Conference on Democratization in Taiwan, George Washington University, Washington, DC, April 8-9.

Chung-kuo shih pao [China Times], Taipei.

Clough, Ralph. N. 1978. *Island China.* Cambridge, MA: Harvard University Press.

Clough, Ralph N. 1993. *Reaching Across the Taiwan Strait.* Boulder, CO: Westview Press.

Copper, John F. 1994. *Taiwan's 1991 and 1992 Non-Supplemental Elections.* Lanham, NY and London: University Press of America.

Democratic Progressive Party. 1994. *Charter and Platform.* Taipei: Democratic Progressive Party.

Feldman, Harvey J., ed. 1991. *Constitutional Reform and the Future of Republic of China.* Armonk, NY and London: M. E. Sharpe.

Gold, Thomas B. 1986. *State and Society in the Taiwan Miracle.* Armonk, NY and London: M. E. Sharpe.

Hsin hsin-wen [The Journalist], Taipei.

Hsia, Tao-tai and Zeldin, Wendy I. 1994. *The Fourteenth Party Congress of the Kuomintang, the Remaking of the Party in Taiwan and the November 1993 and January 1994 Elections.* Washington, DC: Law Library, the Library of Congress.

Hsu, Chung Y. and Chang, Parris H., eds. 1992. *The 1991 National Assembly Election in Taiwan.* Chicago: North America Taiwanese Professors' Association.

Hu, Jason C. 1993. "The Case for Taiwan's U.N. Representation." Paper presented at the Atlantic Council, Washington, DC.

Huang, Kun-huei. 1991. *The Key Points and Content of the Guidelines for National Unification.* Taipei: Mainland Affairs Council.

Huang, Teh-fu. 1992. *Min-chu-chin-pu tang yu T'ai-wan ti-ch'ü cheng-chih min-chu-hua* [The Democratic Progressive Party and Political Democratization in Taiwan]. Taipei: Shih-ying ch'u-pan-she.

Huang, Teh-fu. 1994. "Elections and the Evolution of the Kuomingtang." Paper presented at the Conference on Democratization in Taiwan, George Washington University, Washington, DC, April 8-9.

Kau, Michael Ying-mao. 1989. "Political Challenges of the Post-Chiang Ching-kuo Era," 3-29. Hearing Before the Subcommittee on Asian and Pacific Affairs, Committee on Foreign Affairs, U.S. House of Representatives. Washington, DC: U. S. Government Printing Office.

Kau, Michael Ying-mao. 1991. *Taiwan: the National Affairs Council and Implications for Democracy.* Hearing Before the Subcommittee on Asian and Pacific Affairs, Committee on Foreign Affairs, U.S. House of Representatives. Washington, DC: U. S. Government Printing Office.

Kau, Michael Ying-mao. 1992. "The ROC's New Foreign Policy Strategy." In Denis Fred Simon and Michael Ying-mao Kau, eds. *Taiwan Beyond the Economic Miracle,* 237-256. Armonk, NY and London: M. E. Sharpe.

Kau, Michael Ying-mao and Marsh, Susan H., eds. 1993. *Chian in the Era of Deng Xiaoping.* Armonk, NY and London: M. E. Sharpe.

Lee, Teng-hui. 1994. "Pi-hsu chu-ch'uan tsai-min" [Hold Fast on the Sovereignty of the People]. *Chung-yang jih-pao* [Central Daily], Taipei, April 23, 1994

Lien-ho pao [United Daily], Taipei.

Lin, Wen-cheng. 1993. *Political Integration and Democratization: The Case of Taiwan.* Unpublished Ph. D. Dissertation, the Fletcher School of Law and Diplomacy.

Shiau, Chyuan-jeng. 1994. "Election and the Changing State-Business Relationships." Paper presented at the Conference on Democratization in Taiwan, George Washington University, Washington, DC, April 8-9.

Simon, Denis Fred and Kau, Michael Ying-mao, eds. 1992. *Taiwan Beyond the Economic Miracle.* Armonk, NY and London: M. E. Sharpe.

Sutter, Robert S. 1988. *Taiwan Entering the 21st Century.* Lanham, NY and London: University Press of America.

T'ai-wan kung-lun pao [Taiwan Justice News], Yunlin, Taiwan.

Tien, Hung-mao. 1989. *The Great Transition: Political and Social Change in the Republic of China.* Stanford: Hoover Institution Press.

Tien, Hung-mao. 1994. "The Election and Taiwan's Democratic Development." Paper presented at the Conference on Democratization in Taiwan, George Washington University, Washington, DC, April 8-9.

Winkler, Edwin A. and Greenhalgh, Susan, eds. 1988. *Contending Approaches to the Political Economy of Taiwan.* Armonk, NY and London: M. E. Sharpe.

Wu, Nai-teh. 1987. *The Politics of a Regime Patronage System.* Unpublished Ph. D. Dissertation, Dept. of Political Science, University of Chicago.

Yang, Maysing. 1989. *Political Trends in Taiwan Since the Death of Chiang Ching-kuo,* 35-49. Hearing Before the Subcommittee on Asian and Pacific Affairs, Committee on Foreign Affairs, U. S. House of Representatives. Washington, DC: U. S. Government Pringting Office.

Yang, Maysing. 1993. "The Democratic Movement in Taiwan." Paper presented at the Conference on Forms of Transition to Democracy, Sintra, Portugal, March 14-20.

Yang, Maysing and Hwang, Phyllis. 1993. "Taiwan was Temporarily Part of China, But That Was Long Ago." *International Herald Tribune,* September 21, 1993.

Yuan-chien tsa-chih [Global Views Monthly], Taipei.

NOTES

Chapter 2: The Evolution of China's Policy Toward Taiwan

[1]This complex mix of rivalry, intimacy, and sentiment is illustrated by a letter Liao Chengzhi (son of Sun Yat-sen associate and KMT martyr Liao Zhongkai) wrote in July 1982 to "my younger brother Ching-kuo" (a classmate in Moscow) telling of his "unshirkable responsibility" to act while the leaders of both sides still knew each other (implying the offer was limited to the present generation). Also, Chiang's father's remains should be brought back to rest in his native soil. Not to be outranked, Taiwan responded with a letter not from Chiang but from his father's widow, in which she admonished the younger Liao to obey his father's will and return to the KMT.

[2]As to which elite groupings support which policy mix, it is reasonable to assume based on their bureaucratic interests that the pro-reform faction has supported greater reliance on diplomacy and "peace" offensives while the military and the hardliners have favored a resort to military preparations or threats, and that with the devolution of control over economic policy local authorities in southern coastal China have ardently supported growing economic interdependency and been cool to the prospect of invasion while local leaders in the interior provinces have been indifferent to or even perhaps hostile to economic "opening." But Taiwan policy has been so closely held that the empirical evidence to confirm these hypotheses has not been at hand.

[3]Taiwan succeeded in participating in the 1984 Olympics under the name "Taipei, China" [*Taibei, zhonghua*], and also agreed (under protest) to participate in the Asian Development Bank under the same name in

1988 (after fruitless boycotting the organization for two years when Beijing gained admittance). But when Taiwan then proceeded to try to participate in all possible international organizations or activities under that name, including the Asian Games in 1989 and hopefully later in GATT, the OECD, IMF, the World Bank, even the UN General Assembly, Beijing balked. Insisting that this was not a legal precedent, Beijing demanded that Taipei use the term "Taipei, Chinese" [*Taibei, zhongguo*], and that admission could only procced on a case-by-case basis with Beijing's explicit approval in each instance.

[4]For example, in October 1978 deng Xiaoping said in Tokyo, "If it [sc. the Taiwan issue] cannot be settled in 10 years, or in a century, it will be settled in a thousand years." But at the beginning 1979 *Renmin Ribao* listed a deadline of 12 months, and Deng told a group of American journalists at this time that "ten years...would be too long for reunification." In a speech before the 3rd Session of the 4th NPC (February 2, 1980) he said that "the return of Taiwan to the motherland" was one of the three main goals of the 1980s (listed after realization of the Four Modernizations and before the struggle with hegemonism). This is a rather wide range of terminals within a few months. The most recent estimates seem to have been more patient. In a news conference in September 1990, Yang Shangkun told a group of reports from Taiwan that "it seems improper to be too hasty. It is possible that people my age may not live to see the day when China is unified." A December 1993 national conference on Taiwan held in Xiamen reportedly also concluded that there was no need to hurry, China could wait 30 or 40 years, until the level of development on the mainland approached that in Taiwan.

[5]After Nixon's first visit, Mao criticized Zhou Enlai and Ye Jianying, the two chief negotiators on the Chinese side, for "capitulating" to the U.S. It turned out that Wang Hairong and Tang Wensheng told Mao that Zhou was offering concessions on the nonuse of force on Taiwan. On Nov 7, 1973, Mao told Wang Hairong, Tang Wensheng, and Kang Sheng that "the statement that there are two possibilities to resolve the Taiwan issue is wrong. It has to be fought."

[6]On July 10 he wrote to Zhou Enlai, "We must prepare to attack Taiwan. Besides the army, the air force is a major force. To possess one, we can succeed; to possess both, the success is more secure."

[7]The original schedule was for Beijing to launch its invasion of Taiwan in July, and for Kim to move in August; the reason Kim preempted Mao is unclear. See Jun Zhan, *Ending the Chinese Civil War: Power,*

Commerce, and Conciliation Between Beijing and Taipei (New York: St. Martin's, 1993).

[8]See *Cheng Ming* (Hong Kong), no. 200 (June 1, 1994), pp. 17-18, as trans. in BBC Short Wave Broadcasts, June 11, 1994, pp. 239-140 for a report of military exercises following the recent Qiandao Lake incident.

[9]Deng Xiaoping set the following conditions for the conceivable use of force: if Taiwan leaned toward Moscow instead of Washington, if Taipei decides to develop nuclear weapons, if Taipei claims to be an independent state, if it loses control in succession, or if it continues to reject reunification talks "for a long period of time."

[10]In a lunar New Year's message to Taiwan in February 1980 the offer previously made by the NPC was now referred to as "the proposal of the CCP," changing it from state-to-state to inter-Party negotiation. The message was sent from the CPPCC.

[11]*Los Angeles Times*, Nov 15, 1981.

[12]*Zeng Ming,* July 1, 1982.

[13]Den Xiaoping, *Fundamental Issues in Contemporary China* (Peking: FLP, 1987).

[14]At the 5th Plenum of the 5th NPC (Dec 1982) a rewritten constitution stipulated in Art 31 that the state might adopt SARs when necessary, and the systems to be instituted there should be prescribed by laws enacted by the NPC "in the light of specific conditions." Item 13 of Art 62 stated that the NPC had the power to "decide on the establishment of SARs and the system to be instituted there." *Beijing Review*, December 27, 1982, pp. 16, 19. This makes clear that the SAR will be applied to HK, Macao, Taiwan, with provision for flexibility on specific measures among them; the "when necessary" however opens the interpretation that the SAR is a provisional arrangement to be eliminated in time.

[15]*Renmin Ribao* [People's Daily], 22 April 1986.

[16]Yan Jiaqi, "Yiguo liangzhi de kexue hanyi ji qi tezheng" [The scientific meaning and special features of the 'one country, two systems'], *Honggi* [Red Flag], Sept 1985, pp. 17-19. Yan has continued his interest in drawing out the full ramifications of "one country two systems" since his 1989 exile, moving most recently to a theory of federalism.

[17]*Liaowang zhoukan* [outlook weekly], domestic edition, 15 Oct 1984, pp. 8,9.

[18]*Qishi niandai* [the seventies], August 1983, p. 19. The contingency was not mentioned in the account published by Beijing in *Renmin ribao*.

[19]*Renmin ribao*, July 30, 1983.

[20]Deng Xiaoping, *Janshe you zhongguo tese de shehui zhuyi* [Building socialism with Chinese Characteristics] (Hong Kong: Joint Publishing, revised ed., 1987), p. 83.

[21]By the fall of 1992, the Dutch were again negotiating with the PRC for permission to sell submarines to Taiwan. In fact, Fokker did sell some Fokker 50s to Taiwan—with the quid pro quo that they sold some Fokker 100s to the mainland. *New York Times*, February 19, 1992.

[22]There is some reason for this. October 13, 1991, the DPP made the establishment of a "Republic of Taiwan" part of its party platform for the upcoming National Assembly election in December, 1991. Beijing reacted by threatening force, and Hau Pei-tsun pointed this out to the electorate. As a result of this unusual CCP-KMT collaboration, the DPP got only 23.9 percent of the vote.

[23]The launching of conventional war, even without US involvement, would doom the policy of opening to the outside world, disrupt the schedule for modernization (and for the retrocession of Hong Kong, provided that had not yet occurred), possibly percipitate a break in Sino-Japanese relations, destroy China's good relations with ASEAN and precipitate an arms race in SE Asia. War would also expose China to Taiwanese counterattack: with 70 percent of Chinese industrial capacity on its eastern seaboard, coast, and a rich coastal agriculture fed by a complex system of dams, water reservoirs and canals, Taiwan could do a lot of damage with its air force, severely damaging industrial capacity and putting vast areas under water. The support of the US for a besieged or blockaded Taiwan would revive the diplomatic chances of a two-Chinas policy and lead to re-isolation of the mainland.

[24]At the early stages of commercial contact in 1980 Peking lifted all import taxes for products from Taiwan, but this led to such an increase of imports that tariffs were reintroduced selectively. Still, however, Beijing gives Taiwan investors more favorable treatment than other FDI: "adjustment taxes" imposed on Taiwanese goods are slightly lower than import tariffs and controls on goods elsewhere, supervision of Taiwanese factories less stringent.

[25]After the Sino-British Joint Declaration was initiated and signed in September and December 1984 respectively, the 3rd session of the 6th NPC established a Basic Law Drafting Committee (BLDC) of the Hong Kong Special Administrative Region (HKSAR) in April 1985, consisting of 59 members, only 23 of whom are from Hong Kong. To paper this over a Basic Law Consultative Committee (BLCC) was constituted to solicit opinions from the people of Hong Kong, consisting of the Hong

Kong members of the BLDC plus 180 other Hong Kong notables. It was expected a similar procedure would be followed for implementation of the Sino-Portuguese Joint Declaration for return of Macao in December 1999. The (first) Draft Basic Law of the HKSAR was released in April 1988 for solicitation of opinions in May-September. The BLCC collected 70,000 pieces of opinion from various sources and compiled 5 volumes of consultation reports, which were distributed to the people of Hong Kong and to the BLDC. Based on these suggestions the BLDC made a revised draft, which was submitted to the 6th session of the Standing Committee of the 7th NPC by Ji Pengfei in February 1989. It was decided that Draft II should be publicized to solicit opinions in Hong Kong and other parts of China from February to July 1989. So a second round of consultation was held, leading to final approval of the revised draft at the 3rd session of the 7th NPC in April 1990.

[26]In August 1988, Professor James Hsiung arrived in Taipei claiming to have had high level talks in Beijing in which his interlocutors made new proposals: Beijing would formally eschew reunification by force, rewrite its constitution to downgrade the role of the CCP, and offer the Kuomintang a place in a "coalition government." Taiwan had merely to accept Beijing's sovereignty and foreswear independence. The message was never authenticated, however, and Taipei did not respond. The following year Tiananmen occurred, and the sponsors of these proposals may have been purged or discredited.

Section II Discussion: The Politics of Legitimacy

[1]Helen Siu. "Recycling Rituals: Politics and Popular Culture in Contemporary Rural China." *Unofficial China: Popular Culture and Thought in the People's Republic* edited by Perry Link, Richard Madsen, and Paul G. Pickowicz. Boulder: Westview Press (1989):121-137.

[2]Tu Weiming. "Cultural China: The Periphery as the Center." *Daedelus,* Vol.120 No.2 (Spring 1991):1-32.

[3]Thomas B. Gold. "Go With Your Feelings: Hong Kong and Taiwan Popular Culture in Greater China." *China Quarterly,* No.136 (December 1993):907-925.

Chapter 4: Taiwan and the Mainland: Can Economic Interaction Mute the Conflict?

[1]Details of the dramatic change in cross-straits economic relations since the late 1970s are discussed in many places. A well-done brief

overview can be found in Chia Siow Yue and Lee Taso Yuan, "Subregional Economic Zones: A New Motive Force in Asia-Pacific Development," in C. Fred Bergsten and Marcus Noland (eds.), *Pacific Dynamism and the International Economic System* (Institute for International Economics, Washington, D.C.: 1993), pp. 249-264.

[2]Re-unification was one of the Mainland's three primary goals for the 1980s, and the incentives targeting Taiwan businesses were explicitly part of a strategy to lay the groundwork and build dependency. See Ada Koon Hang Tse, "The Emerging Legal Framework for Regulating Economic Relations Between Taiwan and the Mainland," *Journal of Chinese Law*, [6:137, 1992] pp. 142-43.

[3]Julian Baum, "Chinese Gambit: Talks overshadowed by investment move," *Far Eastern Economic Review*, 30 December 1993 - 6 January 1994, p. 14.

[4]No contact, no compromise, and no negotiation with the PRC.

[5]How better to promote capitalism and the success of Taiwan's policy approach than through the businessmen who have been the driving force of progress.

[6]This legal history is summarized from *Ibid.*, p. 143-157.

[7]Frank Ching, "Taiwan Is Drafting Legislation To Govern Ties With Hongkong," *Far Eastern Economic Review*, 1 July 1993, p. 28. Virginia Sheng, "Bill outlines Hong Kong relations," *Free China Journal*, Feb. 25, 1994, p. 3.

[8]Yoichi Funabashi, Michael Oksenberg, and Heinrich Weiss, *An Emerging China in a World of Interdependence*, A Report to The Trilateral Commission: 45 (May 1994), p. 23.

[9]Allen Pun, "Investment in Southeast Asia leads the way," *The Free China Journal*, August 19, 1994, Vol. XI, No. 32. p. 3.

[10]Christine Lee, "Massive Economic Landing: Taiwan Businessmen Swarming to Mainland," *China Information*, February 1994, pp. 24-25.

[11]"Biggest Mainland Investment," *The Free China Journal*, May 13, 1994, p.3.

[12]*Ibid.*, p. 257.

[13]Jeremy Mark, "Taiwan is Signaling Its Readiness To Expand Contacts With China," *The Wall Street Journal*, March 24, 1993., p. A11.

[14]Julian Baum, "Human Wave: Rise in illegal immigrants from China alarms Taipei," *Far Eastern Economic Review*, 5 August 1992, p. 24.

[15] Data reported in Milton D. Yeh, "Taiwan-Mainland Relations: An Analysis of International and Domestic Factors," *American Journal of Chinese Studies*, Vol. 1:401, October 1992, P. 407.

[16]*The Free China Journal*, August 19, 1994, Vol. XI, No. 32. p. 1.

[17]See for example, Julian Baum, "The Unstoppable Tide: Rapid rise in Taiwan-China trade pressures Taipei," *Far Eastern Economic Review*, 20 May 1993, p. 66.

[18] "Back On Track: After Some Reversals, China-Taiwan Relations Move Forward," *Asiaweek*, August 17, 1994, pp. 26-28. Jeremy Mark, "China and Taiwan Progress On Hijackers, Other issues," *The Asian Wall Street Journal Weekly*, August 15, 1994, p. 3.

[19]The most recent event being Latvia's transfer of official ties from Taiwan to China.

[20]Likewise, the Mainland chose to challenge, and beat back, France's decision to sell fighter aircraft to Taiwan by threatening large scale contracts with French firms. They have not shown the same aggressiveness towards the U.S. over the decision to sell F-16s.

[21]*The Free China Journal*, August 19, 1994, Vol. XI, No. 32. p. 1.

[22]Deborah Shen, "McKinsey draws up 'hub' blueprint," *The Free China Journal*, August 19, 1994, Vol. XI, No. 32. p.8. A recent (December 1993) McKinsey report, commissioned by the CEPD, recommended concentrating in three business areas; manufacturing, transshipment by air or sea, and professional services in finance, telecommunications, and the media. Implementation of some of the reports recommendations are include in the CEPD development plan submitted to the government for approval on August 15, 1994. Premier Lein has given related government agencies two months to offer suggestions on the McKinsey plan to CEPD.

[23] See for example, Kathy Chen, "With China's Own Succession Drama Looming, Leaders Prepare Themselves for the Inevitable," *Asian Wall Street Journal Weekly*, 18 July 1994, pp. 1, 3.

Chapter 5: U.S. Policy Toward Evolving Taiwan-Mainland China Relationships

[1]For an excellent detailed analysis of the agonizing within the U.S. government over the fate of Taiwan, see David M. Finkelstein, *Washington's Taiwan Dilemma, 1949-1950: From Abandonment to Salvation* (Washington: George Mason University Press, 1993)

[2]For a cogent, recent analysis of U.S.-China relations and thoughtful recommendations concerning U.S. policy toward the PRC, see A. Doak Barnett, *U.S.-China Relations: Time for a new Beginning—Again.* (Washington, D.C.: Johns Hopkins School of Advanced International Studies, April 1994.)

[3]Ralph N. Clough, *Reaching Across the Taiwan Strait: People-to-People Diplomacy* (Boulder, CO: Westview Press, 1993)

[4]Fan Liqing, "A New Stage of Non-Official Talks," *Beijing Review,* February 28-March 6, 1994, p. 21; Philip Liu, "Mixed Diagnosis for Mainland Fever," *Free China Review,* Vol. 43, No. 9, September 1993, p. 44.

[5]The DPP expressed firm opposition to a meeting between Tang Shubei, vice chairman and secretary general of the ARATS, and his SEF counterpart, Chiao Jen-ho, scheduled for August 4-7, 1994 in Taipei. Secretary-General Szu Chen-chang of the DPP declared: "It's not the right time for Tang to visit Taiwan. Mainland China still threatens to use violent means to take over Taiwan and people in Taiwan are still suffering in the aftermath of the Qiandao Lake incident." *China Post,* July 21, 1994.

[6]*China Post,* May 2, 1994.

[7]The highest recorded support for independence expressed in public opinion polls was 27 percent in early April 1994, soon after the Thousand Island Lke murders. *China Post,* April 18, 1994.

[8]Note the recommendation by Chi Su that Taipei should promote these two in tandem. He argues that if relations with the mainland develop too rapidly, Taiwan independence advocates will condemn the policy, while if "pragmatic diplomacy" seems to be going too far, unification supporters and the PRC will denouce it. Therefore, Su urges, in order to minimize domestic political controversy and adverse effects on relations with the PRC, neither strand of the policy should get too far ahead of the other. ("The International Relations of the Republic of China" in Gerrit Gong and Bih-jaw Lin, eds., *Sino-American Relations in a Time of Change,* Washington, D.C.: Center for Strategic and International Studies and Taipei: Institute of International Relations, 1994.) Su is a vice chairman of the Mainland Affairs Commission.

[9]*New York Times*, Sept. 8, 1994; *Washington Post*, Sept. 8, 1994; *Washington Post,* Sept. 11, 1994.

[10]*China Post,* June 22, 1994.

Chapter 6: Japanese Policies Toward the PRC and Taiwan

[1]For an excellent survey of Japan's China policy prior to, and during this period, with an emphasis upon the role of the business community in supporting a change, see Sadako Ogata, "The Business Community and Japanese Foreign Policy: Normalization of Relations with the People's Republic of China," in Robert A. Scalapino, ed., *The Foreign Policy of Modern Japan,* pp. 175-204.

²An early statement of the President of Toyota was carried by Kyodo News Agency, Tokyo, 13 July, 1994, and published in FBIS-EAS-94-134, 13 July, 1994, p. 2.

For a subsequent statement after it was announced that China would itself invest $250 million in the Toyota plant, see Joeph Kahn, "Beijing's Decision Excludes Toyota From Auto Project." *The Asian Wall Street Journal Weekly,* September 12, 1994, p. 2.

³Kyodo News Agency report, 23 June, 1994, published in *ibid.,* 23 June, 1994, p. 8.

⁴See the report of the Foreign Relations Committee of the National Assembly, Taiwan, *Conditions in Northeast Asia and Current Conditions and Prospects for China-Japan Relations,* issued June 27, 1994, especially pp. 11-14 (in Chinese).

⁵Deborah Shen, "Foreign investment in ROC up 50 percent," *The Free China Journal,* July 22, 1994, p. 3.

⁶A recent comment after a recent lecture by this author at the Sichuan Academy of Social Sciences in Chengdu, however, might be worth recording. A researcher made a statement, asking for my response. The statement was: "In earlier times, we were exploited by the West; then we were exploited by Japan; today, we are being exploited by Hong Kong and Taiwan." After inquiry, it seemed clear that she was referring to the exploitation of Chinese workers in foreign-owned factories and investments that drove prices—particularly land prices—up.

⁷A very fine analytical article dealing with contemporary Sino-Japanese relations is Robert A. Manning, "Burdens of the Past, Dilemmas of the Future: Sino-Japanese Relations in the Emerging International System," *The Washington Quarterly,* 17:1, pp. 45-58.

⁸For one among many articles and speeches expounding this theme, see Zhou Jihua, "Japanese Foreign Policy: The Direction of the Post-Cold War Adjustment," *Foreign Affairs Journal,* Beijing, No. 25, September 1992, pp. 35-42. Zhou asserts that the real winners of the Cold War were Japan and Germany, the two nations that benefited from sitting on the sidelines and accepting the opportunities given them.

⁹On July 5, 1994, the ROC government issued a White Paper entitled "Explanation of Relations Across the Taiwan Straits," outlining the new policies in detail. This document was published in *Chung Kuo shih Pao,* Taipei, in Chinese, 6 July 1994, pp. 2, 10, and carried in English in *FBIS-CHI-94-132,* 11 July 1994, pp. 50-59.

Chapter 7: ASEAN, Vietnam, and the Taiwan-Mainland China Relationship

[1]For example, in January 1992, a conference on "Greater Chinese Economic Bloc (Circle)" was held in Hong King. The Conference was attended by scholars from Beijing, Taipei and Hong Kong and enjoyed considerable attention in the mass media. Even newspapers in Moscow also reported it. (See China Times, February 19, 1992)

[2]For details see "Policy on Mainland China and the Relationship between the Two Sides of the Taiwan Straits," by Huang Kun-huei, Mainland Affairs Council, the Executive Yuan. Republic of China, December 1991.

[3]The project was subsequently delayed due to government's intervention. But according to the source from the Fujian government, the project is still on and the provincial government in Fujian is continuing its work on infrastructure there.

[4]The figure reported on July 16, 1991 by Beijing's "Economic Daily"

[5]For details see, "[insert foreign title]. July 1991, [see original text]

[6]The total DFI from the entire world as US $1,778 million.

[7]See "The Patterns and Prospects of the Economics Relationships between the Two Sides of the Taiwan Straits" by King Pei and Hsu Chia Xian.

[8]This was estimated by Chung-Hua Institution for Economic Research (May 9, 1991), and quoted in the King paper.

[9]A first hand study on this issues was published by Chung-Hua Institute for Economic Research, June 1990.

[10]There are other non-economic factors (such as respect, satisfaction, etc.) identified by Chinese scholars.

[11]The relocation had sped up since the creation of the Special Economic Zones. The deindustrialization process reduced the share of GDP for the manufacturing sector to less than 20 percent. At present only 670,000 Hong Kong workers are still engaged in the manufacturing industries, while about 3 million Chinese workers are employed by Hong Kong firms operating in the Pearl River Delta. In the immediate past few years, the manufacturing industries has lost about 10 percent of their employment to the service industries each year.

[12]See "Taiwan's Investments in Mainland China and their Implication for the Manufacturing Sectors", Chung-Hua Institution for Economic Research, Taipei

[13]The first meeting of seventeen Asia/Pacific nations plus the European Union in Bangkok to discuss regional security questions and cooperation represents ASEAN's achievement in consolidating regional dialogue process.

[14]Regnier, P and N. Yuanming and Z. Ruijin "Towards Regional 'Integration' in the East?" Paper presented at the national Changchi University, Taipei, Taiwan, August 1992.

[15]Siew, Vincent "The Six-Year National Development Plan and ROC's future Economics Development." paper presented at a conference on the ROC and the New International Order, Taipei, August 1991.

Chapter 9: Alternative Scenarios of Internaction in the International Arena

[1]One manifestation of the possible evolution of Taiwan's approach to legitimacy based on principle, on competition, and now on cooperation is the idea that, "as Premier Lien Chan of the ROC has pointed out, the time has come for the PRC to give up its zero-sum game and begin working for 'win-win' solutions" ("United We Stand," Taiwan Welfare Association in New York, *New York Times*, August 29, 1994, p. A16.).

[2]The Executive Yuan, "Relations Across the Taiwan Straits," (abstract) (Taipei, Taiwan, Republic of China: Mainland Affairs Council, July 1994), p. 3.

[3]Taiwan Affairs Office and Information Office, "The Taiwan Question and Reunification of China," (Beijing, China, State Council, August 1993) p. 20.

[4]Ibid.

[5]Ibid.

[6]The Executive Yuan, "Relations Across the Taiwan Straits," (abstract) p. 5-6.

[7]Ibid., p. 6.

[8]Ibid., p. 10.

[9]See, for example, Hung-mao Tien, "The 1992 Parliamentary Election and Cabinet Reshuffles: Taiwan's Party Politics and Implications for Washington and Beijing," in Bih-jaw Lin, ed., *Sino-American Relations at a Time of Change* (Washington: Center for Strategic and International Studies and Taipei: The Institute of International Relations, 1994) pp. 127-136.

[10]These are admirably detailed in Thomas B. Gold, "Taiwan's Quest for Identity in the Shadow of China," in Steve Tsang, ed., *In the Shadow*

of China: Political Developments in Taiwan since 1949 (Honolulu: University of Hawaii Press: 1993).

[11]Jason C. Hu, "Solid-as-a-ROC: Taiwan Deserves UN Status," *The Seattle Times*, February 14, 1994, p. B5.

[12]Juang Lu Lin, "Myth of Re-unification: Taiwan Should Take Initiative and Apply to Join the UN Body," *The Seattle Times*, March 1, 1994, p. B5.

[13]Hedley Bull, *The Anarchical Society* (London: Macmillan, 1979), pp. 9-10.

[14]See Gerrit W. Gong, *The Standard of 'Civilization' in International Society* (Oxford: Clarendon Press, 1984), pp. 14-21, 238-248.

[15]See, for example, Professor Hungdah Chiu, "The Right of the Republic of China and its 21 Million Chinese People to Participate in the United Nations," as prepared for delivery, ROC-UN Conference, University of South Carolina, April 1, 1994. See also Taiwan Welfare Association in New York, "It's Time to be Pragmatic," *New York Times*, August 22, 1994, p. A13. The *Washington Post* recognized similar realities in "Yes, Taiwan Exists," August 15, 1994, editorial page.

[16]See Ralph N. Clough, *Reaching Across the Taiwan Strait: People-to-People Diplomacy* (Boulder: Westview Press, 1993), p. 104.

[17]These themes are detailed in George T. Yu and David J. Longenecker, "The Beijing-Taipei Struggle for International Recognition," *Asian Survey* XXXIV, 5 (Berkeley: University of California Press, May 1994), p. 475.

[18]Taiwan Affairs Office and Information Office, "The Taiwan Question and Reunification of China," p. 18.

[19]Ibid., pp. 19-20.

[20]Ibid., pp. 20-21.

[21] "Typhoon Kills 700 in China; Damage Is Put at $1.6 Billion," *New York Times*, August 24, 1994, p. A11.

[22]Taiwan Affairs Office and Information Office, "The Taiwan Question and Reunification of China," p. 21.

[23]Edward I-hsin Chen, "Breaking the Wall of Separation through Active Participation in International Institutions," presented at International Conference on Taiwan in a Transformed Global Setting, Cambridge, Massachusetts, U.S.A., April 28-29, 1994, p. 9.

[24]Ibid.

[25]The Clinton Administration's Taiwan policy review seems not unsympathetic to this approach, noting in its initial background briefing

that "Taiwan has a role to play in a number of trans-national issues such as in APEC and the Asian Development Bank, and we support their admission to the GATT."

Further, "We believe it is in the general interest for Taiwan's voice to be heard by some additional international organizations confronting these issues. And, thus, on a selective basis we will look for opportunities for Taiwan's voice to be heard in such organizations." See, Background Briefing on Taiwan Policy Review by Senior Administration Official, Wednesday, September 7, 1994.

See also the statement of Assistant Secretary of State Winston Lord before the Senate Foreign Relations Committee hearing on Taiwan policy, September 27, 1994. In this testimony, international organizations were discussed as follows: "Recognizing Taiwan's important role in trans-national issues, we will support its membership in organizations where statehood is not a prerequisite, and we will support opportunities for Taiwan's voice to be heard in organizations where its membership is not possible" (Testimony, p. 7).

INDEX

ABOUT HUDSON INSTITUTE

Hudson Institute is a private, not-for-profit research organization founded in 1961 by the late Herman Kahn. Hudson analyzes and makes recommendations about public policy for business and government executives, as well as for the public at large. The institute does not advocate an express ideology or political position. However, more than thirty years of work on the most important issues of the day has forged a viewpoint that embodies skepticism about the conventional wisdom, optimism about solving problems, a commitment to free institutions and individual responsibility, an appreciation of the crucial role of technology in achieving progress, and an abiding respect for the importance of values, culture, and religion in human affairs.

Since 1984, Hudson has been headquartered in Indianapolis, Indiana. It also maintains offices in Washington, D.C.; Madison, Wisconsin; and Brussels, Belgium.